Planning Play and the Early Years

Penny Tassoni
Karen Hucker

Heinemann

Inspiring generations

Heinemann Educational Publishers
Halley Court, Jordan Hill, Oxford OX2 8EJ
Part of Harcourt Education

Heinemann is the registered trademark of Harcourt Education Limited

First published 2005
10 09 08 07
10 9 8 7 6 5 4 3 2

British Library Cataloguing in Publication Data is available from the
British Library on request.

10-digit ISBN: 0 435 40119 X
13-digit ISBN: 978 0 435 40119 1

Copyright notice

Typeset and illustrated by Thomson Digital

Original illustrations © Harcourt Education Limited, 2005

Cover design by Harcourt Education Ltd / Peter Stratton
Printed in China by South China Printing Co.
Cover photo: © Impact Photos / Peter Arkell

Picture research by Harcourt Education Ltd / Christine Martin

Acknowledgements

Every effort has been made to contact copyright holders of material reproduced in
this book. Any omissions will be rectified in subsequent printings if notice is given to
the publishers.
Corbis: page 304; **Mary Evans Picture Library:** page 18; **Getty Images:** pages 52, 205;
Harcourt Education Ltd/Gareth Boden: pages 55, 121, 124, 132, 138, 141, 148, 159, 190,
238, 292, 299; **Harcourt Education Ltd/Haddon Davies:** pages 26, 175;
Harcourt Education Ltd/Jules Selmes: pages 75, 79 144, 160, 194, 263, 278;
Harcourt Education Ltd/Tudor Photography: pages 13, 151.

Contents

Acknowledgements

This has been an exciting book to write and I could not have done it without the practical and moral support of colleagues, friends and my family. I would particularly like to thank staff at Kinderquest head office for their patience and support, especially Pat Everett for help with OfSted requirements, Tracy Reading for providing a curriculum plan for older children and Denise Wrenn for giving permission for items to be reproduced. I also need to thank Jo Williams at Beaky's Nursery and Julie Henderson at ABC Nursery for passing me materials to inspire me.

The success of this new edition has relied on the help and input of many. My thanks go to Gill Heseltine, Jennie Lindon and particularly the staff of Oakwood Infants School, Clacton On Sea. I would also like to thank Lucy Hyde and Beth Howard at Heinemann.

Thanks as well to those readers of our first edition who have over the years taken the time to comment on what they had found useful.

Finally, my thanks again to The Tassoni Team, especially my daughters Anne-Marie and Marie-Lise.

Penny Tassoni

Thank you to Martin whose continuing support allows me to be involved in a wide range of activities.

Karen Hucker

Introduction

Since the first edition of this book, there have been many changes in the early years sector. Play is now seen as a major learning tool and increasingly practitioners are asked to look for ways of delivering curriculum outcomes through play. This is excellent news and essential as there is also a trend for babies and young children to spend longer periods in group care. In the period since the first edition, we have also seen the introduction of frameworks for the under threes. We have therefore added in a chapter looking at ways to support play and good practice for this age group.

The debate as to how best to provide play opportunities continues, however, and this book looks at the issues – both past and present – in doing so. As in the previous edition, it also considers planning and how to implement an early years curriculum.

The book is divided into three main sections:

Section 1 – Play

This section looks at the history of play through to the modern day. It also looks at the influences of the early years educators on play as well as considering European provision.

Section 2 – Planning

Planning has become increasingly important and there is a range of planning tools used in the sector. This section looks at the different ways in which early yeas settings might use planning and includes step-by-step approaches to producing plans. We have also included examples of different planning styles.

Section 3 – Early Years curriculum

This section is designed to give students and practitioners the underpinning knowledge required to help children develop their skills in different areas of the curriculum. There are many examples of activities that can used with children to help assist their learning while also being fun and enjoyable. The section begins with a chapter on the under threes as increasingly babies and toddlers are coming into group care.

There is no single curriculum across the United Kingdom for early years. Each of the home countries has produced a framework that best reflects its culture and needs. There are, however, some similarities across the different curricula and this section looks at six areas of learning and the 'core activities' that form the backbone of most early years settings. We have continued to link activities to the Early Learning Goals for England as this proved popular in the first edition.

Chapter 1   What is play?

Children play every day. Play is now seen as being crucial to the development of the child – it is through play that children learn many things about the world around them. Professionals working with children need to understand the value of play and how it helps children to learn. This chapter will look at what play is and explore its purpose or function. It will cover the stages of play as well as looking at the different types of play.

Defining play

Play occurs throughout life, although the form of play varies as a person grows older. Babies play by exploring with their hands and feet, while a young child may dress up as part of pretend play. In an older child, play involves hobbies, games or leisure activities, and this type of play continues into adolescence and adulthood. Even adults play! People who do not take part in any form of play are believed to be more likely to suffer stress, depression or boredom.

A dictionary definition of the verb 'to play' describes it as 'occupying oneself or amusing oneself in an activity or a game'. It includes the competitive aspect often linked to team games or sports. It suggests an activity undertaken for pleasure, especially by children.

Play is considered to be one of the primary needs of a child and is often said to be a child's work. It is a common behaviour of children in all countries and cultures – children naturally want to play, although they also learn to play, so both nature and nurture contribute to the development of the skills needed to play effectively. However, providing for play takes time and effort. The adult is the key to successful play in the early years, both in the home and in a professional situation.

True play has a number of different features. It is:

- initiated by children themselves, for example, role play of mothers and fathers, or playing in a puddle of water in the garden after rainfall

- designed by children themselves – they choose how to play and what to play
- something children choose to do because they like to do it, not for an end product or a reward
- natural, something that all children seem able to do without coaching or lessons
- spontaneous, which means children can involve themselves in it without guidance or instruction from an adult
- voluntary, in so far as children can choose whether or not to join in. Children play because it provides a way in which they can explore their environment, develop communication skills and express their pleasurable feelings. It combines both action and thought, and in so doing gives the child a sense of satisfaction.

Do all children play?

There are circumstances in which children cannot play. For example, studies of children brought up in orphanages where the adults did not initiate play showed that children were not able to play. In this situation, children did not have the experience of being played with to build on. Most of the games played with babies, such as peek-a-boo, are initiated by adults and need an adult to keep the game going. However, once given a toy such as a baby gym, babies will play by themselves. More information on the important role of the adult in play can be found in Section 2, pages 106–9.

ACTIVITY

Observe a baby to see whether he or she initiates play.

Did the adult need to be involved at least in providing the material for play, or did the baby make a game without adult help or materials, such as playing with his or her fingers?

Note exactly what the baby did over a five-minute period. Repeat your observation on several occasions and see if you notice a pattern.

Play has a role in the physical, social, emotional, language and cognitive development of children. Play is a learning experience – some theorists believe it allows children to practise the roles they will need to take on in adulthood. Susan Isaacs (1885–1948) saw play as the way in which children come to understand the world they live in.

CASE STUDY:

Abigail, aged five, comes into the lounge with a string of blue plastic beads wrapped around her lower arm and nestling in the crook of her elbow. 'Would you like to smooth the snake, Mummy?' she asks. 'Make sure you don't smooth its head as it's very poisonous.'

How does this example fit the definition of play?

Free play versus structured play

In recent years, comparisons have been made between the benefits of free and structured play. Whether play is free or structured is influenced by the amount of adult control and guidance taking place.

Free play

True free play, it could be suggested, is seen only in situations where the child has the opportunity to choose the focus of the play without constant interference or involvement by an adult.

Some experts believe that children remember best the free play they have created themselves, because it had meaning for them. It is also often the case that such play will hold a child's interest far longer than an activity organised and controlled by an adult.

Free play takes place when the child is leading the play experience and controlling the way the play develops. The child sets out the rules and boundaries of the play and as the play changes, so do the rules. Free play does not always take place in groups; it can be solitary, in pairs or parallel play. Whatever the type of play, children often become deeply engrossed in the activity because they have developed it themselves.

> **ACTIVITY**
>
> Watch how involved a group of children become in a role play. Observe the characters they put themselves into and how they can continue a game that inspires their imagination for a very long time.

In the past, free play used to take place on the streets as children were given more freedom to play outside and in their local neighbourhood. Nowadays, children are much more guarded and this can limit opportunities.

In free play, children can demonstrate a high level of knowledge and sensitivity towards others. It helps children bring together all they have learnt, and draws on physical, social, emotional, intellectual and language skills. It is holistic, which means it develops all aspects of the child and does not concentrate just on one.

Structured play

Structured play is adult-led, guided and planned. Bruce (1987) suggests that where play is seen as the way a child prepares for life, the amount of adult guidance in the play activity increases. At the same time, a child's role in deciding what to play and for how long decreases. It is often said that such play occurs in more formal situations such as playgroups and nurseries, and often an end product, such as a painting or a model, is produced.

Some studies have shown that children are less involved in the play that develops when an adult is directing, since as the children do not 'own' the experience. With structured play there is often only one way of doing something, for example, completing a puzzle or sorting boxes, and this restricts the way a child can play with a toy. Any pre-structured materials have this effect on play and can limit the child's opportunities to be inventive.

Structured play can be described as the adult teaching the child to play, as the adult may show the child how to do something that the child then develops. An example would be an adult carrying out a structured cooking activity with children, who then role play cooking in the home corner. In this case the adult is giving children the skills and the knowledge they need to play effectively.

ACTIVITY

Watch children playing with structured toys, for example, jigsaw puzzles. Do they try to play with them in different ways? How long is their attention span with toys that offer limited ways to play?

Structured activities, where children play in a guided manner, are valuable learning experiences but it is important that a child is also given the opportunity to play freely. Highly structured timetables do not always allow for free play of the type described above.

Some activities can draw on both structured and free play. One example could be painting. An adult may set up the activity and provide the paints and paper, but may leave children to use the paint how they wish, giving them the opportunity to express their ideas freely. Alternatively, an adult might set up a very structured paint activity where the children are asked to paint something specifically linked to a topic.

THINK ABOUT IT

Are the following activities structured or free? What areas do they develop? Are they holistic?

◆ Skipping

◆ Home corner

◆ Playing ships with cardboard boxes

◆ Marbelling

◆ Clay

◆ Playing on a slide or swing

Can you add others to the list? Is a pattern developing?

How can adults help to extend play opportunities?

Free play draws on all the experiences children have had, whether happy, painful or frightening. However, although the child is very much in charge with free play, this does not mean that a child should be left to play without any support from an adult. Children like adults to help keep their play going. With appropriate involvement, adults can make play experiences much richer for children. Adults need to learn the skill of developing a child's free play without taking over.

For example, children may be playing in the home corner with dolls, pretending they are ill. An adult could help extend this play by suggesting they pretend to visit the doctor. The play experience would then be extended as one child will need to pretend to be the doctor; the children will develop language skills as they explain the problem to the doctor, and so the play continues. Without such a suggestion, the play could have ended as soon as the children's attention span was exceeded.

It is important to remember that it is not the quality of the adult's ideas that is important – adults may find that children do not take up an idea. The skill lies in being able to extend the play in the way children want it to go. Therefore the language used to support the play is crucial.

It is important that adults do support free play, otherwise a child may associate the adult only with work-related activities. This can send the message that free play is not as important as structured play, and this undermines the whole experience for the child. Equally, adults should not tell children that they have to finish their adult-led work before they can play, as this also suggests that free play is less important.

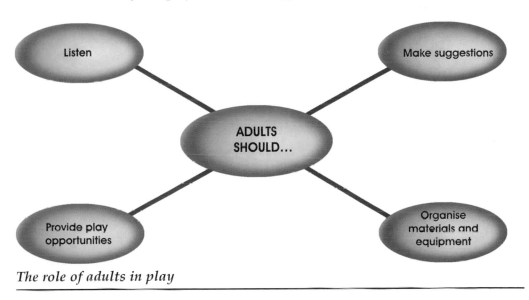

The role of adults in play

Characteristics of play

Whatever definition is used, play has certain characteristics. In the 1980s a psychologist called Burghardt studied the play of animals and noted a list of characteristics. These are common features in all play, although not all features may appear in every play activity.

Burghardt's characteristics of play

- It is common in children.
- There is no obvious, immediate reason for the activity.
- It is chosen by the child.
- It is spontaneous and voluntary.
- It is a pleasurable activity for the child.
- There is a relaxed atmosphere; there is no fear or threat.
- It has no sequence.
- It relies on a stimulus to sustain the activity.
- It involves some active engagement and can be quick and require bursts of energy.
- It may involve the mastery of movements.

THINK ABOUT IT

What early games or play can you remember from your childhood? Jot down your memories on a piece of paper. Compare your memories to those of another student – how would you describe the similarities and differences?

Discuss your findings with the rest of the group – is there a pattern to the memories?

Development through play

Play is the main way in which children learn, and therefore play affects all aspects of a child's development. The spider diagram on page 7 outlines how play contributes to a child's development.

Cognitive development

Through play, children develop an understanding of concepts. They are able to explore different materials such as wet and dry sand, experiment in different ways and solve problems. This exploration begins with the young baby playing with his or her fingers and toes, and continues as the child is able to grasp objects and explore them with the mouth in a more controlled manner. Children will experiment with objects that they can move or make a sound with, and so start to understand cause and effect.

Play helps children to group or categorise objects according to different criteria. Through creative activities, they develop an understanding of shape, colour and form.

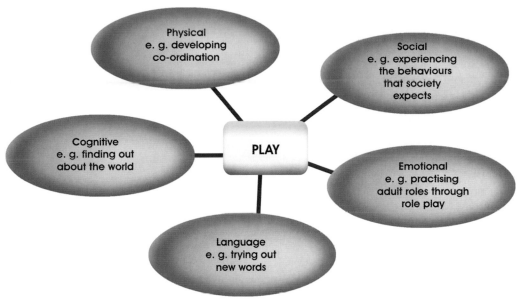

How play contributes to a child's development

CASE STUDY:

In Carousel Nursery, children aged four to five years are given a basket of differently shaped, brightly coloured wooden blocks to play with. How might the nursery staff help the children to develop their understanding of concepts such as shape and form through their use of the wooden blocks in play?

Language development

With each new area of play and each fresh activity or toy, a new set of words will be needed to describe the play that is taking place. Play is a very powerful tool for developing language, particularly as much play in later childhood is based on social relationships and language will be needed to develop and sustain these. All forms of play allow a child to practise language, and role play in particular allows children to try out new words and sentence structures. Adults have an important role to play in extending children's language through introducing new words into the play situation.

Children learn the language for problem solving by asking why, how and what as they explore. The adult can encourage this by answering a child's questions and encouraging further questioning.

As children get older they will use language to explain what they are doing and their intentions for their play. They will use language skills to negotiate with other children. From six or seven years, children use language to explain the rules of their games and ensure that players keep to the rules.

Physical development

Play can develop co-ordination and control of bodily movements as there are often opportunities to run, jump, skip and hop, which develop muscle tone and balance. Catching and throwing help to develop gross and fine motor skills. Physical activities also develop confidence in a child.

Emotional development

Play is often useful as a vent for a child's emotions, both positive and negative. For example, an angry child can let anger out on his or her toys rather than other children or adults, and through this will learn to control anger constructively. Equally, a child may show love and affection through role play.

Quiet activities may prove an effective outlet for a child who needs time and space to be alone.

Social development

Children will learn to interact with others through play. Play situations such as the nursery or playgroup will also help them develop the skills necessary for relating effectively to both adults and children – they will learn social skills such as sharing and taking turns. They will become aware of the feelings of others and begin to be able to take those feelings into account.

Stages of play

The characteristics of play change as different stages of development are reached. All children go through these stages, and although they are linked to ages, children develop at a different pace and some may take longer to go through a particular stage. Also, some children may need greater adult support in order to move from one stage to another. Much will depend on the child's experience; a child from a large family may find it easy to play co-operatively with other children in a nursery situation, whereas an only child may find settling in more difficult. The table on page 9 shows the main stages of play.

The stages are not necessarily separated – a child who is able to play with other children may also like to play alone at times. This means that older children will need opportunities to play by themselves as well as in pairs and groups.

Children who have communication difficulties, such as delayed language development or a sensory impairment, may find it difficult to form social relationships. They may become introverted or aggressive and attention seeking. They are likely to play in a solitary, spectator or parallel fashion for longer, as other children will find it difficult to play with them. Adults have an important role in helping such children to develop the social skills necessary for joining in and in encouraging other children to include them in their play.

Stage	Age	Explanation
Solitary	0–2 years	Children play alone. There is little interaction with other children.
Spectator	2–2½ years	Children watch other children playing around them but do not join in.
Parallel	2½–3 years	Children play alongside others but do not play together.
Associative	3–4 years	Children begin to interact with others in their play and there may be fleeting co-operation between children in play. Children start to develop friendships and the preference for playing with certain other children. Play is usually in mixed sex groups.
Co-operative	4 years +	Children play together with shared goals for their play. Play can be quite complicated and children are supportive towards others in their play. As they reach primary school age, play is usually in single sex groups.

Types of play and their value

Play can take many different shapes and forms. It can include activities intended to be serious learning experiences for children that they find very enjoyable. Play can be classified into four main types, as shown in the table below.

Play type	Examples of materials and resources
Imaginative play	Dressing-up clothes, Playmobil, farm animals, tea sets
Construction	Brio, Duplo, foam blocks, jigsaws, stickle bricks, popoids
Creative play (incorporating play with natural materials)	Clay, paint, play dough, sink modelling, collage, sand, water
Physical play	Slides, hoops, tricycles, balls, skipping ropes

For a fuller discussion of the different types of play, see Section 3. Good quality play provision begins with providing activities to stimulate all the areas of development in the table.

Imaginative play

Imaginative play includes pretend, fantasy and symbolic play; it is sometimes referred to as role play.

- Through imaginative or **pretend** play, children practise and come to terms with different aspects of daily life. You often see young children playing 'schools', acting out the experiences they have encountered. Role reversal is also common in imaginative play – for example, a girl may pretend to be the dad in a game of mums and dads. Children often like to use dressing-up clothes as part of their imaginative play – these are wonderful props and allow children to extend their play.
- **Fantasy** play is common between the ages of three and eight, as children pretend to be something such as a dinosaur or a superhero. This play decreases as reasoning increases.
- **Symbolic** play happens when children use an object in their play but pretend it is something else, for example, pretending buttons are money. Symbolic play becomes role play when a number of objects are used together. For example, children may put chairs in a row and pretend they are in an aeroplane, and use a piece of paper as a ticket or passport. As children play they may explain each symbol.

In symbolic play, children make ordinary objects such as biscuit tins symbolise other things (a drinking cup)

Imaginative play develops self-expression as well as giving children the opportunity to explore their experiences. Children solve problems through imaginative play as they act out things that have happened or could happen. Imaginative play also helps children to see things from others' points of view. It develops social skills, as children often play together for such activities, and fine and gross motor skills – for example, dressing up will require children to use fine manipulative skills, whereas running around as a superhero will help develop co-ordination and balance.

Construction

This type of play can use a range of materials including Brio, bricks and train sets. There is usually an end product but for young children this is not the most important thing as they are more interested in the process of what they are doing and often do not have an end product in mind. Young children will often not decide 'what it is' until well into the work. Older children are more concerned with the end product and will often set out to make a particular thing. Some older children find it difficult to work constructively without knowing what end product they are aiming to produce – they cannot get started until they have a clear idea in mind.

Constructive and manipulative play is suitable for all stages of play. It can be an individual activity such as jigsaws, an activity for children to do alongside each other (in parallel) such as building with bricks, or done in groups such as a large floor puzzle (co-operatively). Children can become fully engrossed in an activity and this strong concentration should not be broken as it disrupts their train of thought and reduces potential satisfaction. It is important that there is adequate time to complete an activity once started.

In this type of play, the adult should offer suggestions and encourage children to complete their task. Adults can develop a child's language skills by encouraging the child to talk about what he or she is doing.

Creative play

Creative play covers a wide range of activities from art and craft work such as drawing and painting to self-expression through music and dance. Like manipulative play, such activities can be carried out alone or as part of a group. A lot of learning takes place through creative play – children learn about the properties of materials, for example, the difference between wet and dry paper. They see and create pictures, patterns, shapes and symbols.

If a wide range of materials are provided, children can learn about different colours and textures. Shiny paper, fabrics with different textures and natural products such as wood chipping or dried leaves are all suitable. Adults can help children produce creative ideas through other activities, stories, outings, or visits from people in the community.

Creative play offers the opportunity for children to develop fine manipulative skills because of the precise nature of many of the movements involved in activities such as painting and colouring. It allows children to experiment and

Children can be encouraged to talk about the feel of clay and describe how its shape is changing as they manipulate it

make discoveries, for example, through colour mixing. It provides children with the opportunity to make decisions for themselves, such as where to start drawing on a page or what colour to use. The end result may not mean anything to an adult, but this is not important.

Work produced during creative activities can also give adults an indication of a child's stage of development; drawing is one area where children develop through similar stages. The results of creative activity can also reveal that a child is upset or distressed.

Adults should not attempt to make a child's creative work seem more acceptable to adult eyes. They should avoid interfering and making statements such as 'if you put this here it will look more like a ship'. This can lead to a child becoming dependent on the adult for ideas, and reduce a child's creativity if he or she is fearful about failing to produce something acceptable to adults. It is important that adults praise children for their attempts and make them feel proud of their work. Work should be displayed without being altered, but by using the skills of display an adult can present the work effectively.

Physical play

Physical play covers many different activities, which can be indoor or outdoor. It can involve the use of equipment like climbing frames, balls or hoops, but may use no equipment at all.

Children enjoy climbing, crawling, jumping and balancing, either in natural environments such as woods or on manufactured large equipment such as climbing frames and tunnels. Not only are such activities healthy, as they encourage children to eat and sleep well, but they also develop self-confidence and physical competence. Physical play develops both fine and gross motor skills as well as muscle control – for example, in a toddler learning to ride a tricycle. It gives children more spatial awareness, offers them challenges and develops the ability to take risks. Outdoor play often involves others so develops skills of co-operation. Physical play can include an element of imaginative play, such as pretending to go shopping.

Physical play is often more suited to the outdoors rather than the indoors because of the space required. Many homes do not have large gardens with space to provide children with swings, slides or a large space for running around. This opportunity can be offered through playgroups and nurseries or at local playgrounds.

It is important to provide opportunities for physical play that are not too challenging for children but not so easy that they quickly become bored. Young children like to be adventurous and climb, but they may need an adult to hold their hand and give extra support as they gain confidence.

Too often, adults supervising outdoor play do so from a distance and

do not become involved with the play. Closer attention would allow the adult to anticipate the next stage of development and make suitable provision for it while ensuring a safe and secure environment is maintained. Adults must ensure that children do not hurt each other during rough and tumble play, and that equipment is safe and well maintained.

Physical play can help build children's self-confidence

Issues in play

Some issues connected with children's play cause much controversy. For example, should children be allowed to play with guns? Is watching television a type of play? What about computers?

Television

Television provides children with second-hand experiences, and while it can be educational in terms of the information it gives, it cannot provide the same quality as real experience. Watching animals on television is not the same experience as going to a farm, seeing the live animals and being able to feed or touch them. This first-hand experience gives children the vivid impressions and the information needed to extend the ideas they incorporate into their play – whether it is a creative activity such as painting, imaginative play such as role playing a visit to the farm, or physical play such as pretending to be a horse.

However, all children need quiet times in their day, so a period of quietly watching a suitable television programme or video can have its place in a play programme. But the time spent watching television should be limited and it should be complemented by active play.

THINK ABOUT IT

What are your views on television for children?

Computers

All schools now have computers, as do many homes and early years settings. More and more information is stored on computer systems and it is becoming an increasingly common method of communication, through email and the Internet. It is important, therefore, that children become familiar with computers and feel at ease with them.

A computer offers children the opportunity to play and learn. Numerous packages are available for children of all ages, which can help children develop confidence with ICT equipment. Many are fun, easy to use and stimulating. Some are interactive and offer reinforcements such as music when an answer is correct, or verbal comments such as 'well done'. Children thrive on this reinforcement and it encourages them to continue. Children also get quite excited when they receive email, and it encourages them to want to use the equipment.

Advantages of using computers

- Children can learn about all aspects of the curriculum through the computer.

- Children can progress at their own pace.

- A game or activity can be repeated as many times as a child wishes, until he or she is ready to go on to the next game or activity.

- Computer activities can challenge children – they can help children work out the right answers to difficult questions or give hints to help them solve problems.

- Many computer games do not have 'dead-ends' that discourage a child. If a child is finding the game difficult, the program will interpret the child's needs and help him or her to progress.

- Children can play on their own or with the support and help of an adult.

- Interactive programs encourage and reassure children.

- Good graphics help to keep a child's attention.

- Children can become familiar with computers and how they are used.

Disadvantages of using computers

- Children can become computer addicts, spending long periods of time at computer games.

- Many of the games available for computers are not particularly educational.

- It is a sedentary activity and children need regular exercise.

It is clear that computers are going to play an important role in the future, so it is important that adults working with children are familiar with computers and effective in helping children to use them.

Guns and war toys

Many adults believe that children should be discouraged from playing with toy guns and other weapons, or warlike games, as they are linked with aggressive behaviour. In playing with such toys, children are encouraged to focus their play on hurting others. Research has shown that watching violence or aggression on film or TV can lead to increased physical aggression or fighting in play. As a result most nurseries and playgroups will not accept toy weapons as part of their equipment. But many children, particularly boys, enjoy play that involves guns, swords, laser blasters or even sticks. If these are not available, they will make them out of Lego!

Geoff Goldstein carried out some research into aggressive play and war toys in 1992. He found that it is often difficult to characterise what is classed as a 'war toy' and 'aggressive behaviour' – practitioners often have levels of disagreement on this. Children appeared to be aware of the differences between real fighting and play fighting. There was also no evidence that playing war games as a child led to long lasting effects in terms of increased aggression, violence or delinquency.

Interestingly, while making war toys available seemed to stimulate the imagination of boys and provoke more fantasy play, it did not have the same effect on girls. This would suggest that the reaction to these toys cannot be just a result of the toys themselves.

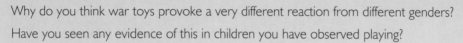

THINK ABOUT IT

Why do you think war toys provoke a very different reaction from different genders?

Have you seen any evidence of this in children you have observed playing?

Chapter 2   History and theory of play

Today we recognise the importance of play in a child's development, but this has not always been the case. Attitudes towards children, their role in the family and their needs have changed over the years. These issues have affected the provision of play. Many of the theories that underpin practice in childcare settings today reflect the development of changing approaches over the past 200 years. It is important that childcare professionals understand these theories, as they will help in meeting the needs of children in their care.

History of play

Various theorists have offered accounts of the origins, functions and pattern of play. The attitudes of society and images of childhood have influenced the care and activities provided for children through the ages.

Until the 1800s, children were largely regarded as small adults and no special provision was made for them. Babies used to be swaddled in close-fitting garments to prevent too much movement. Children had to work to contribute to family income from a young age. Once laws were passed limiting child labour, the average number of children per family went down, as children became a burden rather than an asset.

Jean-Jacques Rousseau (1712–1778), a French philosopher, was revolutionary in his call for children to be allowed to roam freely. Rousseau was probably the first thinker to identify the importance of play. He believed in free play and through his book *Emile* he advocated allowing children to explore freely in their early years and to make discoveries for themselves without constraints. He believed that to learn effectively, a child needed to be isolated from others. He suggested that play and work are all one for children until the age of 10 or 12 years. However, despite his efforts, Rousseau was unable to convince eighteenth-century society of the need for play.

Play became more important in the late-1800s when industrialisation reduced the need for intensive labour and resulted in an increase in

In the nineteenth century children had to work from a young age

leisure time for everyone. Employment laws placed restrictions on children working, and this gave them more freedom than they had ever had before. Nevertheless, society still regarded play and leisure as abnormal activities and work as normal. To make play an acceptable activity, the Victorians focused on play with a purpose, as it was felt that free time should be used for self-improvement.

Rousseau's work influenced other theorists such as Maria Montessori and Friedrich Froebel, although they tended to promote structured rather than free play.

Other early theorists developed some interesting ideas about play. G. Stanley Hall (1844–1924) observed children playing and saw that their play behaviour changed with age. He saw children's play as a reflection of the process of evolution and suggested that through play, children were re-enacting the transitions of the species. He called this the **recapitulation** theory.

Another early theory was the **surplus energy** theory put forward by Herbert Spencer (1820–1903). He observed the boisterous nature of play and suggested that play was the mechanism through which the child expelled the excess or surplus energy that built up as part of a normal, healthy nervous system. He suggested that since this energy was not required for survival purposes such as hunting, play was its outlet.

In 1901 Karl Groos developed the **instinctive preparation** theory, proposing that a child is born with the instinctive ability to play. Groos's view was that play allowed the child to practise the skills needed in adulthood. He believed children would practise these skills without guidance from adults, and suggested that if they didn't have the opportunity to play, the result would be a lack of intellectual progress. When young children are involved in imaginative or fantasy play, they can be heard playing mothers and fathers or pretending to go to work, shopping or on holiday. According to Groos's theory, children are mimicking or acting out the roles and activities of adults as they see them, in order to practise the required skills.

Early theories on play have now been updated or changed but nevertheless had an important influence on the main pioneers of play theory. All theorists have agreed that care and education should be linked and not separately provided. Below, the theories of those who have been the most influential in the UK are described; many of them were born in other countries and developed their theories outside the UK.

Modern theories of play

Friedrich Froebel (1782–1852)

Friedrich Froebel was born in Germany in 1782. His mother died when he was nine months old and he was brought up by an uncle who sent him to school. At this school he learnt about the natural world as well as studying maths and languages. This experience influenced his approach to teaching children – he believed that all children are born good and that to help them develop, adults need to provide the right environment and activities. These protect the child from learning bad habits or 'evil tendencies'.

Froebel worked with three to seven year olds and opened the first kindergarten (literally, garden for children) in Prussia in 1837. This idea spread across the world.

Main ideas and theories

- Children can learn outdoors with other children as well as indoors.
- Outdoor activities should be used to encourage an interest in natural science.
- Children should be able to move around freely.
- Symbolic and imaginative play (such as children pretending that some counters in a pot are food and they are making breakfast) is important and shows high levels of learning.
- Froebel gave items to children to play with, calling them 'gifts'. He would often demonstrate opposites through these gifts, such as a hard and a soft ball, as he felt these developed awareness of concepts.
- He felt that relationships, feelings and being part of a community were important to children's development.

Influences on today's practices

All of Froebel's ideas are reflected in today's approach to childcare and education. Some important ones include:

- the common use of finger rhymes (a concept invented by Froebel) such as 'Round and round the garden, like a teddy bear', as a valuable part of learning from babyhood

- the use of songs to teach children, such as 'One, two, three, four, five, once I caught a fish alive'

- education often designed to be 'child centred', with the needs of the child central to the activities provided

- emphasis on children experiencing things and discovering for themselves.

Free play is often developed from Froebel's idea of 'gifts'. Free play is also covered in Chapter 1, page 3.

Maria Montessori (1869–1952)

Maria Montessori, who was born in Italy in 1869, trained as a doctor and worked as an assistant in a psychiatric clinic for children with learning difficulties. From this, and her experience as the head of a state institute for the education of such children, Montessori formed her own ideas about early childhood education. She felt that children under the age of six years have the most powerful and receptive minds and that this gives them a once-in-a-lifetime opportunity to learn. The Montessori method encourages children to learn about the world around them through exploration. They are given the freedom to move around, manipulate and touch. She developed a number of 'educational toys' and activities to support this process. The equipment and activities were designed to help a child acquire skills, competence and confidence.

Montessori also placed much emphasis on the development of social skills, and these took precedence over early reading and writing. Her methods have been used in thousands of schools around the world.

A Montessori teacher never interferes with play or corrects a child. The teacher assesses a child and presents a suitable piece of equipment. If the child is able to use it correctly, it has been presented at the right time, but if the child is not yet ready to use it, the teacher will put the equipment away for another day. The child is never made to feel inferior or a failure.

Main ideas and theories

- Children pass through particular developmental stages. This is essential for the child to be able to learn.

- Montessori developed a structured education programme based on these stages, including a number of specially devised pieces of equipment that encourage children to develop certain skills. She called these 'didactic' materials – didactic means 'intended to instruct'. They are designed to minimise error, so children can teach themselves in a non-competitive atmosphere.

- Limited emphasis is placed on counting, reading and writing – these will follow once the basic social and emotional development has taken place.

- A child's natural will to learn should be encouraged, to foster a life-long motivation for learning.

- Children should be encouraged to work alone. Montessori felt the best learning occurred when children were focused, silent and completely absorbed in a task.

- Montessori did not believe in free play and did not encourage children to develop their own ideas – play needed to have a learning focus.

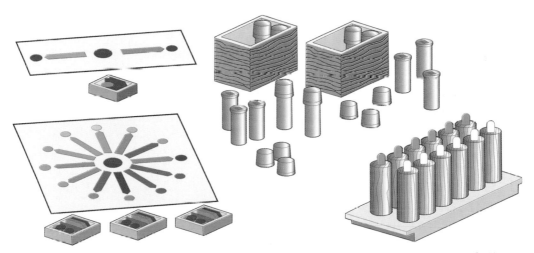

This type of equipment is used in Montessori schools to develop specific skills and concepts

Influences on today's practices

There are many Montessori schools throughout Europe, usually privately run. However, the Montessori approach has also influenced state education, and a teacher with Montessori training is well regarded.

The method promotes a carefully planned environment that neither allows children total freedom nor imposes activities on them. Some nurseries follow the Montessori method completely, while others purchase Montessori equipment and use aspects of her theories within a more flexible programme.

Space inside nurseries is often divided into four areas – practical life, sensorial, mathematical and language areas. Children are encouraged to work alone on tasks as part of the nursery programme.

Rudolph Steiner (1861–1925)

Steiner was born in Austria in 1861. His ideas about teaching young children are known as the Waldorf education system. For Steiner, childhood was a separate period of life and his methods aimed to develop all aspects of the child – the curriculum he designed aimed to provide equal experience of the arts and sciences. Imaginative play, often with natural materials, is central to the Waldorf scheme, and manufactured toys are excluded. Children are free to choose whether to play together or alone.

Steiner placed much emphasis on relationships and the community – children in Steiner schools often stay with the same teacher for the whole of their primary education, and the teacher also gets to know the family well through home visits. The teacher has an important task as a role model for the children, and should encourage a child to think imaginatively through songs, games or activities such as cooking or painting. The teacher also makes up or retells stories, rather than reading from a book, as a way to encourage a child to think. Through close observation of the child, a teacher can decide what material a child might need next.

Steiner felt children should be educated in a happy and joyful atmosphere and not taught about the dangers or less pleasant aspects of society.

Main ideas and theories

Steiner suggested that there were three phases of childhood:

- 0–7 years – the will: the spirit fuses with the body
- 7–14 years – the heart: feelings are important in this phase where the heart, chest and respiratory system beat together
- 14 years+ – the head: the period for thinking.

Steiner believed in reincarnation and that during the early years the child is finding his or her way in the world so needs protection and a carefully planned environment during this time.

Children have different temperaments, which affect their attitudes and behaviour. Steiner believed adults should work with these temperaments, which were classified as:

- sanguine (cheerful and confident)
- choleric (bad tempered)

- phlegmatic (stoic, unemotional)

- melancholic (irritable).

Steiner believed that communities were very important. He felt that brighter children should be encouraged to support their weaker peers. Sessions often start with circle time and all children are encouraged to join in. When, for example, a song is sung many times, this helps the brighter children support the slower ones.

Influence on today's practices

Steiner schools today are privately run and tend to attract many overseas students. However, some of Steiner's theories have influenced the work of both state and privately run settings for early years provision.

Steiner's ideas for circle time, where children of all abilities join in and children wait until others have had a turn, are widely used. More able children are often grouped with slower ones to encourage children to support their peers.

In the education of children with special needs, Steiner's ideas can be seen where there is an element of integration with mainstream children. It is believed that this has a positive effect on the education of children with special needs, because they are cared about and encouraged by their peers.

Margaret McMillan (1860–1931)

McMillan, who was born in New York in 1860 but educated in Scotland, initially designed her approach to the curriculum around toys that developed a child's fine and gross motor skills and manual dexterity – much along the lines of the Montessori method. However, as her ideas developed, she incorporated more of Froebel's theories and gave increasing importance to children experiencing things themselves at first hand. Relationships and emotions were regarded as of equal importance to physical movement. Because play is the way in which children apply what they know and understand, McMillan regarded free play as important.

McMillan introduced the concept of the nursery school. She saw this as an extension to the home and placed great importance on working closely with parents. She even offered classes to parents so that they could develop new skills and learn along with their children.

The outdoor environment was as important as the indoor one to McMillan and she recognised that children could learn a lot from the natural environment. She started the first open-air nursery school in Peckham, London 1914.

One of McMillan's main messages was that children cannot learn effectively if they are hungry, cold or ill – these physical needs have to be satisfied if learning is to take place. She therefore promoted the importance of school meals and medical services for all children.

Main ideas and theories

The main points of McMillan's theories include:

- the development of manual dexterity exercises
- first-hand experience supports learning – free play with opportunities to use various materials offers good learning opportunities
- relationships and feelings are important
- play helps a child apply learning and become a 'whole person'
- good health in terms of diet, housing and physical condition is essential to effective learning
- training for staff is important.

Influences on today's practices

Child centred education offered in many early years settings reflects McMillan's ideas. Today, there is strong emphasis on involving the parent in early years education, and the use of the keyworker scheme in many settings reflects the idea that the nursery is an extension of the home, with one main carer. Also, patterns of care that occur in the home are replicated as far as possible, so as not to confuse a child.

Provision of free school meals and medical services reflect McMillan's emphasis on the importance of good health and nutrition if children are to learn effectively.

ACTIVITY

Visit an outdoor play area in a local nursery or playgroup. Investigate how the play area offers opportunities for:

- discovering nature – flowers, trees, insects
- running around
- climbing.

Susan Isaacs (1885–1948)

Susan Isaacs, a British early education pioneer born in 1885, followed the ideas of Froebel and felt that play gave children the opportunity to think, develop their feelings and learn social skills. Children begin to understand the world in which they live through their play, as it allows them to move from reality into fantasy.

Isaacs felt children needed the space to move and should not be stuck behind desks all the time. This freedom, she believed, allows children to develop an interest in the world around them, and through this the desire to learn. Children need to be encouraged to express their feelings as keeping them bottled up can be damaging.

Like McMillan, Isaacs recognised the important role of parents in the education of young children and promoted an understanding of how to support children through magazine articles and radio talks. Isaacs also felt that the nursery should be an extension of the home. She believed that children should remain in the nursery setting until the age of seven years, as this allows them to develop in the most appropriate environment.

Main ideas and theories

Susan Isaacs believed that:

- play gives children the chance to think and come to terms with feelings and relationships

- classrooms should not force children to sit at tables – children need to be able to move to learn

- parents are important educators

- children need to express their feelings and not bottle them up, as this can interfere with learning

- children should remain in the nursery until the age of seven years – Isaacs' research showed that children often regressed when starting school at the age of five.

Influence on today's practices

In accordance with these theories, some nurseries do not have large areas of formal tables and activities are laid out so that children are able to move freely and choose what they do. However, this is not always the case and some early years settings do have children sitting at formal desks from as young as $2^1/_2$ years.

Parents are now seen as the central adults in a child's life and the ones who know the child best. Modern research has also shown that children do seem to regress on leaving nursery and entering school, but it is still laid down by UK law that children must attend school by the term in which they reach their fifth birthday.

THINK ABOUT IT

Think about the early years education provision in your area. Can you identify in it any of the features mentioned above in the theories of Froebel, Montessori, Steiner, McMillan or Isaacs?

Note which aspects in particular you feel you have seen on placement.

Is there any important aspect you feel you have not seen?

Discuss your thoughts with others. Is there a pattern in the childcare provision you have examined?

Susan Isaacs believed that parents are important educators of their children

Twentieth-century ideas on development and play provision

Besides being influenced by the work of the early childcare professionals discussed above, current practice has also been influenced by more recent research. Twentieth-century theorists have often researched specific areas of development and linked these to the pattern of children's learning.

Jean Piaget (1896–1980)

The major contributor to understanding how a child's intellect develops is Jean Piaget, a Swiss psychologist who studied children in depth. Piaget, who based his theories on his studies of his own children, felt that children are actively involved in developing their own knowledge so they can understand the world around them. To help them do this successfully, Piaget felt, they use a number of thinking processes to allow them to adapt to their environment. The development of these thinking processes is called 'cognitive development'.

> **Key issue — What is the difference between cognitive development and intelligence?**
>
> Cognitive development involves mental functions such as the ability to think logically and abstractly, to reason, to understand concepts, to concentrate, to remember and recall information, and to use problem-solving skills.
>
> All these mental functions are linked. They are also linked closely with language development. When all aspects of cognitive development, including language, are put together, this is known as intelligence.

Schemas

Piaget believed that children develop a number of patterns of behaviour or actions, which they then apply to similar situations. This helps them categorise things into manageable and understandable groups.

Children develop patterns for many different things. For example, a child may always drink from a bottle with a teat. When presented with a beaker with a spout, the child will need to learn that drinks can come from beakers as well, and will amend the pattern of understanding to accommodate this new information. Piaget called these patterns '**schemas**'. As the child grows older, the schema for drinking vessels will be amended to include glasses, cups and mugs.

As children develop, they add more complex schemas to their thinking. Piaget believed that the progression from very simple thinking in early childhood to the more complex thinking of adolescence is achieved through three basic processes, as described below.

1 Assimilation

Assimilation means taking in and understanding new information. The amount of new information a child can assimilate will depend on the level of understanding the child already has. To be assimilated, new information needs to connect to or attach to something a person already knows. For example, a child may have a Collie dog as a pet and think that all dogs are like Collies. The child may then see another species of dog, such as a Doberman. The child will label this 'a dog' and add it to his or her schema on dogs, thereby understanding that dogs can be different shapes and sizes.

It is thought that one of the reasons babies sleep so much is that their brains need to assimilate all the new information they are taking in from the world around them.

2 Accommodation

Accommodation occurs when a child takes in new information that causes a change to an existing schema. An example might be that, to a child who always has juice in a plastic green beaker, all green beakers give juice. If the child is then given water from a plastic green beaker, he or she will accommodate the new information that plastic green beakers do not always provide juice.

3 Equilibration

Equilibration occurs when all pieces of information fit into the schemas that a child has developed. Conversely, disequilibration occurs when the pieces do not link up. Piaget thought this might occur when a child moves from one developmental stage to another, as major reorganisation of schemas occurs. A child may have to abandon an idea because it no longer fits and take another on board.

Influences on today's practice

Chris Athey has developed Piaget's idea of schemas much further and applied the concept to the observation of children's play. Her ideas also give an indication of how adults can support and guide children's play.

Athey described play behaviour as 'enveloping'. She suggested that children have a favourite way of exploring the world at any one time and this approach is repeated in their activities and their actions. For example, a child who is absorbed by 'transporting' may move objects from one place to another while he or she explores them.

There are different schemas which a child may display such as:

- rotation: a child is interested in things that turn and explores objects through spinning or turning

- orientation: a child explores objects by looking at them from another angle, for example, upside down

- connection: a child is fascinated with how things join together and explores objects and ideas by bringing them together.

THINK ABOUT IT

Observe children at play. Can you see any examples of schemas? Jot down the types of repetitive patterns you notice and discuss them with others in your group.

Stages of development

Through his observations, Piaget saw that children make similar mistakes at similar ages. He suggested that a child passes through four stages of development, which are roughly age related.

Piaget believed that these four stages are sequential, which means that a child has to pass through each one in order. Piaget did not believe it was possible to teach a child in one stage about concepts from a more advanced stage. Therefore, activities developed for different age groups should reflect the children's stage of development.

1 Sensori-motor stage (0–18 months)

Piaget thought babies learn about their world through the senses and their physical activity. The baby uses schemas which have been developed using trial and error methods. An example of this is the way that babies explore objects using their mouths. During this phase babies are learning to control their movements and so play involves repeating and varying movements as they acquire more control. Babies also enjoy being able to make things happen and observing cause and effect – you will often see a baby interested in a baby gym because of the repetition that is possible.

A baby will think that something has gone if he or she cannot actually see it – babies do not understand **object permanence**. For example, if when playing ball with a baby you hide the ball under a cloth, the baby will think the ball has gone.

Babies and toddlers in this phase are extremely **egocentric**, which means that they can only see things from their own point of view.

2 Pre-operational stage (18 months–7 years)

During this phase the child uses symbols to represent experiences. Piaget noticed that children would begin to pretend within their play and use objects to represent something else, for example, using a broom as a horse.

At the pre-operational stage, memory begins to develop and a child will mention absent people and things. Children come to understand the concepts of past and future during this phase. They will also try to share knowledge and experiences.

Children at this state are still egocentric – Piaget showed how a child of this age was unable to put himself in someone else's shoes.

Children are still influenced by the appearance of objects. For example, Piaget talks of **conservation**. A child who understands conservation will know that, no matter what shape something is made into, unless it is added to or something is taken away, the amount remains the same. Piaget demonstrated that when a pre-operational child is shown the same number of buttons but presented differently, the appearance influences the child's answer as to whether there are more or fewer buttons. If the experimenter lines up two sets of five buttons equally, then lengthens one line in front of the child, a child who is unable to conserve will say that the longer line contains more buttons.

Piaget showed that this pattern occurs with other concepts besides number. For example, in other experiments two identical glasses were filled with water and one was then poured into a taller, thinner glass; in another, two equal balls of dough or plasticine were shown to a child before one was moulded into a different shape. A young child will believe that the quantities differ according to appearances.

ACTIVITY

Try one of the conservation exercises explained with a number of children of different ages. Record your findings. How do they compare with those of Piaget?

3 Concrete operational stage (7–12 years)

From the age of 7 years, children begin to understand concepts such as conservation and can use mathematical skills such as addition, subtraction and multiplication. A child of this age can understand that things may belong to more than one category and that categories have logical relationships. For example, a child will be able to categorise dogs and cats but also realise that dogs and cats both belong to the category of pets.

Piaget believed that children begin to develop inductive logic during this phase, which means that they can link their own experience to general principles. For example, a child may know that if you add one car to a line of cars and count them, there will be one more than before, so the general principle is that addition always increases something. At this stage children deal best with things they can see or manipulate, and are less successful in discussing abstract ideas or possibilities.

CASE STUDY:

Annie, aged six years, was given four sweets. There were only two left for James, aged four. James made a fuss because Annie had more so she offered to give him one of her sweets so that they each would have three. James still insisted that Annie had more than him, and that he wanted four sweets.

Annie is able to see that after sharing the sweets, both children have the same number and it is fair.

James is unable to apply this logic.

Which stage is each child in, and why?

4 Formal operations stage (12 years–adulthood)

By this stage children are able to deal with abstract concepts and relate experiences to others of which they have no first-hand knowledge. They can imagine themselves in different situations and roles. They can apply deductive logic to solve problems, which means they can think through similar experiences they have had in the past and apply them to an unfamiliar situation.

Children also become aware of abstract ideas, such as fair play. Abstract ideas are theoretical and cannot be physically demonstrated. This is the stage that most adults are in, but it is worth remembering that some people do not reach this stage of development, for example, if they have learning difficulties. It is also true to say that people can have well-developed formal operational thinking in one area of life but not in another in which they are less skilled.

Why is Piaget important?

Piaget's work formed the basis on which many modern researchers have built their ideas. Piaget's work has been criticised for a variety of reasons, but particularly because researchers have since proved that children reach the stages at earlier ages. However, his work is still valued and seen as a breakthrough in the way we understand how children think and learn.

Other theorists

Lev Vygotsky (1896–1935)

Vygotsky was a Russian theorist whose ideas have had great influence since the 1990s. Vygotsky thought that play helps children to understand and accommodate what they have learnt because they are free from any constraints when they play and can explore ideas fully. He believed play allowed children to move from their present stage of thinking to a higher level.

Vygotsky also thought that the role of the adult was important. He believed adults could stretch children so that they further developed ideas and thinking through their play. As well as being aware of a child's current stage of development, Vygotsky looked at what a child could do in the next stage. He called this the 'zone of potential development' and focused play experiences on this.

Jerome Bruner (1915–)

Like Piaget and other early educators, Bruner believed that children needed to be able to move freely and be actively involved in their learning. First-hand experience allows children to develop their ideas and thinking. He called this 'enactive thinking'.

Bruner showed that children often need to be reminded of previous experiences. This may be through pictures, books or interest tables. He called this 'iconic thinking'.

He also felt the role of the adult was important. Adults provide support as children develop their competence and confidence. The adult has an important role in setting up experiences for the child, and in judging what the child needs next in order to develop cognitively. The support from the adult would be reduced as the child gains in confidence.

Play and social and emotional development
Sigmund Freud (1856–1939)

Freud was a psychoanalyst whose work in the 1920s has helped play professionals to understand the role of play in social and emotional development. Freud thought children pass through different stages as they develop and that this is reflected in their play. He believed that every child has subconscious forces shaping his or her personality. These are described below.

- **The id:** Freud thought the id exists from birth, and everything a child does in the id stage is to ensure survival. Children try to get immediate satisfaction for their wants and are therefore demanding and illogical. They are not aware of how their demands might affect others. Freud thought that children in this state were interested only in things which provide pleasure. He called this the 'pleasure principle'. A child in the id phase might want a biscuit but his carer may be busy washing up. The child would demand the biscuit, and if he didn't get it straight away, might get frustrated.

- **The ego:** Between the ages of 1 and 2 years, the id is still guiding the child but the child has learnt to use language to satisfy his or her demands. Adults may not give in to all a child's demands and this can make the id frustrated, but a child will soon learn that this will be a waste of energy. At this stage, a more logical and rational aspect of the personality appears. Freud called this the ego. Freud believed the ego was much more aware of how things function in the world. The ego draws on memories and past experiences in its approach to problem solving. With the appearance of the ego a child will see the importance of negotiation and discussion as a means of getting his or her demands met. A child in the ego phase who wants a biscuit might ask the carer if he or she could have a biscuit after the carer's task is finished. The child has recognised that negotiation is the best way to satisfy his or her needs.

- **The superego:** This is a more a advanced part of the personality. It helps a child know what is right and wrong, and what he or she can and cannot do. The superego tries to make sure that the ego does not make unacceptable demands in order to satisfy the id. The child who is hungry but realises that the carer is not going to meet the demand for a biscuit straight away may think about climbing on a chair and helping him- or herself. The superego would tell the child that this is wrong and it is better to wait. If the child waits, he or she will avoid any punishment that may happen if the child helps him- or herself. The id wants the hunger satisfied; the ego can see it can do this by helping itself; but the superego will judge the appropriateness of the behaviour required to fulfil the demand.

Freud called the knowledge of right or wrong the conscience. He called the part of the personality that guides the child into what he or she should do the **ego ideal**. As an individual matures, the ego has to satisfy the id without upsetting the superego. There are often clashes between the three aspects of the personality – when this happens, a person will feel guilty.

THINK ABOUT IT

Jot down something you have done that made you feel guilty.

What need or want were you trying to satisfy by what you did? This is the id.

How did you satisfy it? This is the ego meeting the demands of the id.

How should you have satisfied the need or want? This would have been clear to the superego.

The id wants the hunger satisfied; the ego can see it can do this by helping itself; the superego can see that this method is wrong

Like many theorists, Freud thought children went through a series of developmental stages. He suggested that as children develop, different parts of their bodies become particularly sensitive. He called these areas **erogenous zones**. He also believed that if children's needs were not satisfied at each stage, they may become fixated or stuck at that stage and not move on. He believed that many habits that occur in adults are a direct result of needs being under- or over-satisfied in an earlier developmental stage.

Age and stage	Erogenous zone	Behaviour and habits	Achievements
Oral: 0–1 year	Mouth	Puts everything into the mouth Satisfaction of the id	Weaning
Anal: 1–2 years	Anus	Ability to control the bowels and bladder The ego starts to influence the satisfaction of the id	Toilet training
Phallic: 2–6 years	Phallus	Pleasure is experienced by playing with the genitals Child is attached to the parent of the opposite sex – the Oedipus and Electra complexes Superego begins to affect how the ego satisfies the id	Child comes to terms with the Oedipus and Electra complexes
Latency: 6–11 years	None	No specific development in this stage Loss of interest in the opposite sex Competition between the id, ego and superego in the child's attempts to satisfy needs	None
Genital: 11+ years	Genitals	Increasing interest in sexual behaviour	Positive relationships with both males and females

Freud's theories of development

Freud's ideas are often disregarded today but he pioneered psychological understanding of child development. He was ahead of his time in many ways, and his ideas are still referred to when trying to understand children's behaviour.

Erik Erikson (1902–1994)

Erikson was a supporter of Freud and based his work on Freud's theories. He was particularly interested in how the demands of society and culture affect a child's development, especially that of the superego. For example, in British culture it is felt that a child should be toilet trained by the age of $2^{1}/_{2}$ years. This is reflected in the expected development of a child of that age and the child's ego is boosted by achieving it. Erikson called these stages 'psychosocial stages of development'.

Age	Aspect of personality developed	Common characteristics of the stage
0–1 year	Basic trust versus basic mistrust	Developing attachment and trust in parents, guardians and main carers. This trust will help a child develop relationships later in life. Children who have not been able to develop trust at this stage have difficulty forming deep and lasting relationships later in life.
2–3 years	Independence versus self-doubt	Developing the skills of doing things on their own without having failures constantly highlighted – this would make a child nervous about trying anything new for fear of failure.
4–5 years	Initiative versus guilt	Constantly trying new things. Children may try out their own ideas or use their initiative in order to solve problems and achieve goals. If children are told off for trying out their own ideas, they may feel guilty and not do so as often.
6–12 years	Competency versus inferiority	Society expects a child to have certain skills such as maths, writing and reading. During this stage, children are trying to meet those demands and if they do not, they will feel they have not reached the required standard.

Erikson's theory of psychosocial stages of development

D. W. Winnicott (1896–1971)

Winnicott's work focused on how young children feel when they are separated from people they relate to closely. He showed how important it is for some children to have comfort objects such as teddies or blankets when they are in situations they are unsure about, for example, going to a new playgroup or nursery for the first time. He called these comforters 'transitional objects'. They help a child feel secure and settled until he or she is back in a familiar place or with a familiar person. In the past, some childcare professionals have not encouraged children to have comfort objects and have even taken them away.

THINK ABOUT IT

Do you still have any comforters?

Make a list of different comforters a child and an adult may have.

Do you think it is necessary to take comforters away from children?

Recent thinking

Reggio approach

The Reggio approach hit the headlines in 1991 although it had been around since 1945. Interest in the approach was sparked by the fact that Newsweek named one of its schools, the Diana School in Reggio Emilia, Italy, as one of the top ten schools in the world.

The approach was inspired by the ideas of many of the early educators and has a philosophy of parental and community involvement coupled with democratic rights, duties and responsibilities.

It has a number of key philosophies. These are:

- *Image of the child*: Teachers of this approach see children as having potential, strength, power and competence. They have the capacity to develop their own ideas and test these with other children and adults. This is how they best learn.

- *Relationships and time*: A mutually supportive relationship is fostered between staff and children and they value each other's opinions and views. There is an emphasis on adults and children learning together. The approach also believes in the effective use of time and that the day should be divided to allow time for all aspects of development including reflecting, debating, eating, sleeping, sharing and just being.

- *Teaching, learning and documentation*: There is no set curriculum with the Reggio approach. The children learn through projects that may be long- or short-term but give them first-hand experience and theories on which they base their learning. Projects may come from the children themselves or from the adults, and together they will discuss where to take a particular project next. Projects are fully documented with photos and records to help this process. All ideas are valued so children feel their ideas are respected. This creates an environment where children are not afraid to make mistakes. In these schools, staff work in pairs supported by a pedagogist who helps structure the next stage of learning the teachers will undertake with the children. Each school also has a practising artist or *atelierista* whose role is to stimulate and nurture curiosity. They are charged with creating waves and moving thinking forward. The key role of the adult is to interfere as little as possible with the children's work but to observe, support and facilitate the work of the children.

- *Reflective practice*: Staff constantly review their work and this enhances understanding of how children learn.

- *Learning environment*: The learning environment is designed to give an impression of space and light. Classrooms come off a central meeting place and the dining room is seen as the heart of the school, which reflects the importance of preparing and sharing food in the Italian culture. The approach sees the environment as the 'third teacher'. Each school has a creativity and discovery area called 'atelier' where extended projects are carried out and investigative skills developed.

While the approach has been inspired by many early educators, it is difficult to transpose the approach into a different culture. However, many aspects have been adapted to make them relevant to the UK.

Play provision in the UK since 1940

Despite the influence of the early theorists discussed in Chapter 2 and their views on how children should be educated, the UK has not been a leader in early childhood provision. In the UK the issue has been influenced by attitudes towards the role of women. Until the Second World War, it was considered that the best place for a young child was in the home. Children from the wealthiest families were brought up and educated by staff such as nannies and governesses. It was not the norm for a woman to work full-time outside the home if she had children.

However, the role of women has changed since 1940. Changing attitudes after the Second World War occurred alongside changes in the structure of the population that resulted in a smaller labour force – and it is now necessary for women to be economically active. A number of Acts of Parliament since the Second World War have laid the groundwork for these changes.

The legal framework

1944 Education Act

Despite the efforts of practitioners such as Margaret McMillan and Susan Isaacs, the government did not acknowledge the value of education for children younger than five years of age until the 1944 Education Act. This Act stated that local authorities should provide nursery education. However, this did not happen as the local authorities devoted their resources to carrying out the requirements for school-aged children (5–15 years). No local authority was challenged on its failure to meet the requirement to provide some early years facilities. Nevertheless, there continued to be a series of reports highlighting the value of nursery education throughout the 1960s and 1970s.

The Plowden Report (1967)

This was the first report that was significant for early years education. It identified Educational Priority Areas and highlighted the value of nursery education for children from these areas and its part in improving their achievement in primary school.

Framework for Expansion (1970)

This White Paper was presented by Margaret Thatcher, the then Secretary of State for Education. It promised an increase in nursery places to accommodate 50 per cent of three year olds and 90 per cent of four year olds by 1980. Unfortunately, the recession of the 1980s prevented this from happening.

Current position

Despite lip service being paid to the value of education for early years children, little has been done to ensure comprehensive provision. Studies such as that of Jowett and Sylva (1986) show that children who attend nurseries staffed by qualified teachers, rather than playgroups, respond better to the demands of school. Nevertheless, until recently, government policy has been to leave provision largely to the private and voluntary sectors.

In 1990, the obligation for local authorities to provide nursery facilities was reduced to an optional power to do so if they wished. As recently as 1991, the idea that mothers should be solely responsible for their early years children was reiterated by a government minister who stated that if a woman wanted to return to work, it was her responsibility to find childcare.

The government has tried to encourage employers to make some provision for care of employees' children, but except for a few leading employers, there has not been a great deal of response. One reason for this has been that free childcare was treated as a perk and employees had to pay tax on its value. This made the option less attractive and, in some cases, more expensive than arranging childcare personally. However, attitudes are changing. The government is now putting resources into a National Childcare Strategy with the aim of ensuring provision of good quality early years and after-school facilities and making childcare more affordable via the working families' tax credit.

Key issue – The National Childcare Strategy

A leading element in the National Childcare Strategy focuses on getting mothers back to work by ensuring the availability of good quality before- and after-school clubs and homework clubs for 5–15 year olds. The government is providing funding to support such developments.

These services will be provided through schools as well as extending the services already offered by nurseries, playgroups, after-school clubs and other day care.

How national policies influence the provision of care and education in early years settings

National policies are produced by central government. Central government sets taxes and determines what is spent on areas such as education and health. The government is divided into different departments. The department responsible for education is the Department for Education and Science (DfES). This department is responsible for all aspects of education.

Many laws and Acts of Parliament have influenced the provision of early years care and education. One of the most important was the Children Act 1989.

The Children Act 1989

This Act of Parliament resulted in a number of changes in the way young children were cared for and protected. It covered care in the home including issues around parenthood and arrangements that were put into place if parents separated. It also covered services provided outside the home, for example, child protection care.

The Children Act 2004

The Children Act 2004 established a new Children's Commissioner for England whose role is to raise awareness of issues relating to children and young people and report annually to Parliament, through the Secretary of State, on his or her findings. The role is to look at how both public and private bodies listen to children and report on improvements. It also calls for co-operation between key agencies to improve children's well-being. It places a duty on people working with children and young people to have systems in place that ensure they safeguard and promote the well-being of children through their work. It also calls for a basic database to hold information on children to help co-ordinate joined-up work between different agencies.

Local Authorities are required to have a Director of Children's Services, who brings together Education and Social Services.

Did you know?
- Wales has had a Children's Commissioner since 2001. This was the first Children's Commissioner to be appointed in the UK.
- Northern Ireland also has a Children's Commissioner who was appointed following legislation passed in 2003 – The Commissioner for Children and Young People (Northern Ireland) Order.
- Scotland's first Children's Commissioner was appointed in 2004.

Every Child Matters – What's Next?

Every Child Matters: Change for Children outlines how the Children Act 2004 will be implemented. It covers all children, from birth to the age of 19 years. Through the National Service Framework for Children, Young People and Maternity Services (NSF), which is an integral part of the programme, the government aims to support parents from pregnancy onwards. The vision is to create a joined-up system of health, family support, childcare and education services so that all children get the best possible start in the vital early years. It is a shared programme of change to improve outcomes for all children and young people. It takes forward the government's vision of radical reform for children, young people and families.

Children and young people identified five outcomes that are key to well-being in childhood and later life: being healthy, staying safe, enjoying and achieving, making a positive contribution and achieving economic well-being. This programme aims to improve those outcomes for all children and to close the gap in outcomes between the disadvantaged and their peers.

Between 2004 and 2014 the government's aim is to offer parents greater help with childcare, which will often be located conveniently in schools and/or provided in partnership with the voluntary and private sector.

The DfES Five-Year Strategy for Children and Learners set an expectation that primary schools should, over time, offer childcare between 8.00am and 6.00pm, 48 weeks per year. This builds on the extended school programme and could be arranged by groups or clusters of schools.

Key concept – Education Action Zones

These are designated areas identified by the government as areas of significant deprivation. The aim is to put additional support into children both in schools and in the family setting to raise aspirations and educational success.

Birth to Three Matters

This is a framework to support children in their earliest years. The guidance provides information on child development, effective practice, planning and resources and how to meet diverse needs. It is aimed at supporting practitioners in their work. This initiative establishes the importance of the development of the youngest child and the role the adult has in this.

Sure Start

Sure Start is a government programme that aims to achieve better outcomes for parents, children and communities by increasing the availability of childcare for all children, improving health and emotional development for young children and supporting parents to achieve their aims for employment. The programme focuses specifically on disadvantaged areas and provides financial support to help parents afford childcare. More information on Sure Start can be found at www.surestart.gov.uk.

Current childcare provision

Current provision can be divided into the following types:

- **Statutory provision** is that which is required by law, and organised and run by local authorities. This includes state-run nurseries, which are usually attached to primary schools and currently provide term-time nursery classes for the year before a child enters reception class.

- **Voluntary provision** is organised by non-profit-making organisations where they feel there is a gap in provision. It is usually funded by grants, public fundraising and personal contributions, and can be staffed by volunteers or paid staff. An example is a church-run parent and toddler group.

- **Private provision** is run for profit as a business. The owner of the facility will see childcare provision as a business opportunity and the main aim will be to make money from providing the service.

The table on pages 43–44 describes the options available, together with their advantages and disadvantages.

Many parents make their choice of childcare based on what they can afford. The opportunity to attend early years education in the UK often depends on the parent's ability to pay, unlike in many other European countries. This has meant that more children in other parts of Europe attend some form of early years care for longer than children in the UK.

ACTIVITY

Consider two children in your workplace who have different patterns of attendance. Give reasons why you think their parents have chosen this instead of a different type of provision.

Type of provision	Age range	Length of provision	Staffing	What is it?	Advantages	Disadvantages
Local authority nursery school (statutory)	3½–4½ years	Often half days, term time only	Qualified teacher plus nursery nurse	Often linked to primary/infant school. Limited availability, often situated in priority areas. Ratios of 1 qualified teacher to 25 children.	Good preparation for school. Develops independence. Encourages social skills. Activities provided are carefully planned to develop the skills of the child.	Does not fit the needs of working parents. High child–staff ratio.
Local authority day nursery (statutory)	3 mths–5 years	Full day care	Qualified staff	Run by social services. Open for the working day most days of the year. Parents may pay fees on a sliding scale.	Meets the needs of working parents. Often linked to a local authority workplace.	
Private nursery (private)	3 mths–5 years	Full day care	Supervisor/manager must be trained to level 3 and 50% of staff must hold a childcare qualification	Fee paying.	High child–staff ratio. Develops independence and social skills. Prepares the child for the routine of school.	Expensive. Higher staff ratios can result in children finding it difficult to adapt to the lower ratios in schools. Some staff may not be qualified.
Playgroups (voluntary and privately run)	2½–4 years	Sessional care	Supervisor and deputy must be trained	Often run by committee. Do not have large budgets and often rely on fundraising. Lower fees than nursery.	Valuable in the development of social skills. Develops links within a neighbourhood between the parents/carers of young children.	May rely on untrained staff/parent help to meet ratio requirements. Often in premises not built to meet the needs of children. Mainly sessions, which may not meet the needs of working parents.
Childminders (private)	Up to school age	Day care in carer's own home	No formal qualifications needed	Childminders must register with the local authority. Childminders often do this job because it fits in with the requirements of their own family.	Can build a relationship which will continue through the early school years. Meets needs of working parents.	Parents have to take the child out of the home for care. Will not always provide the same play opportunities and stimulation that a nursery may provide.

(Continued)

Type of provision	Age range	Length of provision	Staffing	What is it?	Advantages	Disadvantages
Nannies (private)	Any age	Full-time care in the child's own home. Can be daytime only or both night and day.	No stipulated qualifications but often BTEC/NNEB are expected	Care in the child's own home that meets the needs of the parents.	Children remain in their own home. More individual attention can be provided.	Expensive. Parents may not be sure what the nanny is doing during the day.
After-school provision	5–15 years	Sessions 8.00–9.00am and 3.00–6.00pm	Qualified staff – playworkers who are specifically trained for working with 5–15 year olds	Provides care for school-age children at the beginning and end of the day to enable parents to work. Fees are charged although there may be some subsidy through the National Childcare Strategy.	Provides regular care at each end of the school day. Generally reasonably priced. Children are often taken to and collected from school. Can include a homework club.	After a day at school, many children prefer to go back to their own homes.
Holiday playschemes	5–15 years	All day	Qualified staff	Most parents who work full-time do not get school holidays and holiday clubs meet this need.	Organised provision for children during their holidays.	
Crèches (private or voluntary run)	Any age	Sessional	More popular in recent years in shopping centres and other places where care is needed for short periods of time.	Short care that frees the parent to carry out certain tasks such as shopping.	Located in appropriate areas.	Child does not know the carer and a relationship is difficult to build. Because the care provided is usually for under two hours, the provision does not come within the regulations of the Children Act.

The different types of childcare currently available

What are the benefits of pre-school education?

The Effective Provision of Pre-School Education project (EPPE) looked at the effect of pre-school education and care on a child's development between the ages of three and seven years. The longitudinal project collected data from 3,000 children from three years of age until the end of Key Stage 1. The research included data on their developmental profiles, family background, the home learning environment and the pre-school settings attended by each child. The research also included comparing children who did not attend any pre-school ('home' children) with the pre-school group when they started school. The project also looked at the characteristics of effective practice in early years settings through case studies of settings where children had made good progress.

The main findings of the project in relation to the pre-school years were catagorised into three sections, as follows:

1 Impact of attending pre-school

- Pre-school enhances all-round development in children when compared to those who did not have any pre-school education.

- An early start, before the age of three years is linked to better intellectual development.

- Full-time attendance provided better gains for children than part-time provision.

- Children from disadvantaged backgrounds benefit greatly from quality pre-school education.

2 Effects of quality and specific practices in pre-schools

- High quality pre-schooling is linked to better intellectual and social development for children.

- In settings where staff have higher qualifications, the children achieve higher quality scores and make more progress.

- Key quality indicators include warm interactive relationships between staff and children, having a trained teacher as manager, and a good proportion of trained teachers as staff.

3 Importance of home learning

It is the quality of the home learning that is most important for intellectual and social development, not the parental occupation, levels of education or income. The factor that influences achievement the most is the range and quality of the experiences the parent provides for the child, such as taking time to read with the child including visiting the library, singing nursery rhymes and songs together and providing children with stimulating experiences such as visits. Such experiences build a love of literacy in a child.

At the end of Key Stage 1, the key findings were:

- The beneficial effects of attending pre-school remained evident in children's performance throughout Key Stage 1, although some outcomes did not continue to be as strong as at school entry.

- The number of months a child attended pre-school had a positive effect on their academic progress throughout Key Stage 1.

- The quality of the pre-school experience was reflected in children's scores on standardised tests of reading and mathematics at age six years. However, by seven years the relationship was somewhat weaker although still evident.

- The effect of the quality of home learning activities continued to be evident in children's developmental profiles at the end of Key Stage 1.

The project identified a number of key characteristics of early years settings in which children made significant progress. These were:

- high quality adult–child verbal interactions

- a balance between staff and children of who initiates the activities

- high levels of knowledge of the early years curriculum

- high levels of understanding by staff of how children learn

- well qualified staff who support children effectively in their learning

- high levels of parental involvement

- children being encouraged to work through conflicts.

In conclusion, the project clearly showed that the longer a child attends good quality pre-school education, the greater the intellectual gains on entry to school. It also showed that for optimum progress, a child should start pre-school education between the ages of two and three years. This was linked with better social skills.

Early years education in other parts of Europe

Provision of early years education varies across other parts of Europe, but it has been available for more children for much longer than in the UK. The table below outlines provision in some of the other European countries.

Country	Age compulsory schooling starts	3–4 year olds in state provision	Details of provision
France	6 years	99%	State-provided nursery education is available, free of charge, from the age of 2 years. This education is called the 'Ecole Maternelle', and all children from the age of 4 years attend. Remaining places are given to parents of 3 year olds who wish to use them, and in some areas places are available for children as young as 2 years. Studies of this system have shown that children who attend the Ecole Maternelle, particularly under the age of 3 years, are less likely to fail at school. Children attend four and a half days per week, for six hours a day on Monday, Tuesday, Thursday and Friday, and on Saturday morning. They are taught by qualified teachers who have the same status, salary, and duties as teachers in a French primary school. The teacher–pupil ratio is approximately 1–28 and there is usually one classroom assistant per class. Children are grouped according to ages and they follow a curriculum which covers four broad areas of experience: physical activities; communication; artistic and aesthetic activities; and scientific and technological activities.
Belgium	6 years	98%	From 2½ years, children may attend nursery schools and classes. The school day runs from 8.30 am until 3.30 pm but many offer care from 7.00 am until 6.00 pm to accommodate working parents. The out of hours care has to be paid for. Staff must have the Diploma in Nursery School Teaching (a three-year, post-school course). However, the pay for a nursery school teacher is lower than for that of other teachers.

(Continued)

Country	Age compulsory schooling starts	3–4 year olds in state provision	Details of provision
Italy	6 years	91%	The state-run pre-primary system is available for all children from 3 years. This school is called the 'scuole materne'. Schools vary in their opening times, from 4 hours per day over six days to 10 hours per day over five days. Children are usually grouped according to ages in classes of 15–30. In 1991 the state introduced guidelines for the work of these schools. They divided activities into 'fields of experience': the body and motor skills; language and literacy; space, order and measure; objects, time and nature; messages, shapes and the media; and self and others. Planning is seen as being extremely important and the work that goes on in the classroom must fit the whole school plan. Teachers are specially qualified to teach this age group.
Spain	6 years	74%	The early years stage is divided into two cycles, 0–3 and 3–6 years. The Spanish Ministry for Education and Science outlines three areas to be covered: communication and representation; discovery of the physical and social medium; and identity and personal independence.
Sweden	6 years	68%	'Forskola' or early years provision takes a number of forms, including day-care centres for children of working parents as well as part-time groups. It includes an open early years session for children without any other early years experience, where parents accompany the children. Family day care includes state-employed childminders for children under 12 years. For day care, the children are divided according to age. The aim is to develop the whole child by fostering learning via work and play. The areas of experience are called nature, culture and society. Nursery nurses account for 50% of staff and 45% are trained. The remaining 5% have no specialist training.

Early years education provision in some European countries

Comparisons between the UK and other European countries

In the UK children start formal education earlier than in many other European countries, but these countries have more early years state provision and it is commonly accepted that children will attend early years facilities, full-time, from an early age.

Many of the ideas on early years education that are current in the UK reflect practice and guidelines that have been in place in countries such as France for a number of years.

Current government policy aims to increase childcare provision, particularly day-care and after-school clubs. One idea has been to staff these by training unemployed people in childcare. This has been pioneered in Belgium, but there were some concerns in Belgium that training unemployed people for jobs in childcare would lower the status of a very important and responsible job.

THINK ABOUT IT

What do you think are the advantages and disadvantages of these proposals?

Early Learning Goals and Desirable Learning Outcomes

The current approach to the curriculum reflects the way many other European countries organise their curriculum. *Desirable Learning Outcomes*, a major government document published in 1996, set out minimum goals for children's learning and takes on many European ideas. These goals set out what ministers felt a child should be able to do on entering compulsory education at five years of age. They specified a curriculum on which early years childcare providers needed to base their work whether they were voluntary, statutory or private providers.

Why were Desirable Learning Outcomes introduced?

In January 1996, the Conservative government launched the Desirable Learning Outcomes. The document was developed by the School Curriculum and Assessment Authority (SCAA), which is now part of the Qualifications and Curriculum Authority (QCA). It specifies a clear set of learning outcomes covering six areas of learning that children should be able to achieve on entering compulsory education, which starts in the term after a child's fifth birthday. Ofsted, the Office for Standards in Education, checks that providers have an appropriate curriculum to meet the demands of the Desirable Learning Outcomes and that children are being given a sound preparation for the National Curriculum, which starts with Key Stage 1 (Years 1 and 2, ages 5–7 years).

The National Curriculum is divided into four key stages for children aged 5–16 years. It sets out the areas of study in ten curriculum areas and the knowledge and skills that must be covered in each. Like the Desirable Learning Outcomes, it leaves the method of delivery to the teacher and school. The curriculum areas are divided into core and foundation subjects. Core subjects are English, maths and science. Foundation subjects are design and technology, physical education, art, history, geography, music and information technology. Achievement in each of the areas can be measured at eight levels. At the end of Key Stage 1, most children in that phase will perform at level 2, with a few achieving either level 3 or level 1. Teachers often use level 1 as a measure of where children should be at the end of the first year in Key Stage 1.

In developing the curriculum proposals, particular attention was paid to early literacy and numeracy, as the foundations for success are laid at an early stage. The emphasis on these skills is strengthened by the National Literacy and Numeracy Hours in primary schools.

The Foundation Stage

In 1999 the Desirable Learning Outcomes were reviewed by QCA and a draft proposal was sent to providers and interested parties for consultation. The consultation document proposed retaining the six areas of learning but looked at extending the early years curriculum to the end of the reception year when most children are five years old, thus creating a foundation stage for children aged 3–5 years.

The Foundation Stage was introduced as a distinct phase of education for children aged 3–5 years in September 2000. It sets out six areas of learning which form the basis of the Foundation Stage curriculum. These areas are:

- personal, social and emotional development
- communication, language and literacy
- mathematical development
- knowledge and understanding of the world
- physical development
- creative development.

Each area of learning has a set of related Early Learning Goals. The curriculum is designed to help practitioners plan to meet the diverse needs of all children so that most will achieve and some, where appropriate, will go beyond the Early Learning Goals by the end of the Foundation Stage. Personal, social and emotional development is like a thread running through all the other areas of learning.

The Education Act 2002 extended the National Curriculum to include the Foundation Stage. The six areas of learning became statutory, and the Act also specified that there should be Early Learning Goals for each of the areas.

The Act also established a single national assessment system for the Foundation Stage, replacing baseline assessment schemes. The Foundation Stage Profile was introduced into schools and settings in 2002–3. The Profile has 13 summary scales covering the six areas of learning, which need to be completed for each child receiving government-funded education by the end of their time in the Foundation Stage.

Under each of the six areas of learning, there are goals that children will be working towards. The goals are called Early Learning Goals and it is hoped that most children will be achieving these goals at the end of the Foundation Stage (reception year).

It is important to note that the Foundation Stage only applies to England as Wales, Scotland and Northern Ireland all have their own early years curricula (see pages 60–1).

The aim of the Early Learning Goals

The main aim of the Early learning Goals is to provide targets for learning by the time children complete the reception class. As all children develop at different rates, individual achievement will vary. Not all children will fully achieve the outcomes by the time they start school, and some will achieve beyond the minimum requirements. 'Extension statements' are provided for each area to show how older or more able children might progress beyond the goals. Some special needs children may continue to work towards the outcomes throughout their time in education.

Many early years providers already go beyond the minimum requirements, and they did so before Desirable Learning Outcomes or Early Learning Goals came into existence.

Good practice in implementing the Early Learning Goals

Although the Early Learning Goals do not prescribe activities, guidelines are provided which identify good practice in planning how to deliver the outcomes.

- The setting should develop an environment in which children feel secure, valued and confident and can achieve through a learning experience that is enjoyable and rewarding.
- Personal, social and emotional development should be an essential part of the curriculum and run through all the activities in the setting.
- The curriculum, the approach the setting uses, and methods of assessment and recording should be fully understood by staff in the setting. They should also be explained clearly to the parents and the schools to which the children will progress.
- The activities and curriculum provided should encourage children to think and talk about their learning, and should recognise the value of first-hand experiences as a means of learning. For example, a visit to a local farm will provide opportunities for discussion and for different activities such as painting and collage.

Children learn a lot from hands-on experiences

- Adults should recognise when it is appropriate to give help and the level of support that is needed. They should interfere only if absolutely necessary. This helps children to develop independence.

- There should be opportunities for concentrated involvement in an activity over longer periods of time.

- Progress and achievement should be regularly recorded through accurate observations. This information should be shared with parents.

- If a child is identified as having particular needs, appropriate support and intervention should be provided. For example, a child with learning difficulties may be provided with some extra one-to-one help.

- Adults in the setting should recognise the importance of training and be active in identifying and meeting their training needs.

Early Learning Goals identify six areas of learning to be included in the curriculum. Five of these are:

- language and literacy

- mathematics

- knowledge and understanding of the world

- physical development

- creative development.

THINK ABOUT IT

Look at each of the features of good practice described above. Compare them to the ideas of the early educators discussed in Chapter 2 (pages 17–19). Can you identify the influences of those ideas in the current curriculum?

A sixth area is personal, social and emotional development. This is like a thread running through all other areas of learning.

Early years providers have to devise a curriculum that covers all the six areas of learning. Within these areas, spiritual, social, moral and cultural issues must also be covered. Together they provide the foundation for the subjects at Key Stage 1. For details on how to provide opportunities for learning in the six 'areas of experience' in curriculum plans, see Section 3.

Many activities will cover a number of the outcomes. An example is given below.

ME

Description of the activity

Children are asked to bring in a photograph of themselves doing something, for example, on holiday or at a party. The children are asked to talk about their photograph within a small group.

Purpose of the activity

Through talking about photographs showing themselves, children are encouraged to speak about their families and past events in their lives.

Preparation for the activity

Children should be prepared for the activity by talking about their families and things they do together.

Links to the Early Learning Goals

Personal, social and emotional development:

◆ continue to be interested, excited and motivated to learn

◆ be confident to try new activities, initiate ideas and speak in a familiar group

◆ respond to significant experiences, showing a range of feelings when appropriate.

Language and literacy:

◆ enjoy listening to and using spoken and written language, and readily turn to it in their play and learning

◆ use talk to organise, sequence and clarify thinking, ideas, feelings and events

◆ sustain attentive listening, responding to what they have heard by relevant comments, questions or actions.

Knowledge and understanding of the world:

◆ find out about past and present events in their lives, and in those of their families and other people they know.

Working with parents

It is widely known that children's experiences at home and the support they receive there have a significant impact on their learning and achievements. The documents on the Foundation Stage and the Early Learning Goals emphasise the importance of settings working with parents to support children's learning. It has been shown that where parents and adults in the care and education setting work together, there are measurable and long-lasting positive effects on achievement. Therefore partnerships should be developed as fully as possible.

A successful relationship will allow a flow of information in both directions. Suggestions for helping to build effective and supportive relationships are as follows.

- Staff must be aware of the important role parents play in the education of the child and develop an open relationship based on mutual respect.

- Staff must recognise the important role parents have already played in the development of the child to date and appreciate that continued involvement is crucial to the child's success.

- Staff should develop a setting where parents are welcomed and can contribute to the work should they so wish.

- Parents should be invited into the setting at regular intervals such as open evenings, meetings to discuss the curriculum, social events and parents' evenings.

- There should be a recognition of the needs of parents whose first language is not English, with provision of information in different languages, interpreters or other ways to improve communication.

- Parents should be kept fully informed of their child's progress. This can cover both physical and intellectual development. Many nurseries provide a daily record of food eaten, activities done and rest taken.

- Children new to a care setting must be given adequate time to settle in. Parents should also be given time to ensure they feel happy and secure about the arrangement.

- Where possible, activities that take place in the setting, such as the reading of books, should be continued and reinforced at home.

Parents who are kept involved will show more interest in what their child is doing. A child will see that importance is placed on his or her experiences and strive to do well.

Planning the curriculum

Any curriculum in settings for the rising fives (children due to start school) must contain a full range of opportunities, activities and experiences to cover the learning goals. This requires detailed and thorough planning. Any plan must identify not only what the children should learn but also how they will learn it.

In order to ensure the children have opportunities to meet the Early Learning Goals, planning needs to be on various levels. There will need to be long-term, broad planning across the year; medium planning over a term; and short-term, more detailed planning on a day-to-day basis. Only planning on this level will ensure that the children have a well-thought-out curriculum and that the Early Learning Goals are met in full. For more details on how to plan an Early Years curriculum, see Section 2.

Collecting evidence of children's learning

One of the aims of the Early Learning Goals is the assessment of children as they enter school. Staff working with children are required to make a judgement on their skills and competence in relation to each of the six areas of learning. Assessments must be based on evidence, which can be collected in a number of ways, including:

- conversations between staff and children and between the children themselves

- observations carried out by staff

- assessment of the work children have produced

- conversations with parents.

Staff should be well trained and have a good knowledge of child development so that they know what they are looking for in children's work. Observations require tremendous skill. Staff need to know how to observe objectively and be able to interpret what they see. Poor interpretation, perhaps due to a lack of detailed understanding of child development, can mean important issues being missed.

Observations require the skills of objectivity and correct interpretation

Brightlands Day Nursery
107 St. Georges Road
Cheltenham
Gloucestershire
GL50 3ED

Tel: 01242 230938

Progress Report To Parents

Child's name: Alexander	Date: 7th December

On behalf of all the staff at Brightlands Day Nursery

Areas of Learning	
Personal and Social Development	**Knowledge and Understanding of the World**
Experiences: i.e. toileting, personal hygiene, putting on coats Alexander is a popular child at nursery. He is able to mix with children of all ages. Alexander is able to go to the toilet on his own, and understands that he has to wash his hands after going to the toilet. Alexander is also beginning to put his coat on by himself without any help.	*Experiences: i.e. sand, water, trips out* Alexander likes going for walks. He is aware of the environment surrounding him and is very well behaved. He also loves playing in the sand and water. He gets very involved in both of these activities. He enjoys socialising with his friends during this time.
Language and Literacy	**Physical Development**
Experiences: i.e. books, stories, singing Alexander enjoys looking at books and listening to stories. He has now begun to sing on his own but prefers to do this in a small group. Alexander is very good at his Letterland. When Alexander is looking at books he likes to tell his own story from looking at the pictures. He has a good imagination.	*Experiences: i.e. outside toys* Alexander is an energetic child who loves to play outside. He likes to run around a lot letting off some energy in a fun way. He really enjoys playing football with the other children and enjoys playing on the toys provided.
Mathematics	**Creative Development**
Experiences: i.e. construction toys, games, threading Alexander is good with his numbers but prefers to play number games with blocks or Duplo. He does, however, love to build new models with these materials. Alexander also enjoys threading, modelling and making new creations with the beads. He sometimes loses concentration easily and can be distracted if something else is going on in the room.	*Experiences: i.e. painting, colouring, collage, playdough* Alexander loves doing creative play, especially painting or junk modelling. He likes to take great care over his painting and colouring and is always pleased with his achievements. When Alexander is colouring he shows good imaginative skills, and he holds a pencil well.

A progress report to parents showing that staff have carefully observed and assessed the child

It is important to recognise that a child's performance in one activity is not necessarily a reliable guide to competence. It is more valuable to collect evidence over time, as this will give a clearer indication of both achievement and development. Therefore, staff need to observe and assess the children constantly. It is also important to use a combination of evidence in forming a judgement. For example, a lot more can be gained from talking to a child about a junk model he or she has made than from just looking at the finished product. The discussion of the process and why a child used a certain material or stuck it on in a certain way may show more complex thinking than is apparent from looking at the model.

THINK ABOUT IT

Which outcomes might a child's painting give evidence for?

If you talked to the child who produced it, what other outcomes might it contribute towards?

Remember: The **process** not the **product** is important. Talking to children about their work is an essential part of the assessment process.

The requirement for evidence does present a problem. Keeping large amounts of children's work can cause storage problems, as files or folders showing names and dates will need to be kept. Staff in each setting must decide what evidence, if any, is kept and for how long it needs to be kept.

Foundation Stage Profile

The Foundation Stage Profile replaces the Baseline assessment process which previously took place halfway through a child's first term at school. It is a statutory assessment for children in the final year of the Foundation Stage. The word 'profile' has been carefully chosen – it reflects a new approach to assessment. The Foundation Stage Profile is based on the Early Learning Goals and is a picture of what a child has achieved, knows and can do. The profile is built up over a year; there are no tests and no set tasks. The Foundation Stage Profile uses observations as a means of assessing learning. The Foundation Stage and the *Profile* together support early years staff in providing a broad, motivating curriculum which is linked to clear expectations as set out in the Early Learning Goals.

The Foundation Stage Profile provides:

- information on the child's level of achievement at the end of the reception year
- information to help further planning of learning for that child (diagnostic).

The results of the Foundation Stage Profile not only identify a child's strengths and learning needs, thus allowing teachers to plan an appropriate curriculum, but also represent a point against which a child's progress through Key Stage 1 can be measured. Schools now have to show how they have made a positive contribution to a child's development. This is called the 'value added factor'. For example, a child's knowledge and ability is measured at the end of the year and compared with where the child was at the start of that year – a Foundation Stage Profile provides that benchmark.

The profile would also:

- provide information for parents, which will inform discussions with teachers
- provide teachers with information about the different achievements of children born in different months
- provide teachers with information on achievements of children from different socio-economic groups
- allow schools to be more effective in managing their resources in terms of meeting the needs of the children in their schools.

Implications for early years groups

Early years settings are expected to assess children to show how they are progressing towards the learning goals and achieving in terms of the Foundation Stage Profile. This is monitored through inspections by Ofsted. Planning should show how the activities provided build on these assessments.

Children are not legally required to be in school until the term after their fifth birthday. Even if entry to school before the fifth birthday is possible in their area, some parents choose to keep their children at playgroup or nursery until this date. In some areas, children are not able to start school until then. Therefore, settings will want to carry out an assessment which is passed on to the child's first school.

Many schools welcome information from early years groups whatever the age of entry. It is good practice to assess children's progress to ensure that activities are appropriate and will develop their skills and knowledge.

How are children assessed?

The Foundation Stage Profile is compiled over the year and must be completed four weeks before the end of the reception year. Its design assumes a record of ongoing learning that is completed at intervals throughout the year. The profile presents the goals as a set of 13 assessment scales, each having nine points allocated to them.

The first three points describe a child who is still progressing towards achieving an Early Learning Goal. The next five points are related to the goals themselves and capture whether a child has achieved a goal. They are ordered according to difficulty but that does not prevent a child achieving one of the more difficult goals first. The final point is allocated to a child who has achieved all the goals and developed his or her understanding and skills further in terms of breadth and depth.

An example of a completed profile taken from the Foundation Stage Profile handbook is given below.

Information about the child from a previous setting:

Nursery transition record: Began full time in September. Settled in easily and mixed well with the other children. Photos showed he enjoyed a range of activities. Detailed records of language development on file.

Home visit:

Some anxiety shown about starting school; will miss nursery. Asked about lunch times and if there would be painting. Read the Hungry Caterpillar and talked about insects.

Discussion with child:

Likes coming to school to 'play with his friends'. Enjoys learning about weather. Favourite thing is painting as he feels he is good at that and he likes mixing colours on paper. Dislikes playtime as some of the children are fast and knock into him. Pointed out that he can tie his laces now and he knows more songs and stories.

Discussion with parents (1):

Mum and Dad describe him as a balanced, happy child who enjoys mixing with other children. He is quite sociable and has no difficulty making friends. Likes to be busy doing things. Enjoys active activities. Happy to have a go at anything, e.g. cooking, puzzles, outdoor play.

Can be tearful and unco-operative when very tired. Generally a confident child who copes well with new situations.

Discussion with parents (2):

Appears to have settled into school well. Talks a lot at home about what he is doing and the friend he has made. Seems to be far more inquisitive and asks about everything around him. Confidence continues to develop.

Discussed how he can be challenged in his reading to help him develop. Generally happy with his progress at school this year.

A completed profile from the Foundation Stage Profile handbook

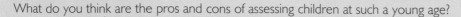

THINK ABOUT IT

What do you think are the pros and cons of assessing children at such a young age?

The profile aims to give a rounded view of the achievements of each child. As the assessment is being used to compare achievements, it is important that it is measured in a consistent and fair way. Practitioners have to be confident that the assessment judgments made of one child are comparable to those made for another. To ensure this is achieved, practitioners work together to moderate their judgments. This may take place within a setting but is also supported by an LEA moderator who will review the judgments made in different settings.

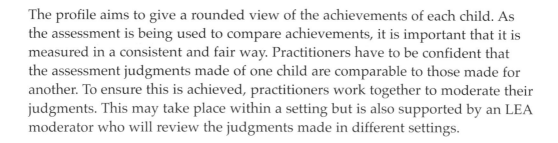

ACTIVITY

How are children in your work placement or setting assessed?

Who is responsible for compiling children's records?

How are parents involved in this process?

Why is it important that records are regularly reviewed and updated?

Early years education in Scotland, Northern Ireland and Wales

Scotland

The Scottish Education Executive Department (SEED) oversees all education in Scotland. Scotland has a flexible approach to the curriculum. There are guidelines for teaching, which are produced by the Learning and Teaching Scotland for SEED, but these are not enforced by law. These guidelines give an outline of what subjects should be covered but do not dictate how or what should be taught. This is left to the individual schools and local authorities.

In Scotland, education is provided free to all three and four year olds. Primary schools cover the ages of 5–12 years.

Compulsory schooling is divided into two age groups: 5–14 years and 14–16 years. Each area of the curriculum in the 5–14 years group is divided into bands from A to F. Children work towards the targets and are assessed by the teachers. Tests are not used to assess levels of attainment but as a confirmation for the teacher of the stage a pupil has reached.

The curriculum is being reviewed at present to develop a curriculum to cover children and young people aged 3–18 years.

Northern Ireland

Northern Ireland has a very complex education system with 10 official bodies involved in the education system. Compulsory education is divided into 4 key stages which reflect the key stages in the British education system. The curriculum in Northern Ireland is set by the Northern Ireland Council for Curriculum, Examinations and Assessments. It is responsible for the assessment of pupils at Key Stages 1 and 2. There is also a requirement for a daily act of worship in all schools although parents have the option of withdrawing children from this if they wish.

Pre-school education is provided in nursery schools and nursery classes attached to primary schools. Northern Ireland has been involved in secular disputes for many years. As a result of this, Northern Ireland has received extra money from the European Union Special Support Programme for Peace and Reconciliation to increase pre-school education. The government's aim is to provide free nursery education for all nursery-aged children.

In the primary stage, pupils are assessed at Key Stages 1 and 2 (ages 7/8 years and 11 years) as in England. As secondary education in Northern Ireland is still selective, the 11+ examination has been retained. Depending on the results of two set tests which children take at 11 years, children are given a place at a grammar or non-grammar secondary school.

Wales

The UK government devolved control over the education system in Wales to Wales when the Welsh Assembly came into being in 1999. The Welsh Assembly Department for Training and Education has full responsibility for all aspects of education in Wales.

Under the National Curriculum, which was established as a result of the Education Reform Act 1988, education in Wales is divided into the four Key Stages as in England.

Pilots of a new Foundation Phase curriculum for 3 to 7 year olds to replace Key Stage 1 have begun in Wales. It is estimated that the Foundation Phase will replace Key Stage 1 in all schools in Wales by 2008.

Children attend pre-school between the ages of 2 and 5 years. Free nursery education is provided for all 4 year olds and an increasing number of 3 year olds through the government's Sure Start scheme. Wales is also developing children's centres, which will bring together early education, childcare and family and health services.

In Wales, all children have to start primary education in the term after their fifth birthday. Primary schools are divided into infants (5–7 years) and juniors (7–11 years). Welsh can be taught as a first and second language from primary school level and may be the only language used in some schools.

Section 2
Planning

Chapter 4   Types of planning

The first section of the book looked at the different theories of play and the major influences on early years provision. This section considers how to **plan** for children's care and education as this is a fundamental skill needed by early years workers in order to carry out their work effectively.

The chapters in this section look in detail at:

- different types of planning

- ways of producing plans

- implementing plans and activities

- the evaluation process.

Planning is an important part of many childcare courses, so specific guidance is included for students and their supervisors. This guidance is aimed at students who need to produce plans as part of their assessed coursework; it can be found in shaded text boxes.

Note: The term 'activities' is used in its broadest sense to include all types of play opportunities and experiences – both structured and unstructured.

Why is planning important?

In many ways good planning is the key to working professionally with children. The first few years of children's lives are the foundation for their future development. It is therefore essential to plan play opportunities and learning experiences in these early years for the benefit of the children's later education and development. Planning is also the key to helping early years workers feel motivated and organised in their work, as simply 'minding' children can be tedious and makes for very unrewarding work. Finally, good planning helps parents feel that their children are in safe hands. It reassures them that they will not only be well cared for but will benefit from being with early years workers.

Routines

Most people have some sort of pattern and order in their lives. They may get up in order to go to work at about the same time each day, and have their lunch break at the same time each day. This pattern or structure is what is meant by a routine.

Routines are important in children's lives as having a familiar pattern to the day helps children to feel secure. Routines form the backdrop to children's care and provide a framework for learning and activities to be added. Planning a routine requires a good understanding of child development, and students on childcare courses need to show that they can devise routines for different age groups and for different settings. A good routine will meet children's needs, allowing them times to eat, rest, play, learn and sleep, while being realistic to follow. Although many settings tend to have a daily routine, some may also develop weekly routines – especially if certain resources or areas are shared or only available at certain times. The routine on page 64 is taken from a nursery that shares some resources and facilities with the primary school to which it is attached.

Flexibility in routines

Routines are important for children. A good routine can help children to feel secure and settled, while still allowing them time to explore, play and learn. But although settings can plan a routine, it is also important that routines are not implemented rigidly as there may be times when this is not appropriate; for example, a routine might include half an hour for lunch, but in reality children may need longer on some days. Routines can also be disrupted because of factors such as a change in the weather, a child not feeling well or a staff member being absent, so it is important that early years workers can be flexible and are able to reassure children.

Devising a routine for children

There are many factors that need to be taken into consideration when planning a routine for children. In general, a good routine should:

- provide a structure and a pattern to children's lives
- give children a sense of security
- meet children's developmental needs – language, social, emotional, etc.
- allow children time when they can explore, play and have fun
- provide opportunities for a range of different learning or play experiences
- give children opportunities to rest and if appropriate sleep
- meet children's hygiene needs

| | Morning children | | | | | Afternoon children | |
	9.15–10.00	10.00–11.00	11.00–11.45	Lunch	12.45–1.30	1.30–2.15	2.15–3.15
Monday		Main hall – movement	Story	Staff meeting		Outdoor play area	Story
Tuesday		10.30 Outdoor play	Story			Main hall – soft play	Story
Wednesday	9.30 Assembly	10.30 Music room	Story			Outdoor play area	2.30 Assembly
Thursday		10.30 Outdoor play	Story	Staff meeting		1.30–2.00 Music room	Story
Friday		Main hall – indoor soft play	Story			Main hall – Movement	Story

A nursery school routine

- meet children's dietary requirements

- provide opportunities for children to spend some time with an adult

- meet parental wishes and requirements

- be flexible and realistic enough to be implemented.

Below is a step-by-step guide to show how a routine might be put together.

Step 1: Identify the children's needs

A good routine must meet children's needs. The first step in devising a routine is to find out as much as possible about the developmental and care needs of the age of children for whom the routine is intended. Parents and other early years workers are often a good source of information along with the 'standard' child development books. Questions to consider include the following.

- How much sleep and rest does this age of child require?

- What are the best times for sleep and rest?

- How many feeds/meals and snacks do children of this age need?

- At what times do the children usually have their meals?

- What types of activities and play opportunities will children need?

- How many times may nappies need changing?

- Do the children have any other physical care needs, such as bathing or caring for a medical condition?

Step 2: Identify practical considerations

In order for a routine to be realistic, practical considerations must be taken into account – such as the times at which other children in the family need taking to school or at which the outdoor play area is available. Below are some practical considerations which commonly affect the structure of routines.

- *Group settings*

    - start and finish times of settings

    - availability of areas and resources, for example, cooking activities can only be carried out in the afternoon because the kitchen is not free until then

    - noise levels: in some settings quiet activities are programmed for older children after lunch as the babies and toddlers in the same setting are then having a nap

- health and safety: can all the children go outside at the same time? Are there enough adults available to accompany children on an outing?

● *Home settings*

- needs of other children in the family; for example, if older children need to be taken to school or if one child needs a rest in the afternoon

- wishes of parents; for example, parents may ask that their children should be ready for bed when they come back from work, or that children are given a substantial snack at 4 o'clock so that they can eat supper later in the evening with their parents

- resources available; for example, where there is no garden for children to play, a routine might include a daily walk or activity where physical exercise can be encouraged

- timings: when is bedtime? When do children have a bath/shower?

As well as taking into account all these factors, early years workers have to think about how long it takes to complete certain tasks; for example, how long it takes a group of five children to put on their coats, hats or gloves, or how long it takes to bath and dress a child. Most early years workers and parents become very experienced at 'allowing' sufficient time for these types of tasks and are often able to advise the less experienced.

Step 3: Put the routine together

A good starting point for putting the routine together is to write down the 'fixed' parameters of the routine such as meal times, sleep times and the start and end times of sessions. A skeleton framework can then start to take shape. The example below shows the sort of timings and fixed points that a nanny caring for a 2 year old and a 4 year old might record.

Time	
7.45am	Parent leaves house. Breakfast time
9.00am	Matthew's nursery session starts
12.15pm	Matthew's nursery session finishes
12.45pm	Lunch
5.30pm	Parent returns. Tea time

Step 4: Other details

Once the fixed parameters have been recorded, other details can be filled in such as where storytimes or bathtime would fit into the routine. Routines for home settings tend to look more detailed than those of group settings as in home settings there are often children of different ages whose needs can be quite varied.

Below are two examples of different routines: one for a playgroup and one for a day in a home setting (on page 68).

Routine for a playgroup

Time	Child initiated	Adult directed	Other information
9.00am		Welcome and register in keyworker groups	
9.10am	Sand, water, dough, small-world play and construction Access to outdoors and physical equipment	Various activities to cover early years curriculum (Tues–Thurs: cooking 11.00–11.45am)	Snack bar open from 10.15am
11.15am	As above but large hall also available		
12.30am	Choice of story or quiet activities including jigsaws, books and construction toys	Story and songs	

Note: Free play includes core activities such as sand, water, dough and painting. Children are encouraged to learn through play, and adults play and work alongside the children. Structured activities might include cooking, sewing and board games as well as activities that specifically cover the Early Years curriculum.

ACTIVITY

Routines

Look at the routine in the setting where you work.

◆ Who designed the routine?

◆ Is it the same each day?

◆ What are the main influences on the structure of the routine?

◆ In what circumstances does the routine vary?

◆ Try to compare your routine to that of another, similar setting. What are the main differences?

Routine for a home setting

There are two children aged 2 years and 4 years. Emily has just started part-time in the infant school. The carer also has responsibility for the household tasks and meal preparation.

	Ian (2 years)	Emily (4 years)
6.45am	Awake, drink and nappy change	
7.00am	Plays near carer	Awake and play
7.20am	Breakfast	
7.45am	Wash and dress – nappy change	Wash, dress and brush hair
8.30am	Prepare to go out in pushchair – coat on, etc.	Pack bag for school
8.45am	Arrive at school – play with other children	
8.55am	Leave school	School starts
9.05am	Arrive home – play while dishes are washed up, beds made and other household chores are completed	At school
9.45am	Visit local shops	
10.45am	Drink, snack and check nappy	
11.00am	Play and help around house	
11.40am	Leave to collect Emily from school	
11.55am	Arrive at school	
12.00pm	Walk home	
12.15pm	Plays near carer	Talks about school day
12.30pm	Lunch	
1.00pm	Nappy change and nap	Quiet time – story, jigsaws, games or television
2.30pm	Wakes up, check nappy	
2.40pm	Drink and snack	
2.50pm	Leave home for park	
4.00pm	Return home–check nappy	Return home – read school book
	Play alongside sister with toys	Play with jigsaw puzzles, duplo, role play with brother
5.00pm	Tea	
5.30pm	Bath time and nappy change	Bath time
6.00pm	Story and bedtime	Look at books
6.20pm	Story and bedtime	

Routines and babies

In many respects, babies create their own routines, and often the role of the adult is to try to accommodate a baby's needs either into the routine of the rest of the family or into that of a group setting. When planning a routine for a baby, it is essential to remember that the routine will need to be very flexible and that it will need to be adapted frequently to meet the changing needs of the baby. Routines for babies are also learning experiences for them. This means that everyday care activities such as feeding, nappy changing and bathing need to be seen as activities (see Chapter 6). The two examples below show how a baby changed its sleep and feeding pattern within one month.

Routine for baby aged 5 months	
6.45am	Milk feed
8.00am	Breakfast – pureed cereal and milk
9.30am	Sleep
11.00am	Juice
12.30pm	Lunch and milk feed
2.30pm	Sleep
4.30pm	Water
5.00pm	Dinner and drink
5.30pm	Bath
6.30pm	Milk feed and bedtime

Routine for baby aged 6 months	
6.30am	Drink
7.15am	Breakfast and milk feed
9.00am	Sleep
10.00am	Juice
12.15pm	Lunch
1.00pm	Sleep
3.00pm	Water and a banana
5.00pm	Dinner and milk
5.30pm	Bath
6.30pm	Small milk feed and bedtime

NOTE TO STUDENTS

If you are devising a routine as part of a childcare course, you will need to add in a rationale. The rationale should provide evidence that you understand the process of producing a routine and that you understand the factors that affect a routine. The rationale should explain:

a the needs of the children – these could also be referenced

b the reasons behind your timings, for example, 'I have chosen to allow 15 minutes for snack time as I would need to put the child into a high chair and put a bib on the child'

c your choice of activities.

The reflective practitioner

It is essential to reflect upon the effectiveness of routines. They are after all the skeletons onto which other planning is hung. It is not uncommon to find that routines that were developed in settings twenty or thirty years ago are still being used without anyone taking a moment to critically reflect on whether they are effective. A good example of this is the timing of stories. Traditionally these have been put at the end of a session, but this may not be the best place for them as children might be tired and a group story time might be hard for them to cope with.

A good indicator that a routine is not quite working is children's behaviour. You may find, for example, that groups of children become restless or show excited behaviour at certain points during a session. When you can virtually predict these points during the session, you must reconsider the effectiveness of a routine. One pre-school, for example, found that tidying away before snack time was always difficult. When they questioned why there was a need to tidy up, or even to have a fixed snack time, they realised that the routine was actually causing the problem. Their solution was to have a rolling snack time when children could self-serve. This meant that there were no longer any queues or the need to clear tables.

◆ When was the routine of the setting last evaluated?

◆ Are there times when children are waiting without anything to do?

◆ Are there times when staff feel stressed and do not enjoy their work?

◆ Does the routine allow times when staff can work with individual children?

◆ Does the routine allow for plenty of outdoor activities?

◆ Does the routine allow children to become independent, for example, to get their own drinks or go to the toilet?

◆ How much child initiated play does the session allow for?

Different types of plans

There are five broad types of plan which form the core of most planning in early years settings (see the chart overleaf). Students on childcare courses will need to show that they can plan using the different planning types, as this demonstrates that they have a good understanding of the needs of children and children's development. Early years workers usually find that they contribute most frequently to the production of curriculum plans, weekly or daily planners and individual education plans.

It is also worth noting that most plans in common use tend to show structured activities, as unstructured activities by their very nature can be harder to tie down in terms of learning outcomes. They are, however, absolutely essential (see page 76).

It is also possible to consider children's daily or weekly routines as a type of background plan as they show the overall structure or pattern of the day or week, for example, mealtimes, storytimes, etc. However, routines are not included here as one of the types of plan but are seen more as a foundation for the planning process.

Type of plan	Periods of time covered by the plan	Purpose
Long-term plans – also known as schemes of work or syllabus	Depends on settings, but often yearly or half yearly	Gives a broad outline of the activities, themes and visits that are planned for the year. The long-term plan may also show how the overall activities and play opportunities will link to the Early Years curriculum or a child's developmental areas.
Curriculum plans – also known as outline plans	Daily, weekly or monthly, although some settings plan for longer periods and call these plans medium term	Shows the activities and play opportunities that are to be provided.
Daily or weekly planners	Daily or weekly	Shows what activities and play opportunities have been planned on a day by day basis. Planners are often used to support curriculum plans and individual education plans. May also show learning intentions.
Detailed plans – also known as activity plans	Short periods of time – the length of time it takes to prepare and carry out the activity	Shows how an activity is to be carried out and the preparation and resources needed. Shows learning intentions.
Individual education plan	Weekly or monthly	Shows the activities and play opportunities that are required to help meet a child's particular requirements or needs.

Understanding how the different planning types fit together

Not every setting will produce all of the planning types shown above but it is useful to have an understanding of how the different plans fit together. The overall process includes different ideas and themes which are planned in more and more detail. The routine of a setting will affect the types and length of activities that can be planned and so tends to act as a backdrop to the overall process of planning activities and play opportunities.

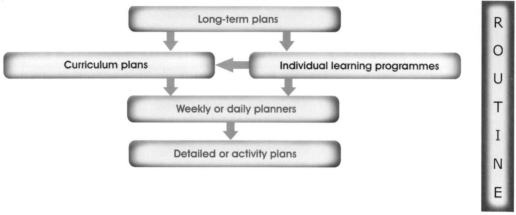

How different types of planning fit together

Planning is a process

It is now generally accepted that planning is part of a process and it is quite common to see this process represented as a cycle.

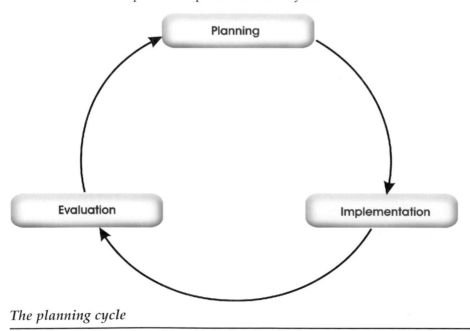

The planning cycle

The planning cycle shows that plans are not produced in isolation, and that the information gained when evaluating plans is used to formulate future plans. This may seem obvious but it is important to remember. Most people do this in their everyday lives – for example, if you are late getting to work, you might plan to try a different route; whilst using the new route, you will consider whether it is better and then decide on this basis which route you should take in the future.

Structured and unstructured activities

There are many ways of working effectively with children and this is reflected in the routines and the planning systems of different settings. Writing about how to plan is always difficult as good planning should reflect the philosophy and approach of the setting. The key difference between settings can be the amount of structured activities that are used and the way in which they are carried out. Structured activities are those activities where adults do a significant amount of guiding, for example, they may show a small group of children how to play a game or take a pair of children to do some cooking. Some settings use the term 'focused activities' instead of 'structured'.

Structured activities have many benefits. They allow the adult to focus children's attention on a specific concept, skill or knowledge. Adults might also find that focused activities can be used to ensure that specific parts of a curriculum are covered. There are also dangers when activities are structured unless adults are very sensitive to children's needs and interests. Highly structured activities can mean that children simply follow instructions and do not learn for themselves. Children may also become bored or restless if the activity does not appeal to them or they do not have any ownership of it. This means that the use of structured activities needs to be carefully thought out.

Unstructured activities are ones where children use and choose materials and equipment and develop their own play ideas and themes. Some settings refer to this type of activity as 'free play' or 'child initiated'. Where children are able to choose what to do and how to do it, they are more likely to concentrate for longer periods and to develop many skills including self-reliance, co-operation and problem solving.

Most settings find that they need to strike a balance between structured and unstructured activities.

Planning structured activities

Most of the planning that settings record is linked to activities and play experiences that adults are in some way structuring. This allows settings to check that all areas of a child's development or parts of the curriculum are being covered.

It can be helpful when recording structured activities to differentiate them further. The terms 'adult directed' and 'adult initiated' can be used to show the degree of structure and the role of the adult within it.

Adult directed activities

Adult directed activities are those structured activities where the adult has a high profile role. The adult may directly show, teach or explain to children what they might do. They may ask questions, play games or direct the children in some way. Adults may, for example, bring in a feely bag and ask a group of three children if they can guess what is in the bag. The adult may then ask children if they would like to take out the items and count them. In Section 3, there are plenty of examples of adult directed activities, although it is important to remember that children will equally need plenty of opportunities for unstructured or 'child initiated' play.

Adult directed activities work best when children come to them of their own free will rather than as conscripts! Children who do not want to take part are likely to show this in their behaviour and while the adult might feel that he or she has been teaching, this is not a guarantee that children have been learning. Children tend to learn best when they are interested and motivated.

GOOD PRACTICE GUIDE

Tips when planning adult directed activities

◆ Use these activities sparingly

◆ Make activities participative, keep them playful and give them a purpose

◆ Think about children's interests

◆ Keep activities on the short side and linked to children's interests

◆ Find ways of giving children ownership of the activities (see pages 75 and 108)

◆ Think about the timing of activities

◆ Remember that not all children may want to take part

◆ Keep group sizes small to accommodate children's needs

◆ Think about how activities can be extended or adapted to suit different children

◆ Remember that the outdoor area can also be used for structured activities

Adult initiated activities

Adult initiated activities are an extremely effective way of providing some structure in children's play without the adult actually directing and controlling the play. Through careful planning and preparation, the adult provides materials

Adults play an important part in initiating learning

and equipment in such a way that children are 'prompted' to play in the way that the adult intends. A good example of an adult initiated activity would be where an adult has hidden some coins in the sand tray and left out a few piggy banks or purses. It is a fair bet that many children will notice the coins and also put them in a purse. The adult can either leave the children simply to enjoy noticing and playing with the coins or might gently ask children about what they have found. Another example of an adult initiated activity is to put an empty suitcase in the home corner. Children are likely to want to open it and begin to pack it.

The role of the adult in adult initiated activities is low key. There are huge advantages to these activities as while they help focus children's attention, they also give children ownership of the activity. This means that concentration, enjoyment and the quality of learning tends to be improved.

GOOD PRACTICE GUIDE

Tips when planning adult initiated activities

◆ Use these activities in preference to adult directed activities wherever possible

◆ Base activities on children's interests

◆ Make sure that other adults know the purpose of these activities

◆ Make sure that staff are available to support and extend children's thinking

◆ Base some activities on previous adult directed activities (see page 76)

◆ Remember that not all children will visit the adult initiated activity

◆ Use the outdoor area for adult initiated play

Moving from structured to unstructured activities

In the ideal world, you should be able to gauge the success of structured activities by observing that children have begun to incorporate the ideas into their own play. Children who have, for example, enjoyed learning a simple game with an adult may wish to get out the same game and then play it. In the same way, a child who has been sitting with an adult sorting through some buttons may want to return to the tray later in the afternoon and carry on alone. This means that children have travelled from learning something with an adult to being able to take on board the idea or skill and make it their own. There are enormous benefits when children do this as it means that they are practising skills and continuing to explore ideas. In terms of planning, this means that the equipment, games and toys that have been used in structured activities should be available for children to use on their own terms.

Planning unstructured activities

It is important that unstructured or child initiated activities are not seen as 'add ons' by anyone in the setting. Child initiated activities are hugely rewarding in terms of children's self-esteem and overall development. They are also in some ways the backbone of childhood itself as children have always been able to play on their own terms using toys and materials that are made available. Child initiated play can also be used effectively to deliver curriculum outcomes and it is useful if adults observe children when they are playing in this way and note those outcomes that have been achieved. The key to providing unstructured activities is to bed them down in the routine of the day. While some settings provide separate times for unstructured play, many settings make this type of play continually available and find that children dip in and out of the structured activities when they are ready for some adult input.

GOOD PRACTICE GUIDE

Tips for planning unstructured activities

- ◆ Aim to make unstructured play continual throughout the session
- ◆ Where opportunities for unstructured play are limited, make sure that children are given as much time as possible when they do occur
- ◆ Make resources available so that children can access them easily
- ◆ Make full use of the outdoor area for this type of play
- ◆ Use staff to carry out naturalistic observations and also to discreetly supervise

This type of play by its very nature is not always 'tidy' as children may want to combine play materials or explore ideas on their own terms. This has to be catered for and so it is important when planning to ensure that there are sufficient resources.

Planning for the outdoor area

A recent and welcome trend is the realisation that the outdoor space offers many opportunities for children's play, learning and development. This means that if you have an outdoor area, you should be planning activities and play experiences outdoors. In the ideal world, every setting should have access adjacent to the outdoor area so that children can move in and out easily. Where this is not possible and outdoor play has to be programmed into specific time slots, it is important that sufficient time is given. Children find it hard to settle into play when they know that very soon they will be called back inside. It is also important to see the outdoor area as being able to deliver more than just outcomes for physical development. Children can enjoy imaginative play outdoors as well as building structures and dens, and creating their own gloopy mixtures.

Advantages of outdoor activities

- There is more space and children can be freer in terms of movements and noise level.

- Water and other messy materials can be made more freely available.

- Children are more likely to concentrate in a sensory environment.

- Activities can be done on a large scale, for example, in a sand area using water.

- Structured and unstructured activities can be carried out side by side.

GOOD PRACTICE GUIDE

Tips when planning for the outdoors

- Look at storage of equipment – consider outdoor sheds and storage that children can access

- Consider buying some rain ponchos and having them on coat pegs by the door

- Think about having themed boxes for outdoors as adult initiated activities, for example, a wind box containing wind chimes, kites, ribbons

- Think carefully about how the outdoor space is to be supervised without children feeling that they are being watched

Keys to good practice when planning

There are some general principles that form the basis of good practice when planning. We will look at each in turn.

Good practice when planning

Individual needs of children

One of the starting points of planning is to consider the needs of children. This means that overall the plans should reflect the different interests and developmental stages of children. Where children have particular needs, an individual education plan may be developed to ensure that these needs are focused on. An example might be a specific plan to help a child to play co-operatively with other children (see page 99).

Planning as a team

Although the quality of plans may be the individual responsibility of one staff member, most settings recognise that planning is more effective if a team approach is taken. Many settings therefore organise planning meetings to exchange ideas and to evaluate the ongoing plans. By taking a team approach, staff can contribute their own suggestions and ideas, which means that they take some ownership of the plan. This is important because then the plan can be implemented more effectively.

Involving parents

Settings which involve parents in aspects of their planning tend to produce effective plans. Working in partnership with parents means that information which relates to children's needs can be fed into the planning process; for example, a parent may mention that his or her child is overtired at the end of the

Involving children is an important part of planning

day. An early years worker may then use this information to plan in some more opportunities for rest in the afternoon session.

Working with parents is also good practice in many other ways as parents can be useful sources of ideas and can offer practical help. For example, parents may have skills or interests that they can share with the children. This will not only benefit the children but helps to build up good relationships.

Involving children

An interesting recent trend in early years and out of school care is to involve children in planning and decision making. Listening directly to the wishes of children is important as children are, in effect, the 'users' of the planning. Many schools have set up school councils in order to try to respond to the comments of children; for example, putting out equipment for children to use at break times as a result of children's feedback. In the same way, listening to what children enjoy doing in nursery settings can provide ideas for activities that will develop the skills of children while they are playing and enjoying themselves.

Anti-bias curriculum and promoting a positive world view

The early learning experiences of children can affect their attitudes in later life. It is now considered to be good practice to ensure that play opportunities and learning experiences encourage a respect and understanding of others. Curriculum plans should reflect this while also ensuring that the routines and activities themselves will not encourage any hidden forms of discrimination within the setting; i.e. that activities will be accessible and benefit all children regardless of their home backgrounds or gender.

In many ways, the promotion of an anti-bias curriculum is one of the hardest tasks for settings to do in a meaningful way as it requires early years workers to be very objective about the routine, learning activities and play opportunities that are being offered. Popular images used in settings, such as Postman Pat, are, for example, 'very white' and 'very traditional' and do not promote and reflect a multi-cultural world. When promoting an anti-bias curriculum it is therefore necessary to take a very hard look at what is taken for granted in settings and to consider whether there are hidden messages being sent out to children. (The attitudes of staff may need some consideration as well.) This is not to say that Postman Pat should not appear in settings, but that it needs to be balanced by a multicultural character such as Little Babaji.

Flexibility and spontaneity

When faced with the task of planning, one of the groans from some early years workers is that it stops them from being creative and responding to children's needs. This should not be true as within all types of plans there should be times and opportunities for activities which are child led. For example, activities should be designed to allow children to approach them in different ways according to the needs and interests of the child.

Plans should also be thought of as guides rather than rules which have to be followed. Plans should not be so rigid that they cannot incorporate an unexpected event. For example, there might be a fire drill or it might start snowing. In these cases the children are likely to be curious and excited, and so will learn more from talking about the fire drill or running outside to see the snow than they would from trying to ignore it. The curriculum plan can be reviewed later to ensure that it has maintained its balance and that no crucial skills development has been missed.

Health and safety

One of the key responsibilities for adults working with children is to ensure their safety at all times. This means that it is good practice to consider the health and safety implications when producing plans; for example, if children are going to carry out a cooking activity the staff will need to check records to find out about possible food allergies. This focus on safety is particularly important when looking at planning routines for babies and toddlers in home settings. For example, how can an early years worker ensure that a toddler is safe while the baby's nappy is being changed?

Long-term plans

For a long time, schools have produced long-term plans to ensure that they are covering all aspects of the National Curriculum. Most long-term plans developed in schools tend to cover the whole school year.

However, only quite recently have early years settings needed to produce long-term plans and this is a direct result of the introduction of the Early Years curriculum. Settings that cater for children over three years old now have to show that they are covering the learning areas.

This is a new approach to planning for many settings that previously only needed to plan for a month or a week at a time. Many early years settings are still exploring the different ways of producing their long-term plans and so a number of different approaches are taken.

Long-term plans are not generally produced for children aged less than three years old as the flexibility required when responding to children's short-term developmental needs means that planning ahead for six months or a year is not always appropriate.

The purpose of a long-term plan

The main role of the long-term plan is to help early years workers and teachers feel confident that their overall curriculum plans for the year or half year will cover the Early Years or National Curriculum. The long-term plan is also helpful because staff can look out for resources, materials and ideas that might help them over the following months.

Devising a long-term plan

It is generally considered good practice for all staff to be involved in some way with long-term planning so that they can contribute their own ideas and suggestions. Most long-term plans give a broad overview of the year or term and are generally schematic. This broad outline allows flexibility over the course of the plan, enabling staff to change direction or to use opportunities that arise during the period. Most long-term plans are translated into curriculum plans a month or so before the theme or topic is scheduled. In most settings, one member of staff will have overall responsibility for the quality of the plans and will need to check that plans meet most of the following requirements:

- topics and themes are appropriate for the age of children
- overall themes cover the Early Years or National Curriculum
- plans make use of the local environment and events such as festivals, seasons, weather
- time allocated to themes is realistic
- plans make the best use of resources and equipment available
- plans reflect an anti-bias curriculum.

The example below shows a long-term plan produced by a school that plans monthly themes that are then divided into weekly topics. The school then produces monthly curriculum plans which link the activities to the Early Years curriculum.

Summer Term	Main themes
April	*Growing*
	Seeds, bulbs and plants
	Gardens and parks
	Babies
May	*Animals*
	Our pets
	What's in our garden?
	Farm visit
June	*Myself*
	My home
	My favourites
	My family

Curriculum plans

Curriculum plans are also sometimes called *outline plans* or *schemes of work*. Their role is to show what activities and learning opportunities are to be provided during a defined period. The length of time that is shown on curriculum plans varies as some settings produce curriculum plans to cover a month whereas others may plan for shorter or longer periods: for example, a one-day crèche will probably produce a curriculum plan which covers that one day period.

The range of content is wide and the format of curriculum plans produced by settings can be very varied, reflecting the different needs and influences of a setting. For example, a school will have to show how the National Curriculum numeracy and literacy strategies are to be delivered, whereas a setting that cares for babies under one year will produce a plan that shows how the developmental needs of the babies are to be considered. It is a good idea to look at curriculum plans from different settings to become familiar with a range of formats and styles.

Curriculum plans: 0–3 years

Babies and toddlers do not need a curriculum that is based on 'learning' so a curriculum with learning areas is inappropriate. Instead, it is a good idea to produce curriculum plans with activities and play opportunities that link to a child's overall development.

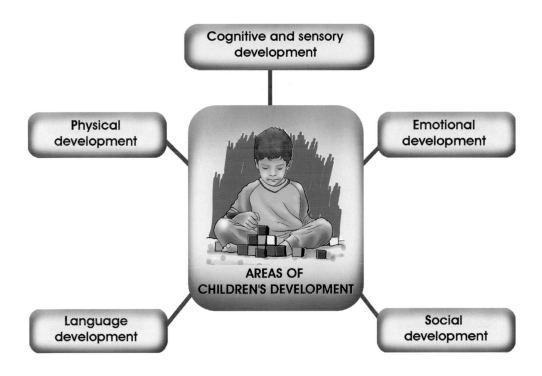

The picture above shows the five key areas which contribute to children's overall development. Cognitive and sensory development in this instance have been grouped together as babies and young children tend to learn through their senses. Stimulating children's development through experiences and play opportunities is the focus of curriculum planning. Although it is possible to plan for this age range in a thematic way, for example, taking 'colours' as a theme, it is not essential for this to happen and some settings take the view that it is not even appropriate.

A more 'holistic' approach understands that children's overall development will benefit from having a range of experiences rather than specifically concentrating on one aspect. The term 'experiences' is particularly relevant to this age range as it implies that children do not have to achieve or produce an end product; for example, a baby may 'experience' water when playing at bath time or a toddler may 'experience' sound by banging a drum.

Curriculum plans: 3–5 years

Curriculum plans for children in the early years age range are likely to show links to the Early Years curriculum. Many settings will plan on a monthly or termly basis and the majority of settings try to use a thematic approach. The topics and themes that are chosen tend to build on children's direct experiences as most early years workers tend to feel that children learn best when experiences and activities are relevant and meaningful. Below is a list of common themes used in early years settings.

Common themes for early years

Ourselves	Colours and shades	Clothes
Growing	Pets	Transport/travel
Families	Animals	Shapes
Boxes	Festivals (these should be familiar to children)	Sea
Water		Toys
Where we live	Friends	
Farms	Holidays	
People who help us	Our food	
Nursery rhymes	Weather	

These themes are often broken down into smaller topics that might last a week, as the diagram below shows.

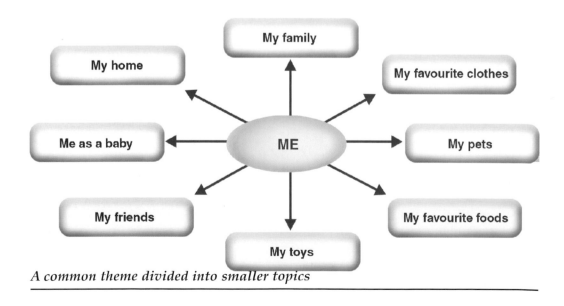

A common theme divided into smaller topics

Monthly Individual Planning Sheet

Month: March 2005   Name of Keyworker: Anne

Child	Current interests/developmental stages	Activities/adult support	Focus for observations
Leman	Out of nappies, although some accidents – needs help with dressing Enjoys gloop, especially with spoons Carries teddy around	Provide support with dressing Remind and put potty near activity Encouragement to feed herself Provide stirring activities outdoors Provide shopping bag for teddy	See if she can pull down trousers and pants by herself Monitor number of accidents See if she talks to teddy
Kio	Nappy dry during naps She points when she needs changing Interested in posting objects Joins in with Humpty Dumpty – beginning to use two word sentences	Opportunities to use potty – adult to observe signs and offer support Shape sorters, posting toys, boxes Sing action rhymes	Response to potty See which shape sorter she can use Record examples of two-word sentences
George	Walking and interested in pushing brick trolley Fascinated with mirror Enjoys peek-a-boo Interested in peeking out of play tunnel	Brick trolley Mirrors Peek-a-boo games and hiding objects Play tunnel Adult to play hiding games with him	See if he can steer brick trolley See if he can recognise himself Notice if he tries to hide objects for adult

There is more emphasis on individual planning for babies and toddlers

Most curriculum plans will only show key learning activities and play opportunities where adult support and interaction play a major part. These tend to be linked to the Early Years curriculum, although it is also possible to produce curriculum plans that show how one particular skill or area of development is to be encouraged. Curriculum plans that show how areas of development are to be promoted or how a skill is to be acquired are particularly helpful when producing plans for home settings, where the links to the Early Years curriculum may not be appropriate. For example, a nanny may produce a curriculum plan for a week that shows how a five year old in the school holiday is going to learn how to throw and catch.

Working alongside Ofsted requirements

All settings which receive the Nursery Education Grant have to be inspected by Ofsted. This means that the quality of the learning experiences are examined and settings have to show that they are giving children experiences that link to the Early Years curriculum.

The table below shows some of the main areas that are looked at during an Ofsted inspection.

Content of the educational programme	Inspectors look at how the Early Years curriculum is being covered and whether the experiences and opportunities offered are appropriate to the age of children. Each learning area of the curriculum is commented on separately.
The planning of the educational programme	Inspectors look to see how the setting is planning the educational programme. It is generally expected that a range of planning methods will be used.
The quality of teaching and assessment	Inspectors will be looking to see that a range of different teaching methods are used – for example, that children are learning through structured activities as well as through free play. Settings will need to show how they monitor and assess individual children's progress. Settings will also need to show how they promote equality of access and opportunity.
Learning resources and accommodation	Inspectors will comment on the equipment and resources that are available in the setting. They will also consider if best use is being made of them.
Partnership with parents and carers	Settings will need to show how settings involve parents and carers. Inspectors will be hoping to see that parents are also involved in the assessment and monitoring of the children.

Curriculum plans: 5–8 years

In schools, curriculum plans are organised around the requirements of the National Curriculum and the numeracy and literacy strategies. Most teachers in schools are responsible for planning, although in some schools students and early years workers are also involved in the planning process.

Curriculum plans can also be produced for this age group that show the activities that are to be offered in holidays, for example, a week's curriculum plan can be produced as part of an out-of-school club. A curriculum plan for this setting would probably be very child oriented and concerned with play and it would not necessarily be linked to any educational goals, as the out-of-school provision serves a very different purpose. It is also good practice for children to be encouraged to identify their own play needs and for their ideas to be used as a basis for planning.

Devising a curriculum plan

Step 1: Gather information

Before a curriculum plan can be devised, it is essential to find out as much as possible about the children for whom the plan is intended. Learning information about a child can help to ensure that the curriculum plan will be realistic. Below is a list of the types of information that may be needed.

- *Children's play preferences*

This is important because you can then build experiences and play opportunities around the children's preferences; for example, a baby may enjoy bath time and so new toys might be introduced. A toddler may have a favourite teddy and so may enjoy making play dough cakes to feed teddy. The need to identify children's play preferences is considered as essential good practice when preparing a curriculum plan for children over five years in out-of-school provision.

- *Children's routines*

Knowing about a child's individual routine is helpful because play opportunities and experiences can be built in; for example, just before nap time a child may wish to curl up and share a book. Children's routines are also affected by their alertness and concentration so some activities, such as going for a walk, are best at particular points in a day when children are not too tired.

- *Children's development*

Information about children's stages of development is essential in order to produce a plan that is realistic and helpful. For example, if a child is crawling it is a good idea to build on this development by providing toys that move and encourage the child to move.

- *Children's needs*

Learning about individual children should make adults aware of their individual needs. For example, if a child has been unsettled – perhaps because of changes at

SPORTS WORLD PLAYSCHEME

Date	Morning activity	Afternoon activity
Monday 26 July Fire & Evacuation Procedures Welcome games	Name Your Sports Team – design your team's crest or logo & make into a giant banner Knex Construction – New Equipment	Sports Team Races & Games Outdoors 'Sports Star Gallery' – draw your sports hero & write a caption about him or her Video Session
Tuesday 27 July Fire & Evacuation Procedures Circus and group games	'Olympics' – make Olympic Rings & torches to display in the playroom Parachute Games & Outdoor Play	'Medal Mania' – design & make medals & ribbons Video Session Badminton
Wednesday 28 July Fire & Evacuation Procedures Circle and group games	'Wembley Towers' – make & build the Wembley Towers or – 'Sporty Stuff' – make your own sports equipment or model	Football & Outdoor Games Video Session Sport Pictionary & Charades
Thursday 29 July Fire & Evacuation Procedures Circle and group games	Bouncy Castle 'Formula 1' – make a Racing Car or a 'Winner's Flower Garland'	Bouncy Castle Video Sessions Outdoor Games 'Question of Sport Quiz'
Friday 30 July Fire & Evacuation Procedures *Circle and group games	'Rattles' – make rattles, poms poms &other 'noises' to cheer with Cheer Leader – make up cheers & dances	Rounders Match & final team games Presentations & Team Winners Video Session

*Children's free choice of play activities, such as board games, construction toys, reading, basic art and team games, will be available throughout the day. There will also be quiet activities during group time, usually at the beginning and end of the day, and during mid-morning and mid-afternoon snack times, when juice and a snack will be provided. Please provide your children with suitable clothing for outdoor activities, which take place each day.

A curriculum plan for a playscheme (5–14 years old)

home – the curriculum plan should provide plenty of activities that are familiar and comforting for this child. Even children of the same age may have very different requirements, including dietary, health and physical needs. A toddler who is starting to express an interest in using a potty may require play opportunities and stories that will help her through this stage of development, whereas another child of the same age will not be ready for toilet training and should not be 'forced' into it.

This range of information can be collected in a variety of ways, for example, by:

- listening to parents
- listening to other early years workers
- talking to children
- observing children directly – either informally noting down what children are doing or carrying out assessments, such as checklists
- researching the needs and stages of child development in 'standard' reference books.

Step 2: Decide on a time-scale and approach

The content of a curriculum plan will be influenced by the time scale and the approach to planning that is taken in the setting. Most settings caring for babies plan on a weekly basis, as babies' routines keep changing and babies tend to make dramatic leaps in their development, for example, learning to crawl, to stand and to walk. Settings with a group of two year olds may decide to plan on a monthly basis and may also decide to use a thematic approach, i.e. planning play opportunities and activities that are linked around a theme.

The approach that is to be taken when planning the curriculum will also depend on the type of setting, for example, a school will have to consider and refer to the National Curriculum while playgroups and nurseries may consider how to cover the Early Years curriculum.

Step 3: Ideas session

Most early years workers find it easier to plan alongside other members of staff and many settings have an ideas session where everyone throws out their ideas, comments and thoughts. Some settings record ideas sessions by producing a spider diagram. Settings that link activities to the Early Years curriculum may consider ideas according to the area of learning to ensure that there are enough ideas to cover the learning outcomes.

Step 4: Organise the plan

After the initial ideas session it is important to do some filtering of ideas and select the content of the actual plan. Practical considerations such as equipment, cost and resources tend to mean that only some of the ideas can be used. This filtering process is important if the plan is to be realistic and useful.

The following types of questions, depending on the age group and setting, should be asked when selecting the final content of the plan.

- Do the play opportunities, activities and learning experiences meet the developmental needs of the children?
- How do the activities link to the Foundation Curriculum or National Curriculum?
- Is any assessment or recording needed and has it been built into the plan?
- Is the curriculum plan promoting a positive world view?
- Is the curriculum anti-bias?
- Can the activities and play opportunities be adapted to meet the needs of all children?
- Are there any health and safety implications?
- Is there a balance of activities?
- Is there some in-built flexibility within the plan?
- What are the resource/staff implications?

NOTE TO STUDENTS

Students may find it helpful to produce a rationale which shows that they researched the needs of children. This can be written as a form of overview to the curriculum plan. Depth of understanding and knowledge can be shown by using references to child development theorists in this overview.

The example below shows a snippet of a rationale produced by a student:

Knowledge and understanding of the world

I have chosen some very practical activities to help children learn about the weather. The type of activities I have chosen should help children to observe and see how the weather affects their environment. For example, by washing ribbons and putting them out to dry, children will learn that wind and sun helps to dry things. The activity may also build on their direct experiences at home when they may have helped with the washing. This activity should also be fun for the children to carry out which is important for this age group. According to Tassoni (1998), 'Children also need to enjoy what they are doing so activities for children must be suitable for their stage of development.'

I have also planned to help the children make their own weather chart. This should help them think about the weather and will be a way of helping them draw and record.

Students will also need to produce an explanation of why they have chosen certain types of activities and play opportunities. It is helpful if they write about how the activities and play opportunities chosen will meet the children's needs. Where a curriculum plan is to be used with children over three years of age in pre-school or school settings, references may also be used to show that students can work with the National and Foundation Curriculum.

Step 5: Present the plan

The style and layout of curriculum plans vary enormously as there is no set way of presenting the information. There are, however, some common approaches and the examples below and on page 92 show two different styles of curriculum plan.

Oakwood Nursery Weekly Activity Plan: 17th January Subject: Friendship		
Area of learning	**Learning objectives**	**Learning opportunities and activities**
Personal, social and emotional	• Separate from main carer with support • Feel safe and secure, demonstrating a sense of trust • Have sense of self as a member of different communities • Express needs and feelings in appropriate ways • Initiate interactions with others • Operate independently within the environment	**Snack time:** go round the circle naming some of our special friends, discussing what friends do for each other and how we can be kind **Friendship corner:** set up a quiet area of the room where children can go with their friends for a chat or to read a book **Buddy system:** pair older child with a younger child to play together
Communication, language and literacy	• Initiate conversation, listen to what others say, use talk to resolve disagreements • Use writing as a means of recording and communicating	**Writing table:** area where children can write messages to their friends or create picture of people being friendly
Mathematical development	• Use mathematical language in play, showing interest in counting and number • Count up to three or four • Show an interest in shape and space by playing with space or making arrangements with objects	**Drawing:** draw pictures of themselves with their friends – name them and count how many there are **Model-making:** use recycled / reclaimed materials to create a model of a friend
Knowledge and understanding of the world	• Show curiosity and interest through facial expression, movement or sound • Gain an awareness of the cultures and beliefs of others	**Water/sand play:** free play, encouraging sharing and turn-taking **ICT:** Drawing pictures of or taking photos of friends and printing these out **Story time:** Friendship stories, e.g. *Krishna and Sudhama Little Red Hen*
Physical development	• Move spontaneously within the space available • Move body position as necessary	**Outside:** play ring games and chasing games, e.g. *Ring-a-ring-o-roses*, encouraging everyone to join in
Creative development	• Use body to explore texture and space • Make constructions, collages, paintings and dances • Choose particular colours for a purpose	**Painting:** pictures of friends (could use a pre-drawn frame) and decorate the friendship corner with these **Handprinting:** cut out different coloured prints to make a friendship tree, sun or person

An example of a curriculum plan

Forward planning programme for the 3 years + children
Date(s) 5–9 September 2005 • 12–16 September 2005

Language and Literacy

Tell us about your family – show photos of your family.

Learn and recite names and addresses. What is a surname and why do we have one?

Listen to different sounds from different rooms in our home – develop an awareness of initial sounds.

Look at different books – babies and children's – discuss the difference.

Make a 'news' book which records events done at home or in the evening with our families.

Make faces using paper plates all with different expressions – discuss feelings – choose an expression and a member of our family and say why they make us happy/sad/laugh, etc.

Mathematics

Put photos of your family members in order of age and size.

Make charts to show hair colour and eye colour.

Look at similarities and differences within the group.

Develop time keeping skills – time ourselves doing an activity that we would do at home.

Use the terms single/double/top/bottom/up/down/upper/lower, etc.

Recite, read and record our phone numbers.

Physical

Make some fairy cakes, pour and stir – take them home for your family.

Move like a baby, toddler, child, adult and old person.

Mime things that we do without families – for example, going to the park, having a bath, mowing the lawn, etc.

Take a walk to the supermarket to do some shopping.

Joggy bear – music and movement.

**THEME
Families**

Personal and Social

How do we care for babies? Ask Melanie to bring Calan in to show the children.

Look at how we have changed since we were babies.

Look at ways to be more helpful at home.

Role play a family outing whereby one of the children misbehaves – the 'parent' then steps in to advise on good behaviour.

Creative

Look in a mirror and draw observational drawings of self.

Make a collage using photos of family members.

Create and respond to noises in the home – make a sounds lotto game.

Musical instruments – sort into noise families – are they blown, struck or shaken?

Make family puppets.

Draw portraits of our family members.

Make clay models of family members.

Make a special gift to give a family member, i.e. decorated paint pot, clay dish, etc.

Knowledge and Understanding of the World

Look at animal families – match old with their young.

Talk about the Mahama family from Ghana (child led) – compare their lives with ours.

Look at pictures of families in the past. Discuss similarities and differences to us.

Discuss family celebrations, i.e. weddings, anniversaries, christenings, birthdays, etc.

Discuss where we live. Learn our address.

Draw a map showing where we live and some important places in the local area.

An alternative style of curriculum plan

Weekly or daily planners

Planners are mostly used alongside curriculum plans to show when activities and play opportunities are to take place. The amount of detail that planners show can vary. Some settings take a simple timetable style approach, whereas others show the key learning intentions of each activity as well as the staff and resources that are to be used (see the tables on page 94).

Devising a weekly or daily planner

Step 1: Decide on the activities to be carried out

This is relatively straightforward where there is a curriculum plan already in place. Activities need to be chosen for the day or week to provide a balanced programme, for example, some activities that require concentrated attention skills will need to be balanced with activities that allow children time to rest and relax. Activities must be programmed in a logical sequence, for example, the 'Jack and the Beanstalk' story needs to be read before children act it out in words and music or make models. In group settings, activities must also be adaptable so that all children can do them at their own level; this is important if you are going to meet individual children's needs. Finally, within the programme there should be opportunities for children to work in small groups and individually with adults. This is important for children's emotional and social development.

Step 2: Look at the routine of the setting

Once the activities have been chosen for the week, they can be programmed into the setting's routine. This means looking at each activity alongside the routine of the setting and considering where best to slot it in. Looking at the routine is essential in most group settings because equipment, resources and space are often shared with others. It is also important to check that children who attend part-time will not miss out on fun or essential activities.

Step 3: Involve team members

The weekly or daily planner may be produced by one member of the team, but it is good practice to make sure that other staff members have the opportunity to contribute – especially if the weekly planner shows which staff members are responsible for leading activities. This means that staff are more likely to be enthusiastic about preparing and implementing activities.

Step 4: Produce the planners

You have seen that planners can vary in the detail they provide. Overall the trend is towards more detailed planners which show staffing, resources and key learning intentions. Planners should, however, be easy to read and show

Red group	*Theme*: Hot and cold
Week beginning 19 September	
Day	**Activity and play experiences**
Monday	Outdoor clothes in dressing up area Make jacket potatoes Cutting and sticking – clothes we wear outside
Tuesday	Ice cubes in water tray Make ice lollies Cutting and sticking – clothes we wear when we are hot
Wednesday	Tasting food cold – mashed potato, spaghetti Watch ice cubes melt on radiator Dressing up clothes – summer clothes
Thursday	Keep teddy warm Melt jelly Paint 'hot' pictures using shades of red paint
Friday	Make bird seed cakes Books about animals who live in cold climates Paint 'cold' pictures

An example of a timetable style approach to weekly planning

Day	Learning activity	Key learning intentions	Target language
Monday	Plant seeds	To make children aware that plants need water and soil	soil, roots, wet, water
	Make seed pictures	Sorting different types of seeds	Names of seeds
	Water garden	To help children share equipment and respect outside environment	Watering can, names of shrubs and weeds
Tuesday	'Jack and the Beanstalk' story	To encourage children to listen	stalk, roots, beans, giant
	Sequence bean growing cards	To practise children's sequencing skills	first, second, third, roots

A timetable showing key learning intentions

everyone in the setting what is happening. It is also a good idea in early years settings to show how 'core activities' are to be used as although children may use these in an unstructured way, they still contribute to children's overall learning.

Activity plans

Activity plans can also be referred to as detailed plans. The aim of an activity or detailed plan is to make sure that an activity runs smoothly. Activity plans are particularly useful if a new activity is being tried out or if an activity needs to be carried out in a specific way in order for children to benefit; for example, an activity plan may be produced for a child with particular needs in conjunction with other professionals, such as a speech therapist. Activity plans can also help volunteers and students carry out an activity in the way the setting had intended. Good activity plans will often include specific guidance on how to implement them.

The format of activity or detailed plans

In many ways an activity plan is a little like a recipe. The aim is that it contains all the information required for anyone in the setting to be able to follow the plan. Some settings have a store of activity plans so that if there are unforeseen changes to the staffing, a temporary staff member can still follow the activities planned for the day.

There are no set formats for producing an activity plan, but the list below indicates the types of information that should be covered:

- name of activity
- age of children the activity would be appropriate for
- maximum and minimum group size
- time that should be allowed for the activity
- preparation time

- resources and equipment required

- learning intentions, i.e. what the children will gain from this activity (learning intentions can be linked to the Early Years curriculum)

- implementation, i.e. how exactly the activity should be carried out – this might include the role of the adult during the activity.

In addition, activity plans might also show how the activity can be extended and adapted to suit children who have particular needs. Some settings also include a section which shows the target language that is to be used with children.

NOTE TO STUDENTS

Activity plans give you the opportunity to show that you are able to plan carefully and choose activities that are appropriate for the age of children with whom you are working.

Activity plans that are produced as part of coursework can be set out using the bulleted headings above (see the example on page 97). They should be as detailed as possible and have a rationale that explains why this activity has been chosen and why it is suitable for the age of the child or children.

You may also use references to show evidence that you have researched the needs of children of this age. It is a good idea to explain how the activity will help children's overall development rather than simply listing the benefits; for example, 'through finger painting the child will learn about the texture of paint and discover how to make marks'. By including a section on health and safety you will also show that you have considered the potential hazards of any activity.

Most courses ask that activity plans should be evaluated (see Chapter 5 on evaluation).

Individual Education Plans

Although activities should always be planned to meet the needs of individual children, there are often times when a child's needs require that activities are planned to support the child further. Staff may notice that a child's progress in one area of development seems delayed, or parents may comment on an aspect of their child's behaviour that is giving concern. Once a child's needs are identified a programme may be put together specifically to help that child; for example, a child refugee may need particular emotional and social support. In England and Wales these types of plans are called Individual Education Plans (IEP) and are a key way in which children are supported. In Scotland and Northern Ireland slightly different terms are used, but the principle of devising a plan to focus on an individual child's needs remains the same.

Plans are usually drawn up using information gained from several people. This will include the child's parents, the person in the setting who has responsibility

Detailed Plan or Activity Plan

Activity	Tray painting

Number of children	4	**Age of children**	3 years

Setting Messy area	**Preparation time** 10 minutes	**Activity time** 10–15 minutes

Resources	**Key Learning Intentions**
4 trays Ready mixed paint – red, green 4 aprons Thin card and A4 paper Large brush Pencil Plastic covering for table	• To learn how to make a print • To share materials • To explore the texture of paint

Links to Early Years curriculum

Knowledge and understanding of the world • Discovery of printing and links to books and other printed materials	*Physical development* • Develop co-ordination and control through placing paper onto tray, drawing pattern and brushing paint
Mathematics • Find out about patterns • Count out pencils and aprons	*Language and literacy* • Talk about feel of paint • Listen to others • Develop primitive writing skills
Creative development • Opportunity to discover feel and texture of paint • Design own patterns and self-expression through paint • Use paint in a new way	*Personal and social development* • Share, take turns • Work as part of a group • Concentration on the activity • Gain confidence in own achievements

Specific language to be developed: descriptive words about the feel of the paint – sticky, wet, cold, tickly – as well as encouraging children afterwards to describe what they have done

Implementation
- Ask the children to put their aprons on
- Show the children a pattern that has already been made
- Talk to the children about printing
- Spread the paint thinly but evenly across the tray with a large paintbrush
- Ask one of the children to draw a pattern in the paint with a finger
- Place a sheet of A4 paper onto the tray and ask one of the children to gently smooth it down
- Lift up the paper and show the children
- Ask the children what they think has happened
- Put another piece of paper over the tray to see if the pattern can be printed again
- Ask all the children if they would like a turn
- Repeat the activity if the children are still interested
- Make sure that children wash their hands thoroughly after the activity
- Mount and display the work when it is dry

Evaluation and comments

An example of an activity plan

for implementing the Special Needs policy (in England and Wales, this post is known as the SENCO – Special Educational Needs Co-ordinator) as well as any other professionals such as speech therapists or physiotherapists. This approach means that an overall picture of the child's needs can be drawn up. It is also important to note that parents are very much part of the process in drawing up a plan and this practice is reinforced by legislation, such as the SEN Code of Practice 2001 in England and Wales. Interestingly, children should also be involved in the process of drawing up the plan.

It is important to bear in mind that Individual Education Plans are not only used for children with severe difficulties. They can also be used with children who have particular strengths in some areas or who have very short-term emotional needs.

Devising an Individual Education Plan

There are clear steps involved in devising an Individual Education Plan. In schools and some nurseries one person (the SENCO in England and Wales) may have the overall responsibility for ensuring that plans are produced, but quite often it is the staff who actually work with the child who will devise the plan using information gained from a range of sources including the parents.

Step 1: Identify the child's needs

Most Individual Education Plans are triggered as a result of an adult noticing that a child has a particular need. This may be through planned assessments, health checks, direct observation or simply by the parents or keyworker having an 'instinctive hunch'. It is worth noting that as soon as some concerns are raised about a child's needs, parents should be informed and then involved.

From this starting point it is essential that planned assessments and observations take place; for example, if a child is thought of as being 'withdrawn' it will be important to discover in what situations the child does socialise and how often the child interacts with adults.

The information gained by carrying out observations and assessments is then used to consider whether a specific programme is required. Plans are normally only drawn up when it is thought that the child's needs cannot be met by ordinary planning and simply extending or adapting activities.

Step 2: Set clear aims

Once a child's needs have been clearly identified, the next step is to set realistic aims for the programme, along with some timescales. This means that everyone working with the programme understands the priorities for that child. Where children have several areas of need it is usual to select only two or three aims at a time. For example, an aim for a four year old who seems withdrawn might be 'to play co-operatively with one other child'.

Step 3: Produce a plan

The next step is to produce a plan which shows how the aim is to be achieved. This means breaking the aim down into small goals; for example, before a child can play co-operatively with another child, the child needs to be able to play alongside other children.

Working out the goals and the activities needed to help the child achieve them tends to come with experience, but referring to standard developmental checklists can be helpful. It is useful to record on the plan who will be working with the child. Most plans also include a section that allows adults to comment on the progress of the child.

There are a variety of formats that can be used to show how the plan is to be implemented. Most plans show the following information:

- name of the child
- age of the child or date of birth
- aim of the learning programme/identified areas for development
- length of the learning programme
- people responsible for planning or implementing the programme

Name of child Josie		D.O.B. 2/11/99		
Keyworker Debra				
Date of plan 13/1/2005		**Date of next review** 14/2/2005		
Aim of programme Josie to play co-operatively with other children				
Goal	**Strategies**		**Date**	**Comments**
To share materials and take turns	• Adults to praise Josie when she takes turns and share materials • Josie's keyworker to work alongside her during group activities such as cooking • Josie's parents to play simple board games at home			
To work with one other child	• Josie's keyworker to provide structured activities such as lotto with Josie and one other child – 2 × 15 minutes weekly			

An example of an Individual Education Plan

- how the programme is to be monitored and reviewed
  - the programme of activities
  - signatures of parents and staff
  - date for the next review.

Step 4: Integrate the plan with weekly or daily planners

In order for a plan to be implemented it is important that it is integrated into the overall plans of a setting. This is often done when weekly or daily planners are being prepared. It is generally straightforward as most Individual Education Plans are looking at the way activities should be focused rather than the curriculum that is to be delivered. Some settings show in their weekly planners how individual children's plans are going to be implemented.

Where specific learning activities are required, for example, exercises to help a child's speech, activity plans might also need to be prepared. This means that other adults working in the setting will be able to follow the activity in the way that will best help the child.

Step 5: Review the plan

Individual Education Plans need to be reviewed and added to regularly. Strategies or goals may prove to be ineffective or a child may 'outgrow' the plan. It will often be the responsibility of the keyworker or class teacher to monitor the plan, but he or she will need to do this alongside colleagues and the parents of the child. Involving parents is considered to be essential as often the same strategies will be used at home, especially where particular aspects of a child's behaviour are being concentrated on.

NOTE TO STUDENTS

Understanding and planning for an individual child's needs is very rewarding. Producing an Individual Education Plan provides good evidence for both observation and assessment and learning activities modules. You should show that you have followed the five steps above by producing an overall rationale to accompany your Individual Education Plan. This **rationale** should explain:

- how you identified the child's needs
- the aim of the plan
- the goals and strategies you included.
- You can also provide some activity plans for the activities and strategies that have been identified on the plan.

The reflective practitioner

◆ Does the routine meet children's needs?

◆ Are there any elements of the routine that create difficulties for staff or children?

◆ Do I refer to the curriculum or frameworks when planning?

◆ How are children's interests and needs reflected in the planning?

◆ Have I seen examples of how other settings manage their planning process?

◆ Is there a wide contribution towards planning from others such as children, parents and colleagues?

◆ How are child initiated activities shown in the planning?

◆ What is the balance of structured to unstructured activities in the setting?

◆ Is the outdoor area being planned for effectively?

◆ How are individual children's learning needs reflected in the planning?

Chapter 5   Implementation and evaluation of plans

Implementing plans and activities

Preparing and carrying out activities with children forms a large part of the day-to-day work with children. It is also the part which many early years workers find the most rewarding and pleasurable, although a lot of hidden work and preparation lie behind successful sessions.

The four elements which form the background to activities are:

- preparation
- layout and timing
- health and safety
- the role of adults.

Preparation

Most experienced early years workers have learnt that good preparation is the key to successful activity sessions with children. Good preparation involves thinking ahead and considering the potential problems; for example, trying out a new recipe for bird seed cakes at home to see if the mixture would become too hot for children, or seeing if a new type of paint stains the hands.

Preparation takes time and this must be allowed for when setting up activities and play opportunities within the daily routine. At the end of sessions, stock needs to be checked as part of the preparation process, as it is frustrating for both adults and children if equipment and resources are unavailable next time.

Layout

The layout of individual activities or whole play areas can affect the success of a session. Children tend to gravitate to tables and play areas where they can instantly see the play possibilities. This means a dressing-up corner with mirrors and a selection of builder's tools, workman's hats and reflective jackets is likely to prompt children into 'fixing' games. In the same way a table with a good selection of interesting collage materials will create an interest just by the feel and look of the resources.

In contrast, it is also interesting to see that young children can be overwhelmed by too many toys – almost as if they cannot focus on the play possibilities because there are too many. This means that in toddler and baby rooms, less equipment may be put out at a time, but it will be changed several times during a session.

Most early years workers also find that when a play area becomes too untidy children begin to become restless and do not play well, so during sessions you should aim to keep play areas attractive so that they remain inviting. You may also 'freshen up' the play possibilities by, for example, topping up the glue on a collage table or putting out some new materials. This needs to be done in a discreet way so that children do not feel that they cannot spread out and explore while they are playing. This is essential as children will find it hard to settle into play if they feel that they are unable to make a mess or that an adult will be constantly tidying up around them.

It is also important when laying out a room to check that there are enough play opportunities and activities on offer for children. Sensory materials are particularly popular with most children and so there needs to be enough of them. It is also important to think about using the outdoor area effectively. While there might not be a huge space indoors for an imaginative play area, creating one outdoors can extend provision and open up new play opportunities for children.

Practical considerations

The layout of activities requires practical consideration. Most settings divide their space into different areas, which allows for messy activities such as paint and water to be placed near sinks and towels. Layouts must ensure children's safety and ease of access and departure; for example, fire exits should never be blocked and there should be room to move between activities easily. If the outdoor space is easily available, some planning must go into how children can move outside from the indoors. Raincoats, for example, might be provided near the door so that children can easily pop outdoors without having first to visit a separate cloakroom.

As well as thinking about the best areas to house activities and equipment, it is also important to think about storage. With the greater emphasis on children taking responsibility and developing self-reliance, this means that some storage needs to be child led. Children will need to be able to reach and serve themselves to equipment as well as put it away.

It is also considered good practice to change the layout of a room from time to time, as this stimulates children's interest and is a way of evaluating pieces of

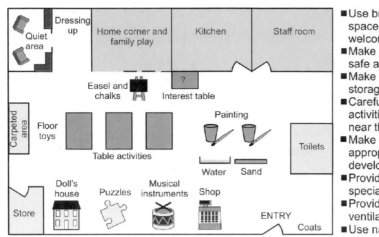

- Use bright colours to make the space look attractive and welcoming.
- Make sure furniture is child-sized, safe and child-friendly.
- Make the most effective use of storage space.
- Carefully plan areas for different activities - e.g. messy play areas near the sink.
- Make sure toys and activities appropriate to children's developmental level are available.
- Provide facilities for children with special needs.
- Provide adequate heat and ventilation.
- Use natural light to best effect.

A nursery layout

equipment and resources. Some settings find that by simply moving a piece of equipment such as a slide, children become more interested in it.

Timing and staffing

When implementing activities it is worth thinking about how to organise staffing. Some activities, such as cooking or physical play with large apparatus, either require close adult supervision or simply benefit from an adult being on hand. This means that some overall thought has to be given to the structure of the session which will enable early years workers to supervise but also interact with individual and groups of children. In general terms a good mix of play experiences and activities that range from the structured to the unstructured works well. This allows children plenty of opportunities to explore and play in their own way while also allowing for one or two focused activities which require adult input.

Timing also needs to be thought about. Children need time to develop their play and really become immersed in it. It is frustrating for children to be constantly interrupted because it is time to change activity or because it is the end of the session. There are also peaks and troughs in children's energy cycles and these affect concentration; these are particularly apparent with babies and toddlers so must be taken into consideration. It means that first thing in the morning is generally a good time to plan activities that will require energy and concentration, while activities at the end of the day may need to be relaxing and allow children to wind down.

Health and safety

Keeping children safe and healthy is a fundamental duty of early years workers. In practice, this means being very vigilant and maintaining high standards of cleanliness and maintenance. New pieces of equipment or ideas for activities should be 'risk assessed' even if this is just a mental process: how might children use/abuse the equipment? Outdoor areas will need to be checked at the start of each session to ensure that the physical environment is safe; for example, that no animals have soiled there and no rubbish has been thrown. Indoors, most settings develop their own cleaning and maintenance routines which form part of the clearing and packing away process.

During a session a constant watch should be kept on children as accidents can happen very quickly; a simple object such as a paint brush could be accidentally poked in another child's eye or a visitor may not shut a gate properly.

The checklist below shows three elements that are important in ensuring children's health and safety during sessions.

GOOD PRACTICE GUIDE

Health and safety checklist

Vigilance

◆ Staff are observant

◆ Staff intervene in potentially dangerous situations promptly

◆ Stimulating activities prevent children from becoming restless

Hygiene

◆ Toilet and other areas are checked during the session

◆ Toys and equipment are routinely cleaned

◆ Floors, tables and other areas are routinely cleaned

◆ The personal hygiene of staff is good

◆ Staff help children with their personal hygiene

◆ Waste products are disposed of appropriately

Safety precautions

◆ Materials, chemicals and medicines are stored appropriately

◆ Safety products, such as stair gates, are correctly used at all times

◆ Outdoor areas are checked before the start of each session

◆ Equipment is checked for damage

◆ Equipment and materials carry appropriate safety marks and are used according to manufacturer's instructions

◆ Heating, lighting and ventilation are routinely checked

The role of adults

The reflective practitioner

The role of adults is critical in working with children. The EPPE (Effective Provision of Pre-School Education) project clearly shows that adults make a significant difference to children's learning (see page 45). Today there is a huge emphasis on adults who work with children thinking about the way that they work. The term 'reflective practitioner' is often used to express this concept. If you are a student, you may be asked to evaluate your own practice in a critical and objective manner. This has huge benefits for both the adult and the children. Children benefit because the practitioner becomes more aware of the needs of the children and tends to respond in increasingly effective ways, while the practitioners finds that as their practice develops, they gain more confidence and enjoyment from their work. Being a reflective practitioner also means keeping up to date with training opportunities and exploring alternative ways of working.

Early years workers have to develop some special skills in order to work effectively with children. Some of these 'key skills' are considered in the table below.

Key skills for working with children

◆ *Judging how best to support children during unstructured activities*

Adults have to be able to gauge when and how to intervene in child led activities – too much intervention can interrupt the flow of children's play and learning, but a lack of support may mean that children's play becomes repetitive or learning opportunities are missed. Sometimes adults need to provide a further stimulus to children's activities by giving them some ideas or equipment and then withdrawing slightly.

◆ *Responding to unexpected learning opportunities*

It is not unusual for unplanned learning opportunities to present themselves – for example, a child notices that the glue turned clear when it dried. Early years workers should try to use these opportunities as they occur even if they are not seen as the key learning intentions. Unplanned learning needs to be seen as valuable as it is quite often memorable for children. The term 'happy accident' is used when an event takes place that looks at first sight to be a problem, for example, when paint drips or when the den collapses. In reality, these can be turned into exciting learning opportunities if the adult is able to respond positively. You might, for example, ask children if they can work out why the paint might have dripped and also encourage them to come up with some solutions as to how to prevent this from happening.

(Continued)

◆ *Encouraging children to persevere*

There are often situations where children need a little help or encouragement from an adult in order to finish an activity, such as a jigsaw or drawing. This may mean giving children a little helping hand or simply a few words of encouragement or support. For some children, an adult who does not actually help but literally spends time sitting with the child and talking to him or her will help the child to persevere. Helping children to persevere to the end of the activity can increase their self-esteem and concentration skills.

◆ *Interacting with children*

A major part of the early years worker's role is to build children's communication and language skills. This is especially vital for babies and toddlers whose language skills will develop according to the amount of input they receive. Early years workers will need to adjust their style of interaction according to the age group they are working with. Babies need to hear running commentaries and experience physical and eye contact. Older children may need questioning and prompts to learn from their experiences, for example, questions such as 'Why do you think that the water is now cold?'

As well as talking, adults need to be able to listen and simply chat to children. This is particularly essential if children have long hours in a setting as by the time they get home, they may be too tired to chat or there may not be enough time. Chatting to children means responding and following the direction of their conversation rather than imposing yours. It is important that opportunities to 'chat' are not seen by adults as a waste of time: they actually develop children's communication skills and help children's self-esteem. They can also help adults get to know a child, and the development of this relationship can have a huge impact on children's responsiveness and behaviour.

◆ *Recognising when to change activities*

Recognising when to change activities is an important skill as once children's interest and concentration have waned, they will no longer gain from the activity and they may become restless. When children are not engaged they are more likely to show behaviours that are inappropriate. Observing children carefully can often be revealing. You might, for example, notice signs that children are no longer engaged through observing body language. They might look around and be easily distracted or they might begin to play with materials in destructive ways. These signals must be noticed and acted upon. You might, for example, go over and chat to a child or remind a child of what else is on offer. Where adult led activities are taking place, it is even more essential to observe children. Persevering with a structured activity when children are not responding is futile and can put children off and teach them that they do not like number, reading or whatever the activity is meant to be about.

◆ *Extending or adapting activities to meet children's needs*

It is important for adults working with children to know how to adapt or extend an activity for a child, i.e. to make a task easier or more challenging. This is the way in

(Continued)

which you can include all children and is a major focus of inclusion policies. Ideally you should think about the needs of children before an activity starts, but in some cases you will need to adapt the activity once you see that it is not meeting a child's needs. For example, during a treasure hunt in which children are outdoors hunting for their names, it might become obvious that one child is looking unsure. The activity needs to be quickly adapted by the adult to avoid a child becoming frustrated or worse still feeling that he has failed. The adult may therefore ask the child if they can hunt together for the names or ask the child if he would like to hide a few more names. As well as adapting activities it is also important to think of ways of extending activities so that children can be further stimulated. A toddler, for example, might be ready to try out a sit and ride toy that can be steered while a group of children might be interested in being shown some new tools and equipment. Varying the activity according to the needs of the children will mean that children enjoy learning and do not get bored or feel that they have failed.

◆ *Encouraging children to take ownership of activities*

Most children will concentrate for longer periods when they have some kind of ownership over an activity or play experience. This means that wherever possible children should be encouraged to be creative and make their own decisions. This requires adults to be confident, and quite often the more confident early years worker is able to find opportunities for children to develop their own ideas or approach an activity in their own way. For example, he or she may choose a cooking activity that lends itself to children making choices and being involved in the preparation, such as making a salad or making pizzas where children prepare and choose their own toppings. Children's ideas might not always be very practical but wherever possible adults should support and encourage them rather than dissuade them. Activities that are very formal and structured can prevent children from using their imagination and are unlikely to stimulate them.

◆ *Recognising and praising children*

All children need praise and recognition. It should be given freely and not tied simply to what a child has achieved or produced. Children need to be recognised simply because they are persevering or playing well alongside other children. While recognition is at its most powerful during an activity or play experience, it is important that you do not disrupt or distract children. This means that you might simply pass by and comment that their game looks fun and that you are pleased that they are playing so well together. It is important that adults praise and recognise children in such a way that they do not simply 'do' an activity to please an adult. The eventual aim is always that children should be self-motivated and that they learn to inwardly recognise their own efforts. This is why you might sometimes ask children if they are pleased with themselves and what they have done. You might, for example, say to a child who has just finished a puzzle, 'Was it exciting to put that last piece in?' This approach still gives children recognition but at the same time helps children learn to appreciate their own efforts.

Stickers such as this give children an enormous boost

Evaluation

As part of the planning process, time should be taken to monitor and evaluate how activities have worked. This should also include some observation and assessment of children's progress and needs. The information gained should then be used to form the next round of planning; for example, an activity that has been very successful may be repeated, adapted or extended.

Gathering information

In order to be able to evaluate effectively, a wide range of information has to be gathered. This will help settings to be sure that they can evaluate objectively. There are many sources of information that can be drawn on, including:

- staff feedback
- parents' comments
- direct observation of children
- children's comments
- comments from other professionals including Ofsted reports
- assessment of children.

Staff feedback

This is the most frequently used source of information as it is easily accessible. The danger of only using staff feedback is that it can be very subjective and some staff can find any evaluation of their own performance threatening. For example, a staff member dislikes supervising outdoor play as she prefers to be inside; she may report back that the time allocated for outdoor play is too long and that the children are becoming restless.

Parents' comments

Comments from parents can be very useful and it is important that they are considered, even though occasionally they may seem negative. For example, a parent may complain that the children never come out of a setting on time. This comment might indicate that the routine of the setting needs altering to ensure that enough time is allocated for children to be ready.

Parents are able to contribute another perspective about the progress and needs of their children, which is why comments should be noted. It is generally considered good practice to involve parents as much as possible as parents know their children well and often understand their needs. They also know what their children enjoy doing in the home; for example, a toddler may at home really enjoy doing simple puzzles. Taking on board parents' observations means that you can build on children's home interests. Good relationships with parents are therefore fundamental to this process. Where parents feel relaxed, this in turn will help them to comment. With older children, parents also get to hear about the child's perspectives. Children may tell their parents what they have and indeed have not enjoyed doing, so working with parents can be quite informative.

Direct observation of children can provide much useful information

Direct observation of children

Directly observing children can help you to evaluate their progress as well as the effectiveness of planned activities. Direct observations can be recorded and used to monitor children's development or they can be done in an informal way to support general feedback on the effectiveness of activities. It is worth observing groups of children as well as individual children during sessions. Observing several children at once can give you a feel as to whether sessions as well as particular activities are engaging children. You may, for example, notice that specific areas of a room are underused or that certain areas are extremely popular. This can help you to plan more effectively.

Children's comments

It is increasingly seen as good practice to involve children as much as possible. Comments from children may help you reflect on what is happening in the setting from their point of view. Where children are too young or do not have the language skills to tell you what they have enjoyed doing, you need to use observations instead. Adults need to look out for activities that seem to really interest children and hold their attention.

Comments from other professionals

A range of information can come from other professionals, including comments relating to a particular child's progress; for example, a speech therapist may comment on a child's language development. Sources of information may also include reports from inspection visits where strengths or weaknesses in areas of provision might be highlighted.

Assessment of children

Assessments of children can provide feedback about your provision and effectiveness. If, for example, you find that many of the babies you work with are not meeting the milestones for language development, it might help you to think about whether the language input is sufficient. On the other hand, if you recognise that the four year olds you work with have good independence skills, you might conclude that you are providing the right opportunities for these skills to be developed.

Building evaluation into the planning process

A good way to embed the evaluation process in an organisation is to build it in as part of the planning process. For example, activities can be identified within a curriculum plan that can also be used to assess ßchildren's progress and therefore to evaluate the effectiveness of the setting's planning.

Sometimes, simply adding a 'comments' column to paperwork such as the weekly planner can provide opportunities for staff to comment on individual children or the effectiveness of an activity (as shown in the table on page 113). Comments can be brief but will provide a focus for further discussion.

Helping staff to assess the effectiveness of activities

You have seen that staff feedback plays an important role when evaluating activities. As part of the evaluation process staff will need to be able to evaluate individual activities objectively and consider their value to the children.

It can be a good idea to have a list of questions to help guide early years workers through this evaluation process. The evaluation checklist on page 114 offers some ideas for such questions.

Weekly planner

Name of nursery:	Kids Galore	Theme:	Families	
Week commencing:	22/11	Age of children:	3–4 years	
Day am/pm	Activity	Key learning intentions	Staff and children involved	Individual children's needs	Comments/evaluation
Mon am	Paint people in our family	Talk about families. Adults are larger than children	Sarah + Jo, Mary, Katie and Tom	Tom's mum due to have baby in December. Use this as an opportunity to talk about this?	Lots of language used. Children counted their family members. Tom did not mention new baby and did not respond when asked about new brothers and sisters.
Mon am	Happy families – card game (simplified version)	Matching sets. Turn taking. Talking about groups	Dave + Greg, Elizabeth, Rajeet, Shirin	See if Shirin can match?	Worked well, although children needed to play through once with all the cards being face up. Shirin matched several cards.
Mon am	Popoids	Make own characters and give them names	Dawn + any children interested		Connor enjoyed this and he stayed with this activity for 20 minutes. He wants to make a house for them tomorrow.

This weekly planner has a section for comments and evaluation

GOOD PRACTICE GUIDE

Evaluation checklist

Overall

◆ Did the children show signs of enjoying themselves?

◆ Did the children concentrate on the activity or were they easily distracted?

◆ Did children have longer or shorter concentration spans than they normally do?

◆ Did the activity stimulate language opportunities?

◆ Did all the children participate fully? If not, why?

◆ What opportunities, if any, for spontaneous learning occurred?

◆ In what ways did the activity fit the planned learning outcomes?

◆ Were there any children who did not largely benefit from this activity? If so, why?

Practical aspects

◆ Was the preparation time adequate for this activity?

◆ Were all the materials and resources available?

◆ Were these the best resources for this activity?

◆ How easy was the activity to supervise, direct or support?

◆ Was the activity appropriate for the time of day/routine of the setting?

Extension and reinforcement activities

◆ How could this activity be developed further?

◆ Were there any children who seemed to be particularly interested in this activity?

◆ Were there any children who would benefit by repeating this type of activity?

◆ Were there any children who did not respond or were not enjoying this activity?

Keeping records

It is helpful if staff keep a running record during activities. This means that if children need further help or reinforcement activities these can be added in or, if an activity has not worked very well, this can be noted. Some settings provide jotters for staff so that they can make notes that can then be transferred to the keyworkers or teachers after an activity. Keeping some form of running record helps the evaluation process as it provides more focused and objective feedback. A note of the children who have spent time in a play area or who have participated in an adult led activity is also useful. This can help you to work out if any children are missing out on areas of learning or skills, for example, a child who never uses the imaginative play area or small world toys but loves playing in the sand might need to be introduced to these activities. You may, for example, put a few dinosaurs in the sand tray.

Assessing children's development

There are many reasons why it is important to assess children's development. Firstly, it helps you to check that you are meeting children's needs and that activities that you are planning are appropriate. In some cases assessments will also flag up that children need additional support from other professionals. Finally, assessments can help you to reflect upon your own practice. If, for example, several toddlers are not meeting the expected development in language, this might mean that you are not providing sufficient language opportunities.

Assessment should not be about labelling children

Some early years practitioners have serious reservations about carrying out assessments. This is because there is a potential for assessments to be used as convenient 'labels' for children. Terms such as 'less able' or 'higher ability' are frequently used in education-speak. In some ways such terms need to be brought into question as they are effectively labelling children in quite global terms. This can in turn mean that from an early age, expectations and therefore opportunities for children might be lowered. Adults who believe they are working with children who are 'less able' might easily plan activities that are not challenging enough and so do not provide children with opportunities to acquire additional skills and concepts.

This means that when assessments are collated, the language that is used needs to be sensitive. It is also important that everyone understands that assessments are temporary. A four year old who is finding it hard to recognise his or her name and count to twenty may three weeks later have cracked those skills.

Assessments should be useful

As well as being aware of the danger of labelling, it is also important that you ensure that assessments are useful. This means that you need to be clear why you are doing them and how they will benefit the child. This is easier to write in some settings than to actually put into practice. However, even if you do find yourself compiling assessments that you feel are not relevant, consider also carrying some out that you feel are important for both you and the child. Taping a child's speech, for example, is likely to give you significant amounts of information.

Involving parents

You have seen that comments from parents can help you to consider the effectiveness of your practice. Parents also need to be involved in the process of assessment. It is useful if you can find out about the interests and skills that children are showing at home as children's responses in the home can be different to those in a setting. The degree to which parents wish to be involved will of course vary, but ideally you should always look for ways of collating and sharing information. It is also worth noting that where practitioners regularly talk to parents about children's progress and interests, it is usually easier to bring up any concerns or make suggestions.

Types of assessment

Assessment tools that practitioners use vary enormously and depend on the setting and the area of the country. Most assessment systems rely on checklists or statements that are divided either into areas of learning reflecting the curriculum areas or into developmental areas. Practitioners look at the checklist or statements and decide whether the child has met them. Observations of the child are usually the evidence which practitioners rely on in order to help them make the assessments.

Assessing children under three years

It is essential to carry out regular and very frequent observations on children under 3 years. Babies' and toddlers' development can be very rapid and unless they are being observed on at least a weekly basis, it can be hard to keep pace. This is important if you are to be able to plan to meet their developmental but also health and safety needs.

Assessing children over three years

While the pace of development is generally slower, the need to observe continues. Children's interests can change and develop, and within each area of development or curriculum area there are many interdependent aspects. Many practitioners find it helpful to carry out holistic observations alongside ones which focus on children's particular skills and interests, in order to pull together an overall view of the child.

Using the evaluation process to inform planning

For the planning cycle to be complete, the evaluation of previous activities and plans must be used to inform future plans. In most settings the information gained from evaluation will be shared and commented on before the process of planning begins again. For example, if an inspection report comments that there are not enough opportunities for children to use musical instruments, staff will probably discuss ways in which musical instruments can be made more accessible.

As a result of the evaluation process, it is likely that some changes will be made either to current or future plans, although these may be minor. If curriculum or weekly plans are changed, it is important that everyone who is involved in these plans is informed about the changes. This may mean making sure that a list is kept of any staff member who was not present at the meeting and also a list of people who come into the settings to help, such as students and volunteers. In the same way, changes to individual education programmes may need to be discussed with other professionals and parents as they may also have some feedback that will make the new plan more effective.

The reflective practitioner

◆ Do I keep a note of children's responses to activities?

◆ Are children's interests noted and used to inform planning?

◆ Is adequate time available for the preparation of sessions?

◆ Do all members of staff understand the purpose and learning intentions of activities?

◆ Do I encourage children to take ownership of adult directed activities?

◆ Is sufficient time available for children to develop their own play themes and ideas?

NOTE TO STUDENTS

As part of your coursework, you may need to produce written evaluations about the plans you have produced. The aim of these written evaluations is to encourage you to reflect on the organisation and usefulness of your plans. This is a major step in being a reflective practitioner and so is an important skill. As you progress in your studies, the chances are that your evaluations will become steadily longer and also more critical. You are likely to be able to reflect more easily on what you have learnt and also work out ways of improving your future practice.

It can be helpful to write up the evaluation in three parts:

1   Review of plan

This part of the evaluation can be descriptive and essentially gives a brief description of how the plan was implemented and how effective it was.

2   Learning outcomes and responses of the children

This section should look at what the children actually gained from the plans.

Were the planned learning outcomes achieved? Did children seem to gain from the activities or routine? It is important here also to think about benefits that you had not planned for. They might include the way in which children co-operated, the development of friendships or the amount of language that was drawn from the activity.

As children's reactions vary it can be a good idea to focus on particular children's learning outcomes. How did they react? What parts of the activity did they enjoy? How did they use the materials? You can use observations taken during the activity to support this section.

It is also a good idea to consider whether any individual children needed extra support and what type of activities they would benefit from in the future.

3   Learning outcomes for the student

This section should concentrate on your performance and what you have learnt from producing the plan. What have you learnt about the children you worked with? How could you improve this activity for them? In retrospect, should you have adapted or extended

(Continued)

117

this activity? If so, how? How could you improve your planning skills? How would you approach this type of planning in the future?

When a plan is successful you may need to think about the reasons why it was successful. Was it because you had researched carefully the needs of the children? Or was it because of the help and guidance you had received from your supervisors?

Evaluation of plans

ACTIVITY

◆ Choose one child in your setting who would benefit from a series of activities in one particular area of development, for example, a child who is ready to learn colours or count to five.

◆ Produce a curriculum plan showing activities that might benefit this child.

◆ Write a rationale that explains your choice of activities and how they will help this child's area of development.

◆ Produce three detailed plans that show how you would implement three of the activities.

◆ Choose one of these activities to carry out with the child alone or within a group of children.

◆ Write an evaluation of this activity.

Chapter 6   Core activities for babies and children under three years

Babies and toddlers have slightly different play needs than older children. One of the key differences is that babies and toddlers needs more adult support and interaction in their play. While children from around three years will be starting to play together, young children need to learn these play skills from being with adults. This means that the role of the adult is crucial when looking at activities for the under threes. This chapter looks at the role of the adult as well as some of the core activities including some traditional simple games that adults can offer babies and toddlers. It covers:

- nappy changing
- meal and snack time
- washing and dressing
- treasure basket and heuristic play
- rhymes and songs
- sensory activities
- traditional simple games.

Adults are the key to successful core activities

The need for adult support and interaction means that the success of any activity is linked to the way in which adults actually work with young children. In this chapter we look at core activities and suggest their learning benefits, although whether children will actually benefit from them relies almost completely on the way in which the adult works with the child.

Consistent emotional care

Babies and toddlers have a terrific need for emotional security. Without this emotional security, they find it hard to learn, concentrate and even physically

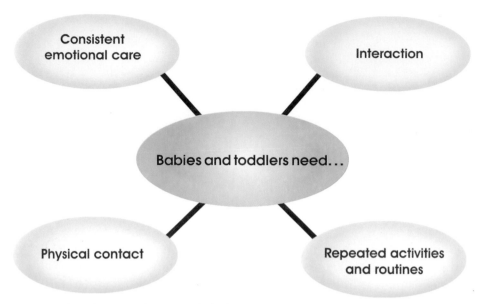

Essentials when working with babies and toddlers

thrive. The basis for providing emotional security is actually quite simple. Babies and toddlers need to spend most or all of their time with the same person. This person or 'keyworker' acts as a temporary substitute for their bond with parents and allows the child to feel secure. Ideally, as many core activities as possible, including aspects of physical care, need to be carried out by a child's keyworker.

Interaction

Babies and toddlers need to pick up the skills of language and communication. In the longer term this will help them to socialise with others. It will also help them to store and use information which is the basis for thought. By interacting well with babies and toddlers, adults help them to break into language and communication. This is easier to do when adults have a close and genuine relationship with a child, which again is linked to the amount of time that they spend with a child.

The term 'running commentary' is often used in connection with the way that adults interact with young children, especially babies. The aim of the running commentary is to narrate what is happening and to draw babies' and toddlers' attention to specific objects or events. Frequent repetition of activities and games means that increasingly children begin to understand the meaning of particular words and phrases. If the same adult repeats activities with children, a language routine develops. This means that the child can begin to anticipate what is about to be said and might try to vocalise. As well as providing a running commentary, adults need also to make good eye contact with children and react instantly to their smiles and vocalisations. Acknowledgment of their early attempts to communicate means that they learn to enjoy the process of communication.

Physical contact

Being held and touched is extremely important for babies and toddlers. It seems to provide emotional reassurance and so when you carry out activities, it is important to think about providing this physical contact. This might mean encouraging a toddler to sit on a lap while looking at a book or gently stroking the hand of a baby who is feeding from a bottle. While you need to offer plenty of opportunities for physical contact, it is also important to note and follow children's needs and desires. It is not unusual for a toddler one moment to have arms outstretched wanting to be picked up for a cuddle and the next moment to be wriggling to get down. It is almost as if once children know that physical reassurance is readily available, the need for it disappears.

Physical care routines can work as core activities

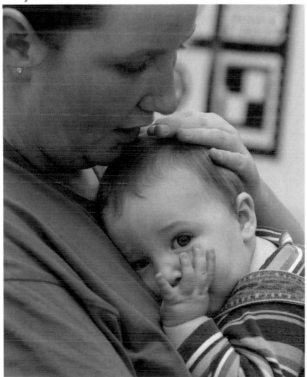

Touch is an essential part of working with babies and toddlers

Physical care routines are essential in helping babies and toddlers to learn. Young children learn best when they can make connections and build on the familiar. Physical care routines are repetitious and it is for this reason that they make excellent learning activities for young children. Ironically, it is their repetitious nature that, in the past, has made adults feel that they are not valued activities. This has created a tendency to see them as inconveniences that need to be rushed through as quickly as possible.

Repeated activities and routines

Young children need stimulation. This comes in part from interaction and physical contact, but also from activities and routines. This might be simply having the opportunity to play peek-a-boo with an adult while dressing or knocking down a stack of beakers. The key for young children is that these activities are frequently repeated so that they can master the physical, language and cognitive skills. This means that you might have to build a tower of bricks six or seven times or to put on a sock that has just been pulled off five times in a row.

Nappy changing

Nappy changing provides a marvellous opportunity for babies and toddlers to have some individual time with an adult. In order for babies and toddlers to gain the most from this experience it is important that the child's keyworker carries out the nappy change. Nappy changing should be seen as a learning activity for the child from start to finish. This means that you need to engage the child before you actually take them for the nappy change. You might, for example, think about how children are collected for the nappy change. Older toddlers are likely to co-operate if you have spent a moment first playing alongside them and interacting with them rather than whisking them away from something that is fascinating them. You might have a song or rhyme that you sing as you carry them or they walk to the nappy changing area.

Setting up

Think about the area that is used for nappy changing. Make sure that it is comfortable but also stimulating. Consider ways in which the room or area can be changed so that the child has something new to look at. Make sure that the area is clean and also everything is to hand so that the nappy change itself can go smoothly. For toddlers who can find it hard to stay still during the nappy change, think about objects that can be safely given to them to explore.

Learning benefits of nappy changing
Physical benefits

A nappy is quite confining for a baby, even the latest compact types. Time spent without a nappy is therefore liberating and is one reason why some toddlers try to do a runner without their nappies. Look out for the way babies and toddlers kick, roll around and try to touch their feet. These movements all increase muscle strength. They also help young children learn more about their body, and you will see an increasing interest in looking at soiled nappies as children become more aware of their bodily functions.

Cognitive benefits

A nappy change gives babies and toddlers a different perspective. It is likely that they will be changed on a raised surface and will by lying on their backs, and you may also change them in a different room from the one they spend the most time in. If seeing the adult from a different height from normal, this gives them a new stimulus to explore. It may be one of the reasons why many babies and toddlers will have a go at pulling hair and touching the person changing them. The new perspective is stimulating, especially if you draw children's attention to different details within the room, such as mobiles or cupboards.

Language benefits

Nappy changing provides the opportunity for one to one interaction. The language used is likely to be of a similar nature each time, especially if the same person carries out the nappy change. The focus of the language during the change is likely to be on the child's body parts, clothes and also feelings of being clean. The familiarity of language and the context means that older babies soon show signs of recognising objects and the routine. If babies and toddlers are normally in group care where there is some background noise, you might find that they are interested in the sounds that they can hear when they are in a quieter room. They may be very quiet or they may take the opportunity to use their voices and explore the sounds they can make.

Social and emotional benefits

Nappy changing provides the opportunity for adult and child to become emotionally closer. It is an intimate experience and one which should leave the child feeling emotionally as well as physically more comfortable.

Nappy changing is also a complex emotional experience for babies and especially toddlers. There is usually some happiness about spending time with the adult and being free of the nappy, but also reluctance to be passive and still. Toddlers might also be interested in their bodily functions and become frustrated that they cannot touch what they have produced and that it is now being taken away from them. This is reflected in their behaviour, which can even change from nappy change to nappy change during a day. You might see frustrated behaviour and resistance but also enjoyment and interest, all in one day of changing.

Meal times

Meal and snack times are core activities and are important for children's care. Babies and toddlers should look forward to these times because they should be pleasurable moments. As with the other activities, children need plenty of one to one interaction with their key worker. This is particularly essential with children under two years old who are not likely to be interacting with other children.

Feeding should be a pleasurable experience

Setting up

It is important that babies and toddlers are not waiting for food and drink as this is a source of frustration for them. Interestingly, quite young babies are able to detect signs that they will be fed soon, such as the arrival of a bottle or having a bib put on. Toddlers may also need some warning that it will soon be time for them to leave a play activity. In some cases it might be worth allowing them to bring the toy they are playing with to the eating area, providing it can be wiped down afterwards.

When planning meal times it is worth understanding that they will take a significant amount of time. Babies and toddlers enjoy exploring the texture of food and will want to play with it alongside feeding themselves.

Learning benefits of meal times

Physical benefits

There are many physical benefits from meal times. Firstly, the nutritional benefits should not be forgotten. Happy and relaxed children tend to eat more and will also digest food easily. This in turn will help them to stay healthy and also to grow.

In addition, the process of actually eating the food is important to the development of the mouth. Sucking and, later on, chewing develops the muscles in the mouth and tongue and this is important for speech. Babies and toddlers also gain hand–eye co-ordination through the opportunity to feed themselves.

By being given a spoon and, later on, a fork, children also learn how to manipulate a tool.

Cognitive benefits

Babies and toddlers are primed to learn through their senses in their earliest years. Babies and young toddlers are particularly interested in exploring using their mouths. Food and drink provides sensory stimulus and babies quickly show that they have preferences for certain tastes and, as they get older, textures. Babies and toddlers also enjoy exploring food with their hands and while this may not be appealing to us, it is an important part of their learning. Properties of foods such as how it spreads, squashes and smears is actually very early science. Babies and toddlers are also learning through trial and error how objects can change shape – thus flattening a piece of bread between the fingers and then sucking it is of great interest. As well as seeing an interest in the properties of food, you will also see an interest in liquids. Most babies and toddlers shake their beakers and are interested in watching drips of liquid appear.

In addition, you will see that babies and toddlers become interested in the objects that are used for feeding such as spoons, bowls and even face cloths. They will learn about sounds, textures and also cause and effect as they attempt to lift, turn upside down or even throw the objects.

Language benefits

Meal and snack times provide opportunities for language. As adults are providing a running commentary in terms of eating style, babies and toddlers will learn the language linked to the event, for example 'last spoon' or 'all gone'. As there are elements of meal and snack times that are constant, babies and toddlers learn the words that are connected with them. Expressions such as 'more' and 'no' are quickly learnt as first words from around 15 months or so.

Emotional and social benefits

Food is a source of great comfort for babies and toddlers. Meal times should be associated with pleasure and can provide feelings of security and intimacy if the adult is engaging with the child. Meal times can also help the socialisation of young children. When they eat alongside adults and other children, they are likely to make eye contact and notice what they are doing.

Washing and dressing

Washing hands, wiping faces and dressing form a significant part of caring for young children. As with nappy changing and feeding, this type of care is also a core activity with learning benefits. As soon as possible babies and toddlers should be involved in their washing and dressing. This allows them to gain a little control over what is happening to them as well as helping them to gain co-ordination. It is also important to see washing and dressing as times when children's relationships with their keyworkers can be strengthened.

Setting up

You should make sure that you have everything to hand before starting. It is important to see washing and dressing in terms of an activity. Consider presenting it as a game, especially to toddlers who can be resistant. Draw babies' attention to their fingers, play peek-a-boo with a face flannel allowing the child to remove it from his or her face, and encourage children to push their limbs through sleeves and trouser legs.

Learning benefits of washing and dressing

Physical benefits

From being active in the dressing process, young children gain co-ordination of their limbs and as they attempt small movements, their hand–eye co-ordination develops.

From being involved in washing their hands and face, children also develop hand movements and become more aware of their bodies.

Cognitive benefits

Washing involves water and so is a sensory experience. Children can learn about the properties of water, especially if they are encouraged to play in a basin of water or with running water. If you play peek-a-boo type games when dressing and washing, children see how objects and people, even when hidden, do not simply disappear.

Washing and dressing helps children to learn about their own bodies and size. They also learn about shape; for example, a sock on the foot takes the shape of the foot and changes from being flat and shapeless.

Language benefits

If a child's keyworker is involved in washing and dressing, the chances are that a familiar pattern will emerge. This means that the language is likely to be repetitive and this helps young children understand and practise it. Children are likely to become familiar with the names of their body parts during washing and dressing. They may also develop an understanding of number if buttons and poppers are counted as they are fastened.

Emotional and social benefits

Washing and dressing represent time alone with an adult and so can help children to feel valued and secure. If adults encourage children as early as possible to be active in the process, they will also be gaining a feeling of independence and self-reliance. This can counter the frustration that toddlers often feel in their third year.

Treasure basket and heuristic play

Treasure basket and heuristic play encourages babies and toddlers to play in a way that promotes exploration and discovery. This is extremely important as it gives very young children opportunities to be in control and to learn that they can have an effect on their environment. The key difference between treasure basket and heuristic play is the type of objects that are given. Objects in treasure basket play are made of natural materials such as leather, wood and metal. Objects for heuristic play are everyday objects from the adult world and can be made of artificial materials such as plastic or nylon. During the activity the role of the adult is to keep a discreet eye on the children to ensure that they remain safe, but not to become involved in the play. The aim is that children are free to play and explore using their own ideas rather than copying those of an adult. This can lead to children making some quite original discoveries.

Setting up

Treasure basket play	Heuristic play
• Select 15 or so objects and place them in a basket that is easy for a non-mobile baby to reach into.	• Select 15–20 objects to put out in groups on the ground for children to explore.
• Choose objects from natural materials that are different in size.	• Choose objects in common use such as corks, plastic bottles, hair curlers, plugs, tins and boxes.
• Make sure that materials are clean and are safe for babies to explore using their mouths.	• Observe children as they play and note what they are particularly interested in.
• Change slightly the combination of objects each day.	• Build on this interest in other play activities.

Learning benefits of treasure basket and heuristic play

Physical benefits

The exploration of objects promotes hand–eye co-ordination. As children will probably play in a sustained way because of their fascination with the objects, they are likely to build muscles and hand strength. Young children who are mobile may choose to carry objects and so this type of play can also help locomotive skills.

Cognitive benefits

There are many cognitive benefits in heuristic play. Concentration levels are particularly high as children are often fascinated with what they are doing. Learning how to focus attention and to sustain attention is an important skill. Children are also learning to explore using a trial and error method. They may, for example, try inserting a cork into a bottle only to find that they cannot retrieve it. In this way, children learn about the properties of materials as well as seeing at first hand concepts such as size, shape and mobility.

Language benefits

Treasure basket and heuristic play are not strong language activities as the adult's role is not to influence and direct the child. Some children will, however, talk and direct themselves in play.

Emotional and social benefits

Treasure basket and heuristic play gives young children the opportunity to be responsible for their own play. They learn from this that they can be in control and independent of the adult. For toddlers this is especially beneficial. They can often have strong feelings of frustration as other elements of their lives are likely to be adult directed.

This activity also helps the child to learn about ownership as children are meant to have their own set of objects. In group care, having the opportunity to play alone with designated materials is important. This is because at other times children might be expected to share or co-operate with others. Having time to play alone in this way can help children's feelings of self-reliance.

Children also gain pleasure by discovering things for themselves and this can often be seen in their facial expressions and by their vocalisations. As children get older they also begin to note how other children explore the materials and begin to imitate each other.

Rhymes and songs

For thousands of years parents, especially mothers, have sung to their children. Singing and playing finger rhymes helps children to feel emotionally secure but also helps them to break into the sounds of the language that they are being exposed to. In addition, songs and rhymes help children learn to play and make contact with adults. A baby may, for example, take your hands and try to make them clap after you have finished playing pat-a-cake with them. In doing this they are signalling that they want to play again.

Setting up

The wonderful thing about using songs and rhymes with young children is that no preparation is required. Singing and rhymes can take place at any time. It is important to remember to think about the children's needs for repetition. This means that you will probably find yourself saying the same rhyme two or three times in response to the child's enjoyment. Building in eye contact and moments of expectation and anticipation is also vital. Watching to see if a child knows what will happen next gives you an indication of his or her understanding. Physical contact is also essential with early rhymes and songs. This means that they work best with individual children and may be used during other activities such as dressing and nappy changing.

Favourite songs and rhymes include: Bye Baby Bunting, Pat-a-cake, Humpty Dumpty, Round and Round the Garden Like a Teddy Bear, Ring a Ring o' Roses, and This Little Piggy.

Learning benefits of rhymes and songs

Physical benefits

Finger rhymes and action songs help babies and toddlers become aware of their bodies. They also help them to master small fine movements with their hands, for example, clapping or grasping fingers. Action songs such as Humpty Dumpty also help spatial awareness.

Cognitive benefits

Songs and rhymes help children to notice patterns and sounds. They help children to concentrate and develop memory skills. Where physical movements are used, children become more aware of their bodies.

Language benefits

Songs and rhymes help children to notice the sounds and speech patterns in the language that they are being exposed to. They also learn about intonation and expression. Children who are regularly exposed to songs and rhymes begin to join in and so learn about interaction and communication.

Emotional and social benefits

Songs and rhymes help children to feel that they belong. They give children feelings of security and emotional reassurance. This is why they are particularly effective at calming babies and toddlers. Socially, they act as an early play tool as the child learns to smile and respond to the adult.

Sensory activities

While young children want to play with food, they can also be provided with other sensory materials to touch and feel. Water, pasta and gloop are good examples of sensory materials that can be used with babies as well as with toddlers. These materials help children to play and explore textures while also helping them with their fine motor development.

Using sensory materials

Setting up

Sensory materials are usually messy and so being prepared is important. Choose moments in the daily routine when children are likely to need changing or washing anyway and protect the floor and yourself. Sensory materials do need good supervision and the best way of ensuring this is to play alongside the child. This helps the child learn how to handle the materials as well as giving you the opportunity to interact with them. Sensory materials can be presented on trays or on a larger scale in paddling pools or builder's mixing trays. In fine weather, they can be taken outdoors (it is important to keep babies and toddlers out of the sun and protected by sun cream).

Water

Supervise babies and toddlers constantly: it is possible for babies and toddlers to drown in very shallow water. Move the water out of reach when the activity is finished or better still pour it away. Make sure that there are cloths on hand to mop up any spills on the floor. Think about partially undressing babies and toddlers and have a spare change of clothes available. Provide opportunities for babies and toddlers to be able to 'go' into the water, for example, a paddling pool, as well as providing water in buckets or washing-up bowls.

Cooked pasta, rice and couscous

Cook pasta, rice or couscous in unsalted water. Small quantities of natural food colouring can be added if wanted. Keep refrigerated until required, but do not store for more than a few hours and do not reuse. Think about providing these activities after meal times so that children are already full and will be less likely to eat large quantities. Do expect that babies and toddlers will put these into their mouths and so be on hand in case of choking. As with all food, check first that children do not have any food allergies. Protect the floor and expect also that these materials might appear in hair and down garments. Provide some props such as spoons, bowls and beakers.

Gloop (cornflour and water)

Mix cornflour and water together to form a thick paste that will flow slowly when held from a spoon. Natural food colouring can be added to the water if desired. Put onto trays or large containers. This is a messy activity, but the mixture can be brushed off clothes and flooring when dry. Consider partially undressing babies. Provide some props such as spoons, small beakers and toys for older toddlers to extend the play. This activity should be suitable for a child who has a gluten free diet, but always check first that children do not have any food allergies.

Sand, gravel and bark chippings

These materials are best used with children over two years old as they are less likely to 'eat' them or to rub sand in their eyes. When introducing these materials, play alongside the children so that you can observe how they handle and use them. This is the best form of supervision as children are also likely to copy your movements. Encourage children to sweep up afterwards. To extend play, provide farm animals, dinosaurs, beakers, cups and small scoops.

Learning benefits of sensory materials

Physical benefits

Sensory materials help children's fine motor movements and hand–eye co-ordination. Children are likely to make repetitive movements and so build the muscles. Where materials are provided on a large scale, children gain whole body co-ordination.

Cognitive benefits

The sensory nature of the materials means that the brain is stimulated and aroused. Children learn about textures and properties of the materials. They do so in a trial and error way and will usually repeat actions to consider what is happening. Where adults are playing alongside children, you might also see modelling. This is where a child tries to copy movements made by the adult.

Language benefits

If adults play alongside children and provide a running commentary, they are likely to associate words and phrases with what they are doing. Older toddlers might also use language to direct themselves and to show adults what they are doing.

Social and emotional benefits

Sensory activities are relaxing and enjoyable for children. They can explore materials easily and are likely to feel in control and competent. Sensory materials are particularly good for toddlers who at other times might be frustrated if they have reached an age when they know what they want to do but are hampered by their physical skills. Adults playing alongside babies and toddlers help them to establish good relationships; in this way they learn to play alongside others.

Traditional simple games

There are a few simple games that babies and toddlers love playing. They require adult input at first, which will help babies and toddlers learn to play and interact. As with many activities, babies and toddlers will often want to keep repeating them.

Building and knocking down

This is a simple game but one that has many learning benefits for children. This game consists of building stacks of beakers, bricks or, with older toddlers, sand castles and then knocking them down. As children's physical skills increase they will attempt to build their own tower of bricks or beakers. From building and knocking down, children go on to become interested in construction play.

Learning benefits of building and knocking down
Physical benefits

This game helps develop babies' and toddlers' hand–eye co-ordination and fine motor skills.

Knocking down games are empowering

Cognitive benefits

From this simple activity children learn the concept of 'cause and effect'. They gradually realise that their actions affect objects. Children also learn about balance and positioning from trying to build their own towers. Babies and toddlers learn using a trial and error method and their skill gradually increases as they learn from their experiences.

Language benefits

Whilst adults are actively playing with children there will be a running commentary. Adults may also develop a language routine, for example, 'ready to knock it down – one, two, three, go!' This helps children to associate words and phrases with actions and events.

Emotional and social benefits

Building and knocking down games help babies and toddlers feel in control and powerful. This is good for their self-esteem. By playing alongside an adult, they learn the skills of how to play and take turns with others.

Enclosing games

Enclosing games are toys and activities where children put objects inside others. Shape sorters, piggy banks and Russian dolls are examples of popular toys that provide this game. It is also possible to use some everyday objects such as small boxes and shells or corks and plastic boxes. Children simply drop or put objects inside another container. At first young babies may appear surprised when they see that an object that has been put into a box is retrieved again by opening the box. This is because they have not developed object permanence, but from around eight months or so babies begin to understand that objects do not 'disappear' but that an object out of sight is still present (see hide and seek games below). It is worth providing some posting activities where the objects might be seen but be difficult to retrieve, such as putting a cork into a plastic bottle.

From these types of games, children often go onto enjoy jigsaw puzzles and other activities involving construction or fitting materials together.

Learning benefits of enclosing games

Physical benefits

Putting objects inside other objects increases children's fine motor movements and hand–eye co-ordination.

Cognitive benefits

Babies and toddlers learn about object permanence (see page 29) as they see that an object that they have 'posted' and may be out of sight is still in existence.

Children learn about shape and size as they will often try to place objects that are too large in a container. They may also learn about rotation and this will develop their spatial reasoning. Most of their learning will be through trial and error, although they will also learn from modelling as they copy the movements of the adult playing with them.

Language benefits

From the running commentary style, babies and toddlers will learn to associate particular phrases and words with events and actions. As with other simple games there is likely to be an element of repetition. This should provide the adult with an opportunity to create a language routine, for example, 'one, two, three – now it's gone!'

Emotional and social benefits

Posting and enclosing objects give children a sense of control and power. They are able to see that they can do things for themselves. This is important in building a good self-concept. Playing alongside an adult also helps the child to learn turn taking and how to play with someone else.

Hide and seek games

Hide and seek games include peek-a-boo and activities where children can place themselves out of sight, such as in tents or boxes or under tables. Peek-a-boo is usually the earliest type of hide and seek game that is played with babies from around seven months. The idea is that the adult covers the baby's head for a moment and then 'finds' the baby. This can happen during the dressing routine or even when wiping the baby's face with a face cloth. This type of game needs to be repeated and eventually babies learn to pull the covering off for themselves. The game can also be played with the adult 'disappearing' and the baby finding the adult. From this earliest game, toddlers go on to enjoy hiding their whole bodies, for example, covering themselves with a blanket and peeping out or crawling under a table and peering out. Eventually this type of play tends to develop into role-play with young children enjoying home corners and creating their own spaces.

Learning benefits of hide and seek games
Physical benefits

Simple peek-a-boo games help children's fine motor skills but, as they graduate into more complex hiding, children use their whole bodies and learn to co-ordinate them. By using, for example, a cardboard box to hide in, toddlers start to learn about their body in relationship to space.

Cognitive benefits

The key concept that babies and toddlers are exploring is object permanence. This is the idea that objects continue to exist, even when they cannot be seen. This tends to be seen from eight months or so, although some babies begin to develop it a little earlier.

This activity also helps toddlers to explore, but not necessarily resolve 'egocentrism' – the idea that your experiences will be the same as someone else's. It is common to find that toddlers put their hands over their eyes and assume that an adult must have disappeared because they cannot see the adult. Toddlers peep out and find that the adult is looking at them and smiling.

Language benefits

This game should be frequently played with children so a language routine develops, as the adult is likely to use similar expressions and vocabulary each time. This allows babies and toddlers to identify key phrases such as 'peek-a-boo' and 'there you are!'

Emotional and social benefits

This is an early game that babies learn to play. Look out for the way in which babies quickly show that they want to play by lifting up their jumpers or vests to hide themselves. This game teaches turn taking and helps babies to enjoy sharing play with others. There are also emotional benefits as children gain reassurance by knowing that they are being 'searched' for and then 'found'.

Throwing, catching and kicking games

Throwing and catching games include rolling a ball over to babies or passing objects to them, for them to drop or throw. Later on these games develop into throwing, catching and kicking. These games involve plenty of repetition as the baby, for example, might drop a spoon onto the ground from the highchair and enjoy watching the adult pick it up and pass it back. Toddlers enjoy simply throwing and running after balls and beanbags as well as kicking objects. Adults need to be patient with children and expect to do quite a lot of retrieving and picking up in the play partnership. The challenge for adults is also to observe children carefully and make sure that activities are kept just inside children's skill level so that while there might be some challenge, the young child does not become frustrated.

Learning benefits of throwing, catching and kicking games

Physical benefits

Simple games involving dropping, throwing and kicking develop babies' and toddlers' gross and locomotive skills. They also help build stamina and muscles.

Cognitive benefits

Children learn about the way in which objects move through the air and across the ground. By dropping things down and throwing things babies and toddlers learn about cause and effect. Throwing, kicking and rolling also develop children's spatial awareness as they quickly learn to aim.

Language benefits

Interaction with the adult will help the child understand language and also encourage vocalisation. Wherever possible, a language routine should be developed so that the young child begins to associate particular words with actions.

Emotional and social benefits

Young children enjoy these types of games because they feel powerful and are pleased to see that they can influence objects. The ability to repeat the same activity several times with an adult builds security. These types of activities encourage turn taking and children also learn play skills.

Chapter 7   Core activities for three to five year olds

This chapter is designed to show the benefits of the most common play activities in early years provision. These activities are:

- dough
- water
- sand
- paint
- home corner
- junk modelling
- construction toys.

It is interesting to visit a variety of early years settings because, although each establishment will have its own identity and style, there will be many common features in the provision of the activities provided. These could be thought of as 'core activities'. The aim of this chapter is to explain their learning potential and how they can be used to support the Early Learning Goals. (Diagrams showing how each of the core activities link to the Early Learning Goals can be found in the Appendix, pages 313–319).

Dough

Dough and other malleable materials have enormous learning potential for children. They are relatively cheap to produce and easy to use with children, making them an ideal activity for many settings. Even adults never grow out of enjoying malleable materials – try to resist stretching and twisting a rubber band or a piece of Blu-tack!

Playing with clay is a very satisfying activity for children

Dough has historical and religious links for many cultures. It might be appropriate to make different types of bread and use dough as a starting point for learning about its significance in different religions. Children have been playing with dough for centuries as traditionally bread was baked in homes and children were encouraged to play alongside adults while learning future skills.

Learning about dough could also be integrated into a topic about harvest. Children could look at the process of making flour and different types of flour could be brought in for them to feel and taste. Older children could try crushing wheat grains with stones to see how the germ contains flour.

Setting up

A table with a surface that is easily wiped or protected with a plastic covering is necessary, and the location of the activity will influence how the children use the dough. If the table is sited near a home corner, the dough will probably travel there and become part of the children's play. There should be sufficient dough available for the children to produce more than one item, as children often enjoy making several pretend cakes or a tray of sausages.

Children will need to wash their hands thoroughly after playing with dough for reasons of hygiene as well as skin care. Some skin conditions can be aggravated as the salt in the dough can dry out the skin.

Equipment: cutters, scissors, rolling pins, spoons, plates, pasta making machines, boards, plastic knives

Learning benefits of dough

See also 'Dough and the Early Learning Goals' on page 313.

Physical benefits

As the child can pound, stretch and model the dough in a variety of ways, small hand muscles are developed as well as hand–eye co-ordination.

The provision of tools can further enhance physical development as the child masters the skills of using cutters and rolling pins.

Cognitive benefits

As children mould and pound the dough, they will explore texture, shape and mass. Dough will also help children to understand the nature and properties of malleable materials, i.e. elasticity.

Allowing children to make the dough will also teach them about measurement, mass and volume.

Language benefits

Most children find using dough a very relaxing experience and adults should use this time to encourage interaction. Shy children may start to talk about what they are making and the adult should use the opportunity to support children in their play. Adults should consider how they can introduce specific vocabulary into the activity. Words associated with dough include 'stretchiness' and 'smoothness'.

Playing with dough should also allow children to interact with each other. Children will compare models, offer each other products and chat about what they are making.

Emotional benefits

There are no 'correct' ways of handling dough and this means that children can enjoy the physical sensations of twisting and stretching the dough, thus providing an outlet for frustration and aggression. The simplicity of dough allows children to use it unaided and children will enjoy creating in an independent way.

Some types of dough can be baked, which can give children satisfaction at having an end product.

Playing with dough can also be a soothing experience for some children and handling the dough can help them to feel in control. (Remember the success of the executive stress ball!)

Social benefits

Dough is a lovely activity as children can be as sociable as they are feeling at that moment. Children of all ages will be seen playing in parallel as they produce models or pound their dough while standing or sitting next to another child, and will look up from time to time to see what another is doing. Some children will use the dough to extend their imaginative play and will collaborate on a project.

Dough is a good activity to provide for a child who is new to a setting or who finds it hard to be part of a group.

Early science

Dough can be a versatile material and the use of different recipes will allow the children to experiment and explore further the properties of dough through direct comparison.

- Children could be asked to 'sort' dough according to its properties. Which type of dough can you stretch the most?
- What happens to dough if it is put in water? Does it float or sink?
- What happens to the dough if it is made with some oil?

Dough recipes

Basic salt dough

This is an ideal recipe for children to make themselves.

- ◆ 3 cups of plain flour
- ◆ 1 cup of salt
- ◆ Just over 1 cup of water to mix
- ◆ Food colouring/powder paint

Mix the colour in with the water and then pour into a bowl.

This dough will not keep for more than a day or so. It will dry out rapidly if left out.

Cooked dough

This recipe is commonly used as the dough can be kept for two weeks in an airtight container. It is similar in texture to commercial doughs. This recipe is not suitable for young children to make themselves as the mixture becomes hot and hard to stir.

- ◆ 2 cups of plain flour
- ◆ 2 cups of water
- ◆ 1 cup of salt
- ◆ 2 tbsp of cooking oil

- ◆ 1 tsp of cream of tartar
- ◆ Food colouring

  Place all the ingredients together in a pan over a medium heat. Keep stirring until the mixture comes away from the sides of the pan and becomes rubbery in texture. It may not look like dough at this point but keep stirring until it all comes together into a ball. Then turn out onto a board and put the saucepan to soak immediately.

  The dough should be kneaded after it has cooled down slightly and children can help at this stage.

Water

Water is essential to life and it provides a source of fascination for people of all ages. Fountains and waterfalls are built in public places as focal points and areas of relaxation. Everyone enjoys running their hands in streams and under taps as well as going swimming and immersing their bodies in baths. For children, water is a medium that can offer a wide range of learning and play experiences and it is therefore found in many early years settings.

Water is fascinating for children

Setting up

Water needs to be provided in a container that is easy to fill and empty. The container should be large and accessible enough to allow several children to use it. Safety must be paramount when deciding on a suitable container, as children can drown in a few centimetres of water. Children should be closely supervised and if the water is to be situated indoors, the floor will need wiping to prevent accidents.

The children will need to wear plastic aprons and sleeves should be rolled up. There should be a good range of equipment available that will allow the children to try pouring and measuring as well as items that will float or sink. As some children find the temptation to pour water on the floor too hard to resist, remember this when putting out equipment: 'the larger the bucket, the bigger the puddle on the floor!'

Equipment for the water area does not have to be commercially manufactured and children will enjoy watching leaves and twigs float or using spoons and cups to measure with.

To prevent any possible infection, it is important that the water is changed after each session and children should always wash their hands after they have finished playing.

Learning benefits of water

See also 'Water and the Early Learning Goals' on page 314.

Physical benefits

Children will be able to master the skill of pouring from one vessel to another. The children will gain good hand–eye co-ordination from moving equipment around in the water. Upper and lower arm muscles will be strengthened during play (a litre of water weighs a kilo).

Cognitive benefits

Water provides an excellent learning experience for children. Through play they should develop the ability to judge volume and capacity as well as discovering some of the properties of water. Children will also understand that some materials are buoyant whilst others sink.

Language benefits

Water can be a relaxing activity and children are likely to interact with each other.

To enrich the language and learning experience, an adult should ask children questions about what they are doing and what they think is happening. Examples of vocabulary include: volume, pour, 'to the brim', overflow, surface, submerge, fluid, liquid.

Emotional benefits

Water play can be soothing and relaxing for children, just as fountains and ponds are for adults. It is an excellent way of integrating a new child into a setting as there is no correct way to play and children can interact with others at their own pace.

Social benefits

Playing with water is fun although play tends to be in parallel, with children of all age groups wanting to have their own pieces of equipment rather than to share. Some children will use the water area for imaginative play and will be co-operative in this, for example, 'My boat is rescuing the princess, your boat is helping mine.'

Early mathematics and science

In the table below are some ideas for themes that could be used to structure water activities in order to allow children to gain some mathematical and scientific concepts (see also Chapter 10 on providing opportunities for mathematics).

Theme	Equipment
Floating and sinking	Boats, plastic bottles with and without lids, twigs, leaves, items made from metal, pebbles, shells
Pouring and measuring	Spoons, cups, jugs, plastic bottles, lids from containers, bowls
Seaside – an indoor seascape	Shells, driftwood, sand, pebbles, seaweed, boats

It is essential that workers allow children to explore the properties of water themselves so that children's mathematical and scientific concepts can be developed.

Good use of questions can help children to gain some understanding. For example:

- What will happen if . . .?
- How can we change this?
- Why do you think this is happening?
- Which one do you think will . . .?

Sand

Sand is a versatile play material which is often to be found in early years settings. A visit to a holiday seaside beach is interesting as there will be adults playing with sand, exploring its texture and making structures with it – even when their children have finished building sandcastles! It is a fascinating material, retaining children's interest into adulthood.

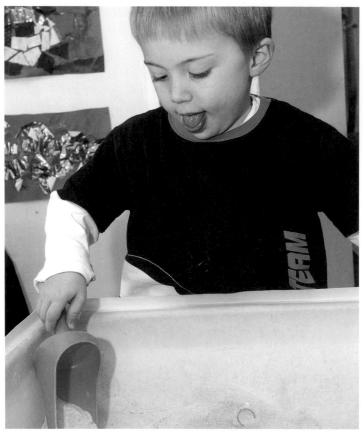

Sand is a versatile play material

Setting up

Although sand is an excellent medium for children, there are some safety factors that must be taken into consideration. Careful checks should be carried out to make sure that the sand is clean and has not been contaminated by animals. Dog and cat excrement may contain worms which can lay dormant and then enter the human body, mostly causing flu-like symptoms. Occasionally the disease called toxocariasis caused by dog's worms can make children blind. If sand is kept outside always remember to replace the lid or covering securely.

The correct grade of sand should be used in the sand area. Fine sand is available from suppliers of early years equipment. Never consider buying builder's sand as it is too coarse and gritty for playing in and could cause skin irritation.

Sand play needs close supervision as children can begin to throw it if left alone. If a child gets sand in the eye, the adult should prevent the child from rubbing it and seek help from a qualified first aider. As sand can irritate and scratch the retina it is essential that children learn that they must never throw sand at each other and appropriate action must be taken by the adult to ensure that the children realise this.

CASE STUDY:

A three year old throws sand at another child. You tell the child that this must not happen again. The child looks at you, smiles and then picks up a fistful of sand and throws it into the middle of the sand tray.

How will you handle this situation?

Most settings will have a sand tray that is at waist height, allowing children to reach into it without becoming covered in sand. Some early years settings will have large indoor pits into which the children can climb. In home settings the sand is likely to be stored in a plastic container in the garden.

A dustpan and brush should also be kept near the sand area as sand can be very slippery on a polished floor. Sand that has been on the floor should either be sifted and cleaned before returning to the tray or simply thrown away.

It is worth remembering that sand is abrasive and that plastic toys will gradually lose their shine. Some work settings will therefore have separate toys for sand play. A good range of equipment will be required to allow the children to pour, scoop and dig. Household items such as sieves, plastic cups and washing-up bottles can be used as well as commercial products such as buckets and spades. Sand is essentially a clean material and children can just be brushed down after play, although many work settings will provide aprons for the children.

Children should be able to play with both wet and dry sand as this will enable them to experience different sensations. Wet sand can be provided in baby baths or trays in settings where wetting the sand tray is not practicable.

Learning benefits of sand

See also 'Sand play and the Early Learning Goals' on page 315.

Physical benefits

The main benefits from sand play will be the development of fine manipulative skills. Children will also learn to master tools and in doing so will develop their hand–eye co-ordination.

Cognitive benefits

Children will learn about the different properties of sand: that, when dry, it can flow like a liquid and is difficult to hold. Children will be able to make prints and solid shapes with wet sand. This activity has sensory benefits and allows children to develop an understanding of texture.

Pouring sand from one container to another will mean that children will learn about volume and capacity in a practical way.

Language benefits

For some children this is such an absorbing activity that they do not chat and interact either with adults or other children. Other children may well talk to themselves and chat to adults while playing with the sand. As this is a relaxing experience for many children it is possible to use this time to communicate with children who would benefit from some adult attention. This can be done by playing alongside children and asking what the children are doing and if they are enjoying their play.

Emotional benefits

This activity is soothing and relaxing. Children can play in their own way and enjoy the sensations of the sand. Many children will play in a repetitive manner, for example, letting the sand run through their fingers. Some children will enjoy being aggressive with the sand by scooping it or by making sand castles and destroying them. This is normal developmental behaviour and allows children to express strong feelings in a positive way.

Social benefits

Children will play with this material in a variety of ways depending on their age and emotional needs. Many children will play co-operatively, devising games such as making roads for their vehicles or pretending to discover buried treasure. For some children this will be an opportunity to develop and explore sand in their own way while remaining near other children. This is a good activity for children who are new to a setting and are just settling down as there will be no pressure on them to join in if they are not ready.

Paint

Paint has been used as a medium of self-expression and as a means of communication for thousands of years. It is possible to trace the history of many cultures through the paintings that have been left behind.

Today paint is used with children of all ages and is a relatively cheap and easy material to work with.

Setting up

This activity needs to be located away from areas and equipment that could be stained. Most settings will put the paint table or easel in an area with a floor that is easy to wipe. If this is not possible a protective covering should be placed on the floor. It is also important to consider what is going to happen to the wet paintings. Some early years settings have specially designed racks; others rely on a clothes line and pegs or a table covered in newspaper. This must be organised in advance otherwise the floor of the setting can become congested with wet paintings. In order to identify the paintings later the adult or child should write a name on the back of the paper as young children will not always recognise a painting that they have produced earlier on in the day. It is good practice to include a date so that parents and professionals can see the progression a child is making. The children should wear aprons and adults can encourage this by acting as role models and wearing aprons or overalls themselves. There are two main types of paint: powder paint and ready mixed paint. It is useful to have both types in stock because each type has its advantages (see below).

Equipment for painting should be varied and allow children to explore a range of painting methods. It is useful to provide a choice of brushes as children should be able to experiment with a range of sizes. Adults would find it difficult to paint a picture if they were only given a wide brush. Some items for the painting area do not need to be expensive; sponges, string and even toothbrushes will make interesting patterns and marks.

Types of paint

◆ *Powder paint*

Powder paint is economical to use because very small quantities can be mixed. It tends to be runnier than ready mixed paint and is therefore particularly good for bubble painting and blow painting. Powder paint can also make an effective 'wash' to put over wax resist paintings. (See Chapter 13 for practical ideas and activities, pages 297–302.)

To make up the paint, water should be slowly added to the powder until a smooth consistency is reached and then more water can be added as desired. Young children should not be left near opened tins of powder paint for safety reasons as well as to prevent mess. (The powder is like fine particles of dust.) Older children can be allowed to mix paint but it is important that they should be adequately supervised.

◆ *Ready mixed paint*

Ready mixed paint is easy to use as it is simply poured from the bottle. It is more expensive than powder paint and towards the end of the bottle there is more wastage as it becomes difficult to squeeze out. It is available in a wide range of colours and is particularly useful for tray painting and printing (see Chapter 13, pages 300–2). Care must be taken with children's clothing if dark colours are used as it can be difficult to remove stains. However, some manufacturers now produce washable paints to help with this problem.

Revisiting work

This is a recent idea which is becoming a popular approach for all ages of children. Children are encouraged to see their artwork as an ongoing process rather than making a single end product in one go. Sponge paintings could become the basis for a collage or, on seeing a painting the next day, a child may decide to add on a new colour or image. Children may have a session just looking at ways of making interesting marks and patterns that they can then incorporate into their designs.

The idea of revisiting encompasses more than just the curriculum area of Art and Design. Children in Key Stage 1 are asked to draft and edit their creative writing in order to understand that the production of work can be a process.

Learning benefits of paint

See also 'Painting and the Early Learning Goals' on page 316.

Physical benefits

Children will develop hand–eye co-ordination as well as control over their hands and upper arms. Using implements will strengthen their grasp and using paint brushes to make marks will help develop the control needed to use pencils.

Cognitive benefits

Painting should help children discover the link between shape, form and colour. Children will learn that new colours can be made by mixing two or more primary colours together. Children will also understand that colours can be lightened by adding white. If children are encouraged to observe items carefully, such as flowers, they will be more sensitive to form and shape. Bringing objects into the

Young children need quality opportunities to paint

work setting and asking children to record them using paint is an effective way of teaching them to look and think. In this way quite young children can produce some extraordinary work (see photo opposite). Using paints will also teach children about texture and the nature of liquids. They will see that if a painting is on an easel and they use too much paint, colours will run downwards.

Language benefits

The adult should try to use paint activities to interact with children as it is a good opportunity to build relationships. Children tend to be relaxed and ready to talk about what they are doing. The adult should aim to extend the learning process by using as rich a vocabulary as is appropriate for the child.

Examples of vocabulary which is linked to painting activities include: shade, hue, tone, dark, light, warm colours, cold colours, rainbow, primary colours, tints, matching.

Emotional benefits

Painting is a relaxing and soothing experience. For children whose language skills are not developed it can be a means of communication. It is often used in play therapy to help children express their anxieties and their anger.

Children can use painting as an outlet for their self-expression and imagination. It is essential to provide a range of colours in order that children can choose a colour to match their mood. A child who seems uncommunicative could be asked to choose to paint a happy picture or a sad picture.

Children will also gain in self-esteem if they see that their pictures are valued. It is worth spending some time framing and displaying their work or putting it into a folder or book.

Social benefits

Painting is a means of self-expression and most children want to paint independently, therefore requiring their own paper and equipment. It is important to make sure that this is possible and to accept that children will get upset if another child puts some paint on to their work. This does not mean that there are no social benefits, as children will often paint whilst chatting to each other about their work.

Home corner

Children of many ages enjoy playing in the home corner or dressing-up area. The traditional home corner with beds, cookery things and chairs can easily be transformed to extend and enhance children's play. It is important to change the area around and to try out a new theme from time to time, otherwise children tend to become repetitive in their play.

The table below shows some examples of ways in which the home corner could be changed, along with possible language outcomes, i.e. extension of vocabulary required for role play.

Theme	Essential equipment	Examples of vocabulary
Hospital	Nightwear, uniforms, charts, medical equipment, crutches	Thermometer, bandages, stethoscope, crutches, visitors, surgeon
Train station	Tickets, timetables, leaflets, uniform, suitcases	Single, return, platform, fare, porter, departures
Newsagent	Newspapers, cards, magazines, sweets, small adverts, wrapping paper	Weekly magazine, customer
Greengrocer	Selection of fruit and vegetables, boxes, scales, paper bags (if possible)	Swede, turnip, ripe, delivery courgette
Toy shop	Cuddly toys, games, skipping ropes, lucky bags, puzzles	Special offer, sale, reduced, gift wrapped, pocket money
Shoe shop	Sandals, boots, trainers, shoes, slippers, foot gauge, shoe boxes	Lace up, fitting, size, width, patent, leather, suede, polish

Setting up

The area to be used should be large enough to accommodate several children as this is often a popular activity. It should also be well stocked with equipment that will allow the children to play without squabbles. Care should be taken when selecting items, taking safety into consideration as well as how robust they are. The children might be encouraged to bring in items from home or make things for the area. Local shops can be a good source of materials, for example, providing brown paper bags or unwanted posters.

At first adults may need to play with the children so they can assimilate new vocabulary, for example, selling tickets so children learn that there are different types of tickets for trains. New vocabulary can also be reinforced with appropriate books and television programmes. Outside speakers, such as nurses or postal workers, can be invited to the setting in order to bring the project to life.

(Continued)

A good supply of dressing-up clothes that are attractive and easy to use is essential. Velcro fastenings can help children who have difficulty in dressing. It may be appropriate to have a selection of clothes from a variety of cultures or countries so that children can experience wearing different types of garments. It is important that hats and other types of head wear are not put out if there is a problem with head lice in the setting.

Role play is very popular with children!

Learning benefits of the home corner

See also 'Home corner/dressing up and the Early Learning Goals' on page 317.

The provision of a good range of equipment is particularly important for children who have more than one language. They may only know the home language word for some items, such as mattress or pillow, so will have the opportunity to learn the English word for these items. It may be appropriate to ask children to bring in items that are important to them at home, i.e. fruit and vegetables that are used in the preparation of their favourite foods.

Physical benefits

This is not primarily an activity that is designed to promote physical development, although children will gain manual dexterity from using the dressing-up materials and small pieces of equipment.

Cognitive benefits

There are some themes that will help children explore such basic concepts as shape, mass and number, for example, shops. Young children will enjoy using money and will gain an understanding that it is used to buy things. Children under five years are unlikely to have a strong feel for the value of money and the number of coins will be more important to them than their worth.

Language benefits

The home corner provides children with an excellent opportunity to develop their language skills. Children will imitate adult speech patterns and will assimilate new vocabulary by taking on different roles.

It is always interesting to spend some time listening when children are playing in this way, as through their play they are showing their view of the adult world.

Emotional benefits

As there is no correct way of playing in this area, it allows children to explore a variety of roles. Some children enjoy having pretend power and this is often reflected in their speech: 'If you do that again I will be cross', a child might say to a teddy.

It is often suggested that role play helps children to understand the world in which they are living and sometimes children who are having difficulties at home will express this through their play.

Social benefits

The home corner allows children to play in a variety of ways. Older children will play co-operatively, choosing roles and suggesting ideas, for example, 'You be the shopkeeper and I will come in and say that I want some eggs.' Younger children will be found playing in parallel, sharing equipment but not always playing together.

Early mathematics

Turning the home corner into a shop will allow children to explore number and counting. The adult can play the role of the customer or shop assistant and through play can count money or objects and, if appropriate, encourage the children to count or to use 'one to one correspondence' (i.e. one for me, one for Daisy, one for Rajeet, etc.). Children can also begin to understand the significance of price tags and receipts in the adult world.

ACTIVITY

Choose one child playing in the home corner and record the number of times the child interacts with other children.

Does the child tend to interact with the same children? How long are the interactions? Does the child try to speak using adult phrases or inflections? Does the child talk to him- or herself?

Junk modelling

In many homes among most parents' collections of objects will be a model that their child proudly presented to them. Made from assorted items glued together and held together by sticky tape it represents the child's own work and effort. Many early years settings recognise the value of junk modelling and provide it as a regular activity.

Setting up

Junk modelling is a cheap and effective way of allowing children to create three-dimensional objects and is an activity which is easy to prepare. It is important to collect a good range of materials which are varied and attractive. Parents and shopkeepers are particularly good sources of interesting materials.

Tip! Some printers will donate off-cuts of card and paper to early years settings.

Ideas for materials for junk modelling and collage include the following:

◆ *Sewing box*: lace, buttons, cotton reels, sequins, fabrics, zips, wool.

◆ *Kitchen*: washing-up bottles, cardboard tubes, cereal boxes and all types of lids, i.e. jam jar, milk bottle, etc.

◆ *Tool box*: wire, screws and knobs, small pieces of wood or cane.

◆ *Paper*: tissue paper, tin foil, wrapping paper, cellophane and sweet wrappers, crêpe paper, different thicknesses of card.

(See also pages 304–9 in Chapter 13.)

Using glue

One of the essential ingredients for junk modelling besides boxes and paper is glue. Children will need to have access to PVA glue and possibly sticky tape. If appropriate a stapler can be used, but the adult must supervise its use carefully.

When providing junk modelling as an activity, enough time and space must be available. Children like to collect lots of items and have them around while they are busy building. Storage space is vital as children will often need to come back to their projects.

It will be important for the adult to support and supervise the children who otherwise can become frustrated, for example, if they cannot make an item stick or stay together.

Learning benefits of junk modelling

See also 'Junk modelling and the Early Learning Goals' on page 318.

Physical benefits

Children will gain skills in cutting, gluing and using equipment. Hand–eye co-ordination and fine manipulative skills will be developed through handling and using materials and tools.

Cognitive benefits

Children will be working with three-dimensional shapes. Problem-solving skills will be developed as children come across difficulties in making their ideas come to life. (Adults too may find the experience challenging!) Through handling materials and cutting items to fit, children will develop the concepts of size and shape. By checking to find if something will fit, children will learn about measurement and comparison. If the materials provided are varied, children will explore texture as well as the properties of these materials.

Language benefits

Junk modelling is a wonderful activity for enriching children's language. Children will have to ask for help and will be keen to explain their ideas. They will need at times to follow simple instructions and will learn some specific vocabulary. Children will be enthusiastic to show other children their models and some older children will be able to co-operate together in producing an item.

There is an opportunity to ask children open questions such as:

- 'Why do you think this will not stick?'
- 'What do you think you need to do now?'
- 'Which materials do you feel will work the best?'

It is good practice for the adult to help children evaluate their work even at this young age:

- 'What are you most pleased with?'
- 'If you had to make this again, would you do anything differently?'

Emotional benefits

Children should enjoy this activity as it will allow them to express their imagination and creativity. If the adult can take a supporting role and allow the child to make most of the design decisions, the child's self-esteem and sense of independence will be enhanced.

This activity also lets the child see that sometimes time and patience are important in producing something worthwhile. This is an essential lesson for children as coping with things that do not go to plan is a life skill. Finished models can be put on display and so will add to the child's feeling of achievement.

Social benefits

Most children will enjoy junk modelling by themselves. They will learn to share equipment and materials with other children. Some children will want to chat as they are modelling and will be genuinely interested in each other's models. Older children in this age group will be able to construct something in pairs, but may well need an adult to guide them.

Construction toys

Being able to fit something together can be very satisfying for children as well as enabling them to learn a useful life skill. (You may well have experienced putting together a piece of flat-packed furniture!) Construction toys are pieces of equipment that children fit together to make objects when they are playing with them. There are many types of construction toys available. Most early years settings will have plastic bricks that link together, train sets and puzzles.

Setting up

There is little preparation required when providing this activity. Children will need enough floor space if they are working with bricks and train sets in order for them to spread out. Most children seem to play with these toys on the floor. Children also need enough time to construct their model or circuit and will become very frustrated if they have to leave this activity before they are ready.

It is important to choose construction toys which the children can manage to work with easily and yet will find satisfying. If the jigsaw puzzle is too complicated or the bricks are too stiff to put together the child may well give up or in extreme cases throw the items in frustration.

Remember that enough materials need to be provided to prevent children squabbling and taking each other's pieces, although there are always some children who seem never to have enough.

Note: As children can choke on small parts it is important that toys are chosen that are suitable for the child's age and stage of development.

THINK ABOUT IT

A four year old declares that she 'needs' all the yellow bricks to finish off her house and starts snatching other children's bricks.

How would you deal with this situation?

Learning benefits of construction toys

See also 'Construction toys and the Early Learning Goals' on page 319.

Physical benefits

As children try to fit pieces together they will develop their hand–eye co-ordination and gain control of their hand movements. In twisting and turning the pieces they will be using their fine manipulative skills.

Cognitive benefits

These types of toys offer great opportunities to develop concepts of colour, form and dimension. Playing with these toys encourages children to develop attention control and to solve problems. There may also be opportunities to design projects and to foster imagination. The other major area of development is spatial awareness.

Spatial awareness

Research shows that this area in the brain seems to be more developed in men than in women. It has been suggested that this may be due to the types of play materials given to the different sexes. Girls have traditionally been given toys for nurturing, i.e. dolls, which encourage language skills, while boys have been encouraged to make things, such as models, with construction toys.

ACTIVITY

Observe a boy and a girl playing with some bricks.

Do they approach the task in the same way?

Can you see any difference in their ability to put the pieces together?

How long do they stay at this activity?

Language benefits

The amount of language used will depend on the activity that is being provided. Children tend not to chat much while they are piecing together parts of a puzzle, although they will often enjoy an adult watching and encouraging them.

Older children will enjoy playing co-operatively with bricks and train sets. They will use language as a way of communicating ideas to each other as well as giving out instructions: 'Don't put that there! I said that we were going to make the train stop here!'

Adults may find it appropriate to ask children open-ended questions such as, 'How are you getting on?' However, this needs to be finely judged as some children will be so absorbed that they will not want to break off from what they are doing to reply.

Emotional benefits

Children gain a sense of achievement when they have finished a puzzle or they have made a model. This helps with self-confidence and gives an inner satisfaction. Children gain in independence from doing these types of activity and the adult should praise children for their effort.

Tip! If a child is struggling with a puzzle the adult might say, 'Can I do this with you because this is one of my favourite puzzles?' This approach allows children to feel that they are doing you a favour in letting you join in and yet they are still in control of the activity.

Puzzles are sometimes used in play therapy as doing a puzzle is thought to be symbolic of the child's attempts to 'sort things' out and to reconstruct.

Social benefits

Children will play in a variety of ways with this type of equipment. Some children will use it in a solitary way, enjoying being in control and finding it restful. It is also possible to see groups of children each working by themselves yet commenting on their progress: 'I am making mine big so that all the trucks can use it.'

Children will also play co-operatively; for example, designing tracks and houses and then going on to use them as part of their imaginative play. Early years children will tend to play in this way in pairs and will find it difficult to work in larger groups.

(Schematic diagrams summarising all the core activities and early learning goals discussed in this chapter are provided in the Appendix on pages 313–9.)

Chapter 8 Providing opportunities for personal, social and emotional development

Personal, social and emotional development forms the foundation for children's learning and development. The development of independence, concentration skills and the ability to follow simple instructions are essential for children to be able to settle and to achieve later in their school career. The personal and social development of children is now recognised as a key issue and consequently has become a key curriculum area in the Early Years curricula in England, Wales, Scotland and Northern Ireland.

Main areas for planning activities

There are four main strands within personal, social and emotional development as a learning area:

- developing self-confidence and independence
- developing positive attitudes towards learning
- learning to work with and respond to others
- caring about and respecting others.

This chapter looks in turn at each of the four strands and suggests activities that will encourage children to develop the skills needed to eventually meet the learning goals. It should be stressed, however, that personal, social and emotional development cannot be neatly parcelled up into one curriculum area, which means that other activities that are carried out in early years settings should also be seen as tools to promote this whole area of development.

Meeting children's individual needs

In this area of the curriculum, more so than perhaps any other, children will have very different and individual needs. This means that in some areas, such as dressing and undressing, some children may need extra support. It is also essential that early years workers check that their expectations of children are age appropriate; remember that a three year old may find it difficult to work in a group, but will be able to play more easily with one other child.

Developing confidence and independence

Personal, social and emotional development forms the foundation for successful relationships later in life

Self-esteem

The way children feel about themselves affects how they behave, how they relate to others and how successful they are in their learning. One of the keys to helping children learn is to make sure that children feel good about themselves and have confidence in their abilities.

Self-esteem and confidence are directly related to the praise and encouragement that adults can give. Children who know that they are loved and hear their efforts praised will have a high self-esteem. Encouragement and praise leads to children being more confident in other aspects of their lives, such as relating to others and taking on responsibility.

Adults caring for children must therefore create a good 'emotional' environment around them. This can be achieved by putting up displays of children's work, giving children stickers and badges for effort, but most importantly by supporting and consistently praising children in an unconditional way.

Self-reliance and independence

Children gain in confidence and self-esteem once they become more independent and self-reliant. Children who are given opportunities to be self-reliant tend to develop a 'can do' attitude.

Praise and encouragement are essential to build a child's self-esteem and confidence

The role of the adult

Children develop a sense of self-reliance and independence when they are given plenty of adult support, encouragement and praise. The key to a child gaining independence is often the time spent alone helping an adult or being encouraged by an adult. Many of you will remember learning a practical skill, such as being able to tie shoelaces, as a result of having had a small amount of time with an adult.

The best way of giving children this independence is to allow them to take on as much responsibility as they are ready for. This means asking children if they would like to carry some paint or pour out their own drink. However, having given children permission to take on this responsibility, adults need to be patient and make them feel good about their attempts to be self-reliant. It does not matter if tables are wiped with the wrong cloth or books put on the wrong shelf; what matters is that children are having a go at being independent. Criticism will make such tasks feel like a chore and undermine a child's confidence – the very opposite of what needs to be achieved.

Providing opportunities for self-reliance and independence

Children need to gain independence before they enter school. There are practical reasons for this, such as the difference in the adult–child ratio in a school setting. Less individual attention and help is possible in school, where a teacher may have 30 children in the class. Helping children to become self-reliant should therefore be a priority in the way early years settings plan activities. Once children have gained confidence in their own abilities and skills they soon learn to take the initiative. The daily routine of settings can provide early experiences of becoming independent, as the spider diagram below shows.

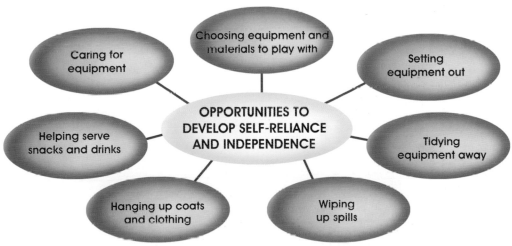

Opportunities to develop self-reliance and independence

These common activities provide plenty of scope for children to gain the confidence they need so that they can take on more responsibility. For example, children can help to lay out newspaper on tables before painting, have a go at wiping a table or put books back on the shelves. Help and guidance from adults is, of course, needed and children must not be put into situations in which they may fail, as this will set their confidence back. At first an adult may need to give a child quite a lot of direction, but if a child successfully repeats a task such as washing a brush, then next time less guidance will be required.

Giving children opportunities to select and use activities and resources independently

One of the ways in which adults can build children's confidence and independence is by encouraging them to make choices. Children who make choices can learn to think for themselves and so wherever possible choices should be built into most activities and daily routines; for example, asking children to choose their pieces of paper or decide which materials to use in a collage. Remember that young children may need to be given guidance or a restricted selection as too much choice can be rather bewildering.

It is also important to look at room layout and consider how children can be helped to choose and put away equipment easily. This may mean investing in good storage systems as well as showing children where things go and using labels or pictures.

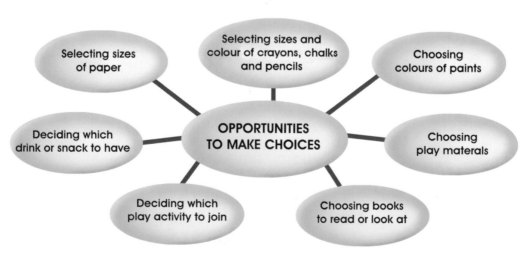

Opportunities to make choices

ACTIVITY

Teddy wants to . . .

Teddy needs some help getting himself organised! He wants to do some painting with his friends, but can't work out what he needs to do to get ready – can the children help him?

Aim: The aim of this game is to help young children think through and collect resources that would be needed to carry out Teddy's activities. Teddy might wish to draw, play with the dough, paint or even cook.

Resources: Everything that Teddy will need to get ready.

Activity: Tell the children about what Teddy is hoping to do. Ask the children to think about what Teddy will need to carry out the activity. A list of the materials that Teddy needs can also be written down at the same time by the adult to introduce the children to the idea of recording words. Some children may wish to do some writing of their own for Teddy.

Varying this activity: Pairs or individual children can prepare a box or bag of toys that they would like to take outdoors to play with or get ready for the next day.

OUTCOMES FOR CHILDREN

This type of activity links to the following Early Learning Goals

It encourages children to select and use activities and resources independently.

Dressing skills

Children need to be able to dress and undress themselves confidently and reasonably quickly before they enter school. Watching a child managing to put on a tangled jumper back to front, it is easy to understand why some parents and early years workers decide to undress a child themselves! But a vicious circle is soon created when children who are slow are helped, as this in turn prevents them from practising the very skills that are making them slow.

There are many ways in which early years settings can help children to learn these dressing skills as part of play activities and as part of the everyday routine. The most important factors in a child learning dressing skills are the amount of time that the child is given and encouragement from an adult. Dressing requires a fair amount of co-ordination and children can easily become frustrated, so it is important that early years workers are able to gauge accurately the amount of help that is needed; too much help can be as bad as too little.

Opportunities to help children learn dressing skills

● *Dressing up clothes*

Children love dressing up and should be provided with a variety of clothing to try on. Velcro fastenings and elasticated waists can help children to dress independently.

● *Asking children to put a coat on another child*

Children can dress each other. This is often a useful way of helping young children fasten buttons and learn to do up zips, as it is easier for them to see what they are doing. It also makes it fun for them.

Teddy's dressing muddle

ACTIVITY

Teddy has got dressed by himself this morning, but nothing seems to feel right on him. Can the children see why and can they help him?

Aim: To help children gain dressing skills and to build children's confidence in their own abilities.

Resources: Large teddy, very badly dressed – for example, hat on the wrong way, two legs in one trouser leg, etc.

Activity: Ask the children to say what is wrong with Teddy's clothes. Ask the children if they can sort out Teddy.

Varying this activity:

Children can choose teddy's 'favourite' clothes from his wardrobe.

Children can 'teach' teddy how to use buttons, zips and buckles.

Children can help to hang up teddy's clothes on coat hangers.

OUTCOMES FOR CHILDREN

This type of activity links to the following Early Learning Goals

It encourages children to:

◆ dress and undress independently and manage their own personal hygiene

◆ continue to be interested, excited and motivated to learn

◆ be confident to try new activities, initiate ideas and speak in a familiar group.

Personal hygiene

The ability to care for oneself also gives children confidence. Personal hygiene is a part of caring for oneself and is therefore an important part of personal and social development.

There are some elements of personal hygiene, such as bathing and caring for hair, that are the responsibility of home, although early years settings can reinforce them by doing topics such as 'ourselves' or 'our day'. There are two main areas of personal hygiene that can be practically reinforced in early years settings, i.e. handwashing and toileting. By the time children go to school, it is essential that they are able to take responsibility for washing their hands after going to the toilet and before meal times. Children will also need to be confident in asking to go to the toilet and for managing to cope alone in toilets.

Adults can give children the confidence to carry out these tasks by gradually giving them less and less support and more praise when they are able to manage by themselves. It is helpful if children are told why they need to wash their hands so that they can see the reason for it. Stickers or stars can be given to children who have managed to clean their hands properly after a very messy paint or sand session. In this way children can see that adults are valuing personal hygiene.

ACTIVITY

Handwashing experiment

What is the best way to wash hands?

Aim: To show children that using warm water and soap is the most effective way of washing hands. (Remember to check if there are any children who are allergic to soap products or who have any special skin care requirements.)

Resources: Bowls of warm water and cold water, soap, paper towels, brush and dark coloured paint.

Activity: Paint children's hands with a dark-coloured paint and ask them to wash it off using only cold water and soap. How long does it take? Does all the paint come off easily?

Repeat the activity, but ask the children to use warm water and soap. What happens now? Is it quicker to remove the paint?

Varying this activity: This activity can be carried out as a race between two children – one using cold water and the other using warm water.

This activity can also be repeated with the soap being omitted, so that children can discover that soap helps to wash hands.

OUTCOMES FOR CHILDREN

This type of activity links to the following Early Learning Goals

It encourages children to:

◆ dress and undress independently and manage their own personal hygiene

◆ continue to be interested, excited and motivated to learn

◆ be confident to try new activities, initiate ideas and speak in a familiar group.

Helping children to follow simple instructions

The ability to follow instructions is a skill that children will need to develop. There are two elements to following instructions:

- self-reliance
- memory.

When given a simple instruction, such as 'when you have finished your drawing, you will need to put it in the middle of the table', many adults assume that children have forgotten it if they then ask what they should do; but this is not always the case. Sometimes children do not carry out instructions because they lack confidence and self-reliance. By checking what they need to do, they are hoping for reassurance. Early years settings therefore need to provide children with activities that will encourage them to follow instructions independently, and ensure they receive lots of praise when they do so.

As memory is also required in order to remember instructions, you might also need to think about the way in which you deliver instructions. Adding a visual memory cue is usually effective. This means that you might use a teddy to show children what they need to do or to act out what happens. Repetition is also important in memory and so you might need to find ways of helping children repeat instructions. For very young children or those who find it hard to follow instructions, you may also need to do some gentle prompting.

Types of activities that help children learn to follow instructions

These can include:

- *Finding a hidden object*

An object is hidden and children have to find it by listening to whether the others say they are getting 'hotter' or 'colder' as they look for it.

- *Origami*

This traditional paper-folding craft can be used even with young children. It develops their fine manipulative skills and teaches them to listen and follow instructions carefully. It is a good idea to demonstrate at the same time, so that children are seeing as well as hearing what they have to do next. Simple shapes should be chosen at first so that children do not become frustrated.

- *Simon says*

This type of game is very good for helping children to listen to instructions. 'Simon says' can be played outdoors as well as indoors – 'Simon says jump three times' – so is useful for children who need to work off some energy.

Teddy's treasure hunt

ACTIVITY

Teddy has hidden a story that he thinks the children would like to hear. Can the children find the book? He has left them a series of clues.

Aim: This type of treasure hunt is very exciting for children and helps them to concentrate and listen. It is ideal to carry out at the end of the day or when children seem to be flagging or unsettled, such as on a rainy day.

Resources: A book or object that Teddy has hidden.

Activity: Give the children a series of instructions via Teddy that will lead them to the hidden object. These instructions can include tasks that children have to do – Teddy says that the children have to put away the pencils in the pencil drawer or Teddy says the children must turn three times on the spot. Actual instructions/clues can also be hidden if preparation time allows.

Varying this activity: Take this activity outdoors. Ask children to hide objects for other children or adults to find.

OUTCOMES FOR CHILDREN

This type of activity links to the following Early Learning Goals

It encourages children to:

◆ maintain attention, concentrate and sit quietly when appropriate

◆ continue to be interested, excited and motivated to learn

◆ be confident to try new activities, initiate ideas and speak in a familiar group

Developing positive attitudes towards learning

Links to the Early Learning Goals

By the end of the reception year most children should be:

◆ interested, excited and motivated to learn.

This Early Learning Goal recognises that enthusiasm and the motivation to learn will affect children's progress. The desire to learn is often present when children are about three years old and so one of the tasks of the early years setting is to preserve and encourage children's enthusiasm.

You can help children with this desire to learn by making sure that the activities you provide are fun and interesting, as well as by your own enthusiasm towards the activities. Children's desire to learn must also be matched with the ability to concentrate on and to persevere with activities.

Helping children to concentrate

Concentration and perseverance are skills which affect children's ability to learn. Children need to be able to finish tasks and to cope when they meet a problem. Some early years settings feel that, in order to help children to concentrate, they must set them 'desk bound' tasks, where they have to sit down. However, children who are given activities and then become bored are more likely to acquire poor learning habits. They may feel that activities which require sitting down are boring and that they are not good at this. Today the early years curricula across the United Kingdom emphasise the importance of using play to help children learn how to focus and concentrate.

Factors that help children to concentrate

You can learn how to help children concentrate by considering situations where children do concentrate. Some very young children are able to concentrate for as much as 20 minutes on one activity, if it interests them. They may be playing in the sand or playing in the home corner. If you look at the factors which influence their ability to stay focused you may find:

● the children have chosen the activity themselves

● they are setting their own play goals

● the equipment they are using is attractive to them and easy to use

  – the equipment can be used in different ways and this allows children to extend their play

  – children are given enough time to settle down to play

  – adults support rather than direct children's play.

Considering the factors that influence children to stay with an activity of their choice can help adults to plan activities.

● Activities need to be stage- or age-appropriate if children are to stay 'on task'. Children generally concentrate on activities that they have chosen for themselves, because they know what their limitations are. If an activity is too hard, a child will soon become frustrated and give up.

● Activities need to be interesting and contain within them the possibility of further development. Children tend to concentrate most on activities that hold their attention and have many learning possibilities. Once most children have mastered an activity and there is no challenge for them, they may become bored. Construction toys can often hold children's attention for longer than an activity such as cutting and sticking, because there is scope for play development. Sensory activities such as sand, water and dough are also good at helping children to concentrate as they stimulate the senses; children who may not enjoy sitting down to worksheets will often be very good at concentrating with these materials.

The role of the adult

The role of the adult is vital when encouraging children to concentrate. Adults are able to encourage children to stay on task by giving them praise and by being involved with children. Adults may help children by playing alongside and with them, or by developing learning by asking them questions or setting them mini-tasks. For example, an adult might ask children who are playing with water if they can work out how many cups of water will fit into a jug.

However, adults need to be able to judge at what point children are becoming frustrated and the activity is reaching its natural conclusion. Making children stay at an activity when there is no further challenge or development. This is likely to make children resentful and wary of carrying out similar activities in the future (although see below on perseverance – it is important to judge the right moment to stop).

Helping children to persevere in their learning

Children will need to understand that patience and perseverance are valued skills. Many skills in life need to be practised and the ability to see a project through is important. Instant success is rare and so children need to learn that patience and perseverance can pay off. However, young children can easily become frustrated and so adults need to encourage them to persevere at some activities for a little longer. Adults can do this by praising a child's efforts so far and then staying while the child finishes an activity. It is essential that praise is used and that children are told how well they have done to see an activity to its conclusion. Children, of course, should not be left to finish an activity if it is too difficult for them or if they are too tired.

Activities that will help children to learn perseverance may also have some element of waiting rather than instant success. This helps teach children that patience is needed. The spider diagram below shows the types of activities that might help children to gain perseverance and concentration skills.

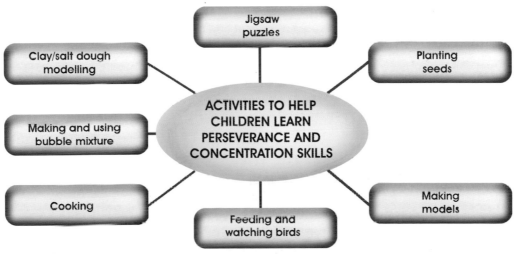

Activities to help children learn preseverance and concentration skills

ACTIVITY

Bird seed cakes

Aim: This is a lovely activity to do in the winter time with children. It makes them think about others, and helps them to develop physical skills while giving them a fun experience where patience is needed.

Resources: Aprons, yoghurt pots, lard, bird seed, peanuts, raisins, other dried food suitable for birds, 30cm pieces of knotted string.

Activity: Help the children tie a knot at the end of their piece of string. Pierce a hole in the bottom of each yoghurt container and thread the string through so that the knot is on the outside of the pot and the string goes down through the inside of the pot.

Put bowls of different dried seeds on a table and ask the children to take scoops and mix them in their own bowls. They can do this with their hands as this is an interesting tactile experience. This can be an opportunity to talk about the names of different nuts and why birds need feeding. Once each child has mixed his or her seeds, an adult adds melted lard to each bowl (lard melts down very quickly in a microwave or in a saucepan and gets very hot). Once the melted lard is in the bowl, the children mix the seeds and lard together using a spoon. The children then put their mixtures in the yoghurt pot and pack the mixture down firmly. The yoghurt pots can then be put in the fridge for the mixture to become hard. Once the mixture is hard, the children can snip off the knotted end of the string and turn out the seed cake. It can then be taken home and hung up outside where the child can watch the birds eat the cake.

Varying this activity: Provide a mixture of seeds to put on the ground or on a bird table.

OUTCOMES FOR CHILDREN

This type of activity links to the following Early Learning Goals

It encourages children to:

◆ continue to be interested, excited and motivated to learn

◆ be confident to try new activities, initiate ideas and speak in a familiar group

◆ maintain attention, concentrate, and sit quietly when appropriate.

Learning to work with and respond to others

Helping children to work as part of a group

Working as part of a group is a skill which children need to learn for life. Some children can find this hard to do as it requires them to be able to take turns, share ideas and understand that they cannot always do as they wish. Most children under four years old will find it difficult to work in groups without the supervision and direction of an adult as other areas of development, such as language, affect children's ability to wait their turn and express thoughts.

As with many other areas of development, learning to co-operate with others is a gradual process. Most children will start by playing with one or two other children in an unstructured way. This is a good starting point for learning to co-operate with others. Gradually, with the help of an adult, children are able to take part in more structured activities until eventually the direction and guidance of the adult is minimal.

There are many benefits for children when they are able to work as part of a group. They may develop friendships, share ideas and feel a sense of belonging. Working as a group also provides opportunities for social and language interaction.

The role of the adult in helping children work together

Children of all ages need plenty of praise when they are managing to work together. It can be easy for adults to intervene only when they hear that children are starting to squabble rather than when children are working well together. Adults need also to make sure that groups of children are balanced and that the activity that they are doing allows all the children to be involved. Sometimes one or two children are always left waiting or are not able to contribute, which can cause problems.

Adults must also make sure that they are giving enough guidance and supervision. This may mean that with younger children, an adult works with a group of children and directs an activity. Where children are working as an independent group, an adult may need to keep checking that no member is frustrated or bored. Early intervention, support and praise can prevent conflicts and keep children feeling happy and motivated.

There are many activities that can help children to share and work in pairs or in groups. The spider diagram below shows the types of activities that will help children to learn to work and play together. It is also worth thinking about providing opportunities for children to show other children a new skill or simple game. Children can also set up activities for other children to try (see activity overleaf).

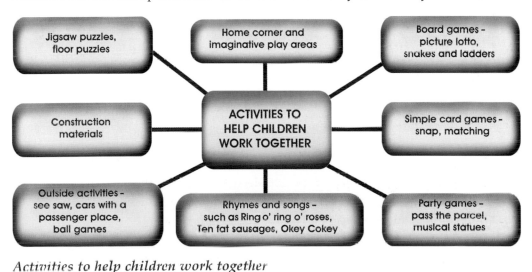

Activities to help children work together

Find the long straw

Aim: For pairs or small groups of children to enjoy playing a simple game together.

Resources: Sand tray or small quantity of sand in a tray, straws cut into different lengths.

Activity: One child pushes the straws into the sand tray. The other child has to guess which one is the longest.

Varying this activity: Children cut the straws into different lengths using scissors.

Children can choose other objects to hide such as shells, plastic animals and buttons.

OUTCOMES FOR CHILDREN

This type of activity links to the following Early Learning Goals

It encourages children to:

◆ continue to be interested, excited and motivated to learn

◆ form good relationships with adults and peers

◆ work as part of a group or class, taking turns and sharing fairly, and develop the understanding that there need to be agreed values and codes of behaviour for groups of people, including adults and children, to work together harmoniously.

Helping children to express their own feelings

Links to the Early Learning Goals

By the end of the reception year, most children should:

◆ have a developing awareness of their own needs, views and feelings

◆ respond to significant experiences, showing a range of feelings when appropriate

◆ understand that people have different needs, views, cultures and beliefs, which need to be treated with respect

◆ understand that they can expect others to treat their needs, views, cultures and beliefs with respect.

Children are more likely to accept and respect other people if they are able to express and accept their feelings. Children with high self-esteem are more likely to be generous towards others than those who are fundamentally unhappy or insecure. This is often shown in situations where children are bullying others or are unpopular. This means that children need to learn that they can expect others to meet their needs and listen to their ideas, feelings and thoughts.

There are many activities which can help children to express and explore their feelings. Some are core activities such as water, sand, dough and dressing up (which are covered in Chapter 8), but in addition activities can be planned specifically to encourage children to talk about themselves and their feelings.

Adults may need to understand that some children experience such a mixture of feelings at some points in their lives that they may not be able to pinpoint them or express themselves clearly. Adults can help children both by giving them the opportunities and the language to express themselves.

It is also important that children are given the chance to express negative feelings. Sometimes, adults can dismiss children's feelings by trying to cheer them up, distracting them or by making remarks such as 'it's not that bad really'. Failing to actually acknowledge children's feelings in this way can mean that children learn that being anything other than happy is not acceptable. This can drive feelings underground, which then results in unacceptable or inappropriate behaviours.

Opportunities to help children talk about their feelings

- *Reading stories*

Reading stories which encourage children to talk about their own feelings is a useful way of helping children realise that they are not the only ones who feel this way. For example, a story about a new baby in the family or a child who is afraid of going to school, or perhaps a child who is unhappy because her parents have separated, can provide appropriate openings for children to share their experiences with adults.

- *Making books with children*

Making books with children can also be a good way of encouraging children to share their feelings, as well as promoting literacy. A group book may be called 'things that make me happy' or 'things I don't like' and children can contribute by doing a drawing, with an adult writing down what a child wishes to express.

- *Imaginative play*

A good home corner can often help children to express their feelings by allowing them to act them out. An adequate range of equipment and plenty of opportunities to go into this area will be needed. Adults can help some children by asking if they can 'play' a part, thus allowing children to share their experiences with someone they trust. Children may also need opportunities to act out their feelings by themselves, away from others.

ACTIVITY

Teddy's paintings – happy, angry and sad

Teddy is not able to speak very much but wants to let the children know how he is feeling. The children are going to paint some pictures for him so that he can tell them how he is feeling.

Aim: To help children learn to express their feelings.

Resources: Paints of different colours, chalk, aprons, paper.

Activity: Ask the children to choose a 'feeling' that Teddy might wish to let them know about and then ask them to produce a painting for Teddy. Use this opportunity to talk to children about what makes them happy, angry or sad.

Varying this activity: Use teddy or a puppet to encourage children to show or talk about what they are feeling.

OUTCOMES FOR CHILDREN

This type of activity links to the following Early Learning Goals

It encourages children to:

◆ continue to be interested, excited and motivated to learn

◆ have a developing awareness of their own needs, views and feelings, and be sensitive to the needs, views and feelings of others

◆ respond to significant experiences, showing a range of feelings when appropriate

◆ understand that they can expect others to treat their needs, views, cultures and beliefs with respect.

Caring about and respecting others

Helping children to realise that their actions affect others

In order for children to be able to co-operate and work in a group, they need to understand that their actions affect others in both positive and negative ways. Children can learn this by being encouraged to do things that are positive. For example, they may give one of the cakes that they have made to a member of staff. This helps them realise that they can give pleasure. Other activities, such as singing 'Happy Birthday' to another child, will also teach groups of children about how their actions affect others.

It is good practice to talk to children about how their behaviour may make other people feel. This should happen when children have done or said something positive as well as after negative behaviour. Children need to learn what they can

Children need to learn to care for others

do to help others respect and like them, for example, 'Sharing your book with Toby was very helpful'. When dealing with unwanted behaviour, adults should, wherever possible, explain to children *why* their behaviour is unhelpful and how it might affect others.

Opportunities to help children learn how their actions affect others

There are also activities to help children learn about the consequences of their actions with regard to others. These include:

● *Books and stories*

Books and stories can be chosen which may help children discuss how others might be feeling. For example, in *Kipper's Birthday Party* (Mick Inkpen, Hodder and Stoughton: 2000) no one turns up because Kipper has not written the invitations carefully and this could be used to make children think about how Kipper might be feeling.

● *Home corner*

Children tend to use imaginative play to act out their feelings and ideas about the actions of others. Children may act out events that have recently happened at home, or stories that adults have read to them might be transformed into mini-dramas.

ACTIVITY

Teddy's got no one to play with

Teddy has a new skipping rope, but none of his friends want to play with him. Teddy admits to calling his friends names and not always sharing his toys.

Aim: The aim of this activity is to make the children think about how Teddy might be feeling because he has no friends and also to explore why no one will play with him.

Resources: Teddy and some of his 'friends'.

Activity: Teddy, via the adult, explains to the children that none of his friends will play with him. The children are asked to say how Teddy might be feeling and also to think of reasons why no one will play with him. Teddy is asked if he knows why his friends are not playing with him. Teddy tells the children that he has not been a very good friend. The children are asked to give Teddy ideas for how to win back his friends.

Varying this activity: This type of activity can help children explore situations that they have themselves experienced. The activity can be varied so that children can consider other problems, for example, Teddy has snatched a friend's pencil because he can't join in.

OUTCOMES FOR CHILDREN

This type of activity links to the following Early Learning Goals

It encourages children to:

◆ understand what is right, what is wrong, and why

◆ consider the consequences of their words and actions for themselves and others.

Helping children to care about and respect other people

Part of a child's emotional and social development is to develop an awareness of other people and their feelings. Children who are able to respond to others are more likely to make friends and to be able to co-operate with others. There are many elements in helping children to achieve this, although adults have an enormous responsibility. First, children have to see good role models in the people who are around them. This means that adults working in early years settings must make sure that they are working well as a team, and that they are showing positive attitudes and open mindedness towards others. This is easier to write than to do! However, it is essential as research shows clearly that children imitate the behaviour and attitudes of those around them.

Children need to experience respect in order that they can mirror it with others. This means that adults need to make sure that they are using appropriate language with them, for example, remembering to say please and thank you.

Adults must also realise that, at first, young children are egocentric and find it hard to grasp the concept of sharing and to understand that others have needs. By the age of three years, most children are starting to take turns, although they will still be inclined to impatience. By the age of five years, children are still developing the skills of sharing and co-operating with others, but you should expect that most children will now be starting to empathise with others and have a sense of fairness.

> **Links to the Early Learning Goals**
>
> By the end of the reception year, most children should:
>
> ◆ have a developing respect for their own culture and beliefs and those of other people
>
> ◆ understand that people have different needs, views, cultures and beliefs, which need to be treated with respect.

Learning to respect others

Children need to learn to respect others whose lifestyle and culture are not the same as theirs. A significant cause of prejudice and discrimination is people's ignorance about the lifestyles of others. It is now generally thought to be so important to address this ignorance that it has become a learning outcome in most curricula both for early years settings and for schools. It is thought that if children are taught from an early age to respect differences, the discrimination and prejudice that troubles society will be lessened.

Learning about the lifestyle and culture of others needs to be handled sensitively, as stereotypes should not be reinforced by adults. A prime example of this 'tourist culture' teaching is when photos of children from other countries show them in their national dress. This often only serves to reinforce stereotypes and can give a false impression of childhood in other countries. Adults also need to make sure that they are not sending out hidden messages which suggest that cultures or religions other than their own are in any way inferior. Often adults do not realise that this is happening when making remarks such as, 'this food tastes funny, doesn't it?' or 'that doesn't look very nice to wear'. Essentially, such comments suggest that your way of life is in some way better.

In the same way, adults need to be sure that the way they present people with disabilities does not just elicit sympathy as most disabled people want equality of rights not charity.

Opportunities for learning about other people

There are many ways in which early years settings can develop children's awareness of others.

- *Using everyday opportunities*

Adults can help children to learn about others by helping them realise that they also have their own differences. This needs to be done during everyday activities such as snack time and choosing books and toys. For example, during a sorting activity you might ask children to tell you about their favourite object and gently point out that you actually like different things. This is a good starting point for children as it helps them begin to understand that people are not all the same and that they may have different likes, dislikes and opinions.

- *Using visitors*

Visitors to settings are possibly the most effective way of helping children to learn about others. The novelty of having a 'new person' ensures that children are more likely to remember what they have learnt. As accuracy is also important in combatting ignorance, a visitor is ideally placed to answer questions and give explanations. Some voluntary organisations, such as Guide Dogs for the Blind, can be keen to promote their work and have speakers especially for children.

Themes can be planned to coincide with festivals and 'awareness weeks' such as New Year. This can extend learning opportunities and allow you to integrate learning about others into other curriculum areas. For example, a nursery may invite a representative of the RNLI to come and talk to the children. Following on from this visit, children can make cards and cakes to sell and so raise money for the organisation's work – thus involving children in maths and cooking activities. Sessions where children are learning in this way can be recorded using videos and photos, which is always a good way of letting parents know what their children are doing.

- *Cooking activities with children*

Cooking is a good starting point for helping children to learn about other people's lifestyles. Food is an important part of most cultures and religions and by helping children to cook and taste different foods, they can appreciate that not everyone eats or likes the same things. Most children also love to play 'cafes', where they can eat the food they have made, thereby extending the theme.

- *Dressing-up props*

The word 'props' has been used here rather than just clothes as children also need to use equipment to learn about others in their play. One nursery has a wheelchair and crutches as part of its imaginative play area, so that children can feel what it is like to be in a wheelchair. This can bring about the realisation that children on crutches or in wheelchairs are still children and have similar feelings to them.

It is important to remember that clothing that is supposed to represent a variety of cultures should be accurate and children may need to be helped in putting it on correctly.

● *Books, posters and other resources*

Stories and books are a good way of helping children to learn and think about others, providing that the source material is accurate and not patronising. A conscious effort to seek out books which promote positive images needs to be made, because despite a strong appreciation of equal opportunities as an issue, there are still few books with a good storyline showing race, disability and age in a positive way. (Try to find books that have images of Chinese children or children with facial birth marks in them – this is still a challenge!)

Helping children to respect their environment

Learning to care for and respect their environment must also be included as part of children's emotional and social development. It is worth noting that children are more likely to care for their environment if it is attractive and well maintained. This means that early years settings that work hard to put up displays and show an obvious pride in the way the environment looks are more likely to foster the idea of valuing and caring for an environment. Children will also need to see that the adults around them care for their environment. They need to see that adults tidy away, fold paper carefully and pick up debris from the floor. Tidying toys and equipment away with the children must become part of a daily routine as this will establish in children the idea of caring for their environment.

These sorts of tasks also allow children to feel more confident and self-reliant. Although respecting the environment should be part of the regular day-to-day routine, specific activities can also be planned for. A good example of this is giving children responsibility for particular tasks, such as collecting up crayons or sweeping up sand. Children can either be given responsibility as individuals or work in groups.

Children can also care for plants and wildlife outdoors. They can make bird food in winter (see page 170) and check that birds have water to drink. A bird table close to a window can allow children to look out and observe birds and other wildlife. Children can grow seeds and plant bulbs outside. Caring for plants and animals in this way can develop in children the desire to care. Eventually children can take pride in their environment, be it indoors or outside.

Ways in which children can take responsibility and care for their environment

These can include:

● planting seeds and bulbs

● putting out and tidying away activities

● being responsible for areas of a setting, such as a book corner

- contributing to an interest table
- caring for a pet
- observing wildlife.

Taking responsibility for possessions

Children need to learn to take care of their own possessions and again there are many opportunities for this in the daily routine. Children can hang up their coats, carry their pictures on to a table to dry and collect their things at the end of the session. Sometimes early years workers find that parents and carers are keen to 'help' children with these things and children just stand while coats are taken off them and hung up. In situations where this is happening it is helpful to remember that sometimes parents and carers do this as it is their way of settling a child in (it is part of the welcoming or parting routine). Tactfulness is therefore required if early years workers are to broach with parents the child's need to gain independence. A badge or sticker can be given to children who, for example, are able to hang their coats up, as it is not only a way of reinforcing the habit with children, it also signals to parents that these types of skills are valued.

Giving children ownership

Children do need opportunities to take some ownership and responsibility of toys and equipment. By, for example, creating environments where children can choose what they would like to play with and where they are able to serve themselves, children gain ownership of the activity. This in turn means that they are more likely to use the materials more carefully and also find it easier to understand why they should tidy them away.

The reflective practitioner

Do I routinely mention how our and children's actions affect others' feelings?

Do I thank children for their time and help during activities?

Are children given responsibility for specific tasks, areas or equipment in the setting?

Are children encouraged to choose, take out and put away toys and materials?

Do I readily give children praise as well as unconditional recognition?

Do I look for ways of encouraging children to take ownership of activities by building in choices and providing activities that are exploratory in nature?

Do I encourage children to get out and put away equipment?

Are children encouraged to find and put on their own clothes?

Are children involved in clearing away, preparing snacks, wiping up spills and other everyday tasks?

(Continued)

Do I find time to listen to individual children?

Do I acknowledge children's negative feelings rather than feeling the need to solve them?

When children are showing sociable behaviour such as turn taking, do I praise them and also explain how their actions might make others feel?

Do I model social behaviours such as waiting my turn or asking if I can join in before doing so?

Do I use props such as puppets and teddies to help children talk?

Chapter 9 Providing opportunities for communication, language and literacy

In recent years, increasing emphasis has been put on the need for all children leaving school to be articulate and literate. Some commentators suggest that these skills have declined, although this apparent need for an articulate and literate workforce could also be seen more as a reflection on the types of skills required by modern employers, with the increasing use of computers and multimedia.

Communication, language and literacy can be divided into three areas:

● speaking and listening

● reading

● writing.

Speaking and listening

This is a key area for early years settings, not just for its own sake but because reading and writing is dependent on a child's ability to understand the process of communication.

> **Early Learning Goals for speaking and listening**
>
> By the end of the reception year, most children should be able to:
>
> ◆ use language to imagine and recreate roles and experiences
>
> ◆ use talk to organise, sequence and clarify thinking ideas, feelings and events
>
> ◆ sustain attentive listening, responding to what they have heard by relevant comments, questions or actions
>
> ◆ interact with others, negotiating plans and activities and taking turns in conversation
>
> ◆ extend their vocabulary, exploring the meanings and sounds of new words
>
> ◆ retell narratives in the correct sequence, drawing on the language pattern of stories
>
> ◆ speak clearly and audibly with confidence and control and show awareness of the listener, for example, by their use of conventions such as greetings, 'please' and 'thank you'.

The importance of speaking and listening skills

There is a strong developmental link between language and social interaction. Understanding others and expressing oneself are essential skills that children need to acquire before they can share and play with others. Without these skills, children's social and personal development can be critically affected. It could be argued that the social aspect of language is even more important than the academic need for children to be articulate, as the consequences of poor social interaction affect the actual fabric of society! Aggressiveness, social isolation and even marital breakdown are often linked to poor communication skills among adults.

Language is linked to thought

Children also need to develop good language skills as there is a strong link between cognitive development and language. This can be particularly observed in young children as they often talk out loud and use language as a way of directing themselves. Activities such as painting, where children are trying to communicate, or using building blocks, which requires problem solving, are rarely done in silence as children often talk as a way of guiding themselves.

This means that in large group situations, young children find it difficult not to shout out an answer or interrupt when thoughts come into their heads. This is why individual and small group activities are best suited to young children as their thoughts and subsequent language can be heard!

The need for children to develop a strong language base is essential if they are to be able to reason and concentrate. The strong link with cognitive development means that activities that enrich children's vocabulary and expose them to different ways of using language will enable them to develop more complex ideas and thought processes.

Uses of language

In order to understand how adults can provide opportunities for language, it is necessary to look at the different ways in which language can be used. Language is not just about talking; it is also about listening, interpreting and conveying messages in different situations. If children are to become skilled communicators, they need opportunities to experience different uses of language (see spider diagram overleaf).

The role of the adult

Although there is an academic argument as to whether children are born with an instinctive ability to learn language, all psychologists agree that the role of adults is crucial in the development and acquisition of a language.

Children need opportunities to experience different uses of language

Children need to hear language being used around them and be encouraged to join in from babyhood onwards. The importance of pre-school language experiences is not completely understood, but studies have shown that children with developed language skills are more likely to learn to read, socialise and concentrate later on in their school lives, than those with poor language skills.

Developing these language skills requires adults not only to provide activities but also to spend time talking and listening to children. This section looks at the ways in which early years workers can encourage the development of speaking skills and then describes some practical activities for encouraging children to use language in different ways.

Providing opportunities for sustained conversations

Children need to have sustained conversations with adults and to have opportunities for developing their ideas during a conversation. For example:

'Why can't we play outside?'

'Because it is raining and you will get wet.'

'If I put a coat on, I won't get wet.'

'You would get wet because it is raining so hard that the rain would come through your coat.'

'But I can see other people outside with coats on.'

'I think that those people's coats will be waterproof and thicker than yours and they might not want to be in the rain. They might be feeling cold.'

'My cat doesn't like to be in the rain. My mum puts him out at night even when it's raining.' And so the conversation continues.

In this conversation the child is trying to explore further why it is not possible to go outside. The child is demonstrating a sense of reasoning, although it would be easy for an adult to cut the conversation off by telling the child to be quiet and find something else to do!

If the language in this type of conversation is examined, you can see that the child is being exposed to a range of vocabulary, tenses and grammatical structures. Short interactions cannot give children these opportunities and restrict the ability of children to reason and think further. They also fail to give children an opportunity to use their listening skills and develop the ability to concentrate.

In the normal pattern of conversations, people develop ideas and move from subject to subject and ideally this is the type of conversation that you should be aiming to provide with children.

Extending vocabulary

● *Introducing vocabulary in context*

Adults need to provide opportunities for children to hear and use vocabulary that extends them. This can be planned for in a formal way by making a list of words that will be used during a topic or theme. When words are identified in this way, you are more likely to remember to use them with children. New vocabulary is often better introduced in context, for example, an adult might say, 'the water has made the sand quite damp.' The word 'damp' can be understood to have an association with water and children are likely to understand that this word is almost like the word 'wet'. Hearing the word again in other contexts will allow the child to assimilate its meaning. While it is rarely appropriate for pre-school children to be taught vocabulary in a formal way, it is important that adults working with children actively look to use words that will develop and build on a child's basic vocabulary. In this way children's vocabulary can be enriched and extended.

● *Using books to introduce vocabulary*

Books offer many opportunities to extend children's vocabulary. However, adults might need to stop and explain the meaning of a word to children if they feel that the context in which the word appears will not be sufficient for children to understand its meaning. Children also enjoy hearing the same story repeated and tend to develop favourite books which enable them to absorb the vocabulary and pattern of language used. Displays and activities that link to a book can help children to re-tell a story. The process of re-telling a story in their own words helps children to learn the skill of sequencing, as well as often extending their vocabulary.

Use questions as a way of extending children's language and thought processes

Questions can be a means of extending children's language but it is important that they are used appropriately. Adults can easily over-use questions and make children feel that they are being interrogated, whereas the good use of questions can be the start of a conversation or can help a child to think about and develop ideas. Look at the two sample conversations below:

Conversation A

'What are you doing?'

'Making a tower.'

'What are you going to do with the tower?'

'Don't know yet.'

'What colour bricks are you going to use for the top of the tower?'

'Red.'

Conversation B

'That looks fun. What are you doing?'

'Making a tower.'

'I wonder what sort of a tower it's going to be? Some towers are part of castles and sometimes people make houses in towers.'

'My tower is having people in it.'

'It will be nice and cosy in your tower for them when you have finished building it. What colour bricks will you use for the top?'

In conversation A, the adult is using open questions and trying to draw responses from the child, but the questions are not being used as part of a normal conversation. A few questions fired at a child cannot be a substitute for sustained interest and conversation. Good use of questions should help sustain the conversation and provide the child with opportunities to develop his or her ideas.

Conversation B is not an interrogation but gives the child more 'food for thought' regarding the construction of the tower. Obviously, conversation B takes more time and effort!

GOOD PRACTICE GUIDE

Checklist for helping children to develop their language skills

◆ Try to get down to the child's level.

◆ Sit with the child, so that the child can feel that you are not going to rush away.

◆ Make eye contact with children.

◆ Allow time for children to respond and to elaborate their answers.

◆ Encourage children's speech by showing that you are listening and interested.

 – Follow up a topic of conversation with a child on another day.

 – Do not correct children's speech. Recast what they have said so that they can hear it correctly instead.

 – Avoid situations where children have to compete against each other to talk and do not allow children to talk over each other.

Activities to encourage children's oral skills

These can involve using the 'core activities' as well as specific activities to encourage **descriptive language skills**.

In early years settings, the core activities such as water, sand and the home corner lend themselves to developing children's oral skills. This means that when planning for the Early Learning Goals, the importance of the core activities should not be overlooked (Chapter 7 shows how each activity links to the Early Learning Goals.)

Other activities to encourage the use of descriptive language include:

● feely bags

● interest tables

● displays

● games in which one child has to describe a hidden object for others to guess where it is.

ACTIVITIES

Picture description

Aim: The aim of this activity is to help children use language to describe what they are seeing. This activity can be carried out with one child or a group of children, when it can become a simple game.

Resources: Several interesting photos or pictures where there is a lot of detail such as a crowd scene or a street picture.

Activity: Children take it in turns to pass around a picture and choose one thing to say about it. They have to listen to the other children, repeat what they have said about it and then add in one thing for themselves.

Teddy on the telephone

Teddy wants to tell his mother all about his new coat. He picks up the telephone but doesn't know what to say. Can the children help him talk to his mother about his coat?

Aim: This activity helps children to look carefully at an object and describe it. Most children love helping others and particularly enjoy using a telephone, even if just in play.

Resources: Toy telephone, Teddy's coat or other object.

Activity: The children are shown Teddy's new object and then asked if they can help Teddy to describe it. The words used to describe the object can be written down by the adult, to help older children begin to see the shapes of words.

Extension: This type of activity can be extended by asking the children to draw the item so that Teddy's mother can see a picture of it.

Tasting tables

Aim: Children often enjoy tasting items and this type of activity can help children to learn new vocabulary and use descriptive words. Such an activity fits in with the curriculum area of knowledge and understanding of the world. The types of food used can also be linked to finding out about different foods, for example, tasting different types of bread.

Resources: Plates or cups of different food substances for children to taste, for example, different types of apples that have been cut up or a selection of different types of cooked rice.

Activity: The children are given the opportunity to taste and comment on different types of tastes. They can talk about their likes and dislikes and can learn the names of the foods as well as specific vocabulary that is used in connection with food, for example, sweet, sour, bitter, tart, sugary, lumpy, etc.

OUTCOMES FOR CHILDREN

These types of activities link to the following Early Learning Goals

They encourage children to:

◆ extend their vocabulary, exploring the meanings and sounds of new words

◆ speak clearly and audibly with confidence and control and show awareness of the listener

◆ use talk to organise, sequence and clarify thinking, ideas, feelings and events.

Activities to encourage **social language skills** can include:

- a greeting song or routine at the start of a session
- home corner or imaginary play area (see Chapter 7 on core activities, pages 149–53)
- construction toys and equipment
- songs and rhymes.

ACTIVITIES

Teddy's paper hat game

Teddy wants to go to a party. His invitation tells him that he must be wearing a hat. The only problem is that he has forgotten his hat. Can the children quickly make him a hat so that he can go?

Aim: This activity helps children work together in pairs and builds the language skills needed to co-operate on a project. Where children do not have the necessary co-operative skills or fine manipulative skills, this activity can be done with a child working with an adult.

Resources: Teddy, different types of paper, sticky tape, scissors.

Activity: The children are told that they have only a little time to make a hat for Teddy. Can they use the resources provided to make a hat for him quickly? This type of activity, in which children are encouraged to solve problems together, helps children to work together. Having only a small amount of time can help children focus clearly on the task.

Teddy's going on holiday

Teddy's going on holiday but he hates packing. He has brought in many things that he wants to take with him on holiday, but there are too many to fit into his suitcase.

Aim: This activity helps children to work together in pairs. They have to discuss what Teddy will need to take with him and also pack for Teddy. Packing helps with children's fine manipulative skills as well as spatial awareness. Children who do not have the necessary language skills can work alongside an adult.

Resources: Small vanity case or bag to act as Teddy's suitcase; items that could be put into the suitcase, including items that do not fit or would not be needed.

Activity: The children are told that they must sort through the things that Teddy has brought with him and together decide on the items that should be packed. Afterwards, the children can explain to the adult why they have chosen certain items. This activity can be extended so that children talk about holidays or moving house. Stories about holidays can also be read to the children to complement this theme.

OUTCOMES FOR CHILDREN

These types of activities link to the following Early Learning Goals

They encourage children to:

- use talk to organise, sequence and clarify thinking, ideas, feelings and events
- interact with others, negotiating plans and activities and taking turns in conversation.

Providing opportunities for listening to others

Listening is an important skill, as communication is not one-sided. Very young children find it difficult to listen to others as they are egocentric. By the age of three years, children should be learning to share and you can encourage children to listen to others. You do, however, need to remember that children will not be able to listen easily for long periods or in group situations when they cannot actively participate. Often activities which require children to listen to others need to be carried out in small groups or even pairs, so that children are not waiting for long periods before everyone has a turn to speak. The other advantage of carrying out activities in small groups is that children can make eye contact with each other more easily and respond visually.

Adults should remember to praise children when they listen to each other and must show by example that this is a valued skill. You need to make sure that you act as a good role model and listen yourself when children are talking to you. It is often too easy to look distracted or put in words for children so as to speed them up.

Games and activities that encourage children to listen

These can include:

- musical activities (see Chapter 13 on creative development, pages 288–94)
- sound lotto
- songs that have actions
- games such as 'Simon says'.

Children need opportunities to chat to adults

ACTIVITY

Teddy's shopping list

Teddy has been shopping. What did he buy?

Aim: This variation of a traditional game helps children to listen to others and use their memory skills. It also encourages children to speak with confidence in front of others. This is a good game to play with young children because the items help children to remember what Teddy has bought. Unusual items can be used to help children extend their vocabulary.

Resources: Items that Teddy has bought at the shop.

Activity: Items that Teddy has bought are put in the middle of the floor and one by one the children pick up an item and say what Teddy has bought and what he will use it for. They must repeat what the other children have said before them. For example, 'At the shops, Teddy bought some toothpaste to clean his teeth, an apple for his lunch, a bag of sugar to make a cake and . . .' The children can look to see what the other children in the circle are holding to help them remember the sequence of what Teddy has bought.

OUTCOMES FOR CHILDREN

This type of activity links to the following Early Learning Goals

It encourages children to:

◆ sustain attentive listening, responding to what they have heard by relevant comments, questions or actions

◆ extend their vocabulary, exploring the meanings and sounds of new words

◆ retell narratives in the correct sequence, drawing on the language patterns of stories

◆ speak clearly and audibly with confidence and control and show awareness of the listener.

Reading

Reading is a process

It is important to understand that learning to read is a process; children are not simply non-readers (or pre-readers) one day and readers the next. Also, there is not one particular way of making this process happen and so there are different methods that can be used to teach children to read.

Reading books is not just about decoding text, it is also about interpreting and enjoying text and pictures. There has to be a clear understanding that although children can be given opportunities to read simple words and look at letters, in the end most children will learn to read at their own pace.

The main purpose of literacy in early years settings should be to develop in children a love of books. Being able to read involves having the ability to decode the symbols. It must be remembered that symbols are abstract representations of sounds and words and that most pre-school children have not reached a stage of cognitive development where they can understand this link. (Early years workers in most other European countries concentrate on pre-reading skills and do not formally teach children to read until they are six or seven years old, in the belief that children are not ready to learn until they reach that age.)

Helping children to learn to read

Understanding the process by which children learn to read

At the start of the process of learning to read, children enjoy listening to stories; by the end of the process, children should be fluent, independent readers enjoying a range of reading materials.

The early stage of reading is often called pre-reading. Most children in early years settings are in this pre-reading stage. It is generally accepted that pre-reading skills are essential and are a cornerstone of an Early Years curriculum.

The starting point for helping children to read is to build their pre-reading skills. The diagram below shows these skills, which form the first layer of the process by which children learn to read.

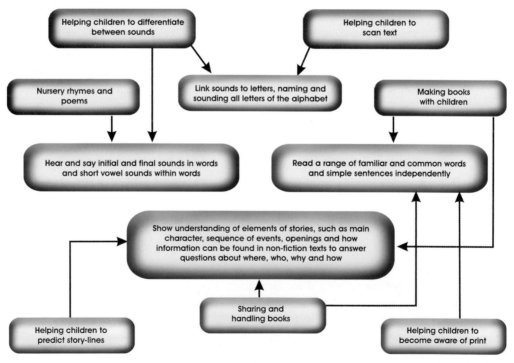

Helping children to develop pre-reading skills

Pre-reading skills involve:

- enjoyment of books

- understanding that text is made up of words

- recognising sound patterns and rhymes in words

- ability to handle books, i.e. turn pages, knowing which way up the book should be

- ability to use pictures and other clues to predict storylines

- awareness of print

- knowledge of nursery rhymes and songs.

Helping children's pre-reading skills

There are many ways in which adults can help to develop children's pre-reading skills, from reading stories and poems with them to making books of their own. But the starting point must be to make children realise that reading is fun.

Helping children to understand that reading is fun

In many ways the most important thing adults can do in early years settings is to give children the desire to read. Young children need to find out that reading is fun. It is a pleasurable activity that can be shared with others or carried out alone. This means that early years settings need to invest in a range of books. A book corner or area that is not attractive or has shabby books is unlikely to make children want to spend time there. In recent years the market in children's books has grown enormously and there is now a wide range of books available. Books should be chosen from many categories as children's tastes vary considerably, and it is good practice to expose them to as many different types of books as possible.

Different categories of children's books

- Picture books
- Feely books
- Factual books
- Story books
- Pop up books
- Poetry and rhymes
- Joke books
- Big books

Sharing and handling books

In order for children to be able to handle books confidently, they will need to have plenty of opportunities to choose and share books. Time spent in small groups or in one-to-one situations with adults will be particularly valuable as children need to feel and hold books while being guided by adults. They may wish simply to look at the pictures or to turn the pages while an adult is reading. This allows children to look at books at their own pace which is particularly useful. Many adults find that children develop favourite books in this way and that children go on to become so familiar with them that they are able to recite the text accurately and word for word; an adult who tries to miss out a line will certainly be corrected! This is the idea behind sharing books with children. It is a good idea that alongside group story sessions, children have opportunities for this type of intimate reading experience.

Children need to enjoy books

Reading stories to groups

Storytime can be a pleasurable experience for children and adults. Most early years settings put storytime at the end of a session or at times when they need children to rest. This type of regular programming should allow settings to plan for different types of stories over a few weeks. Books can be chosen to fit in with different themes and it is possible to ensure that children listen to a range of different books. This can be achieved by using different authors, styles of illustrations and storylines.

Books that are factual or information-based can also be shown to children so that they become aware of the wide range of material available. Sometimes adults may decide to let the children choose which book to read, as groups of children often develop a favourite story and are able to remember the words to it. This can mean that a particular book becomes a starting point for a theme or topic.

Although storytime helps children's literacy, it can also increase children's sense of togetherness as a group when they smile or frown at the same moments. This has a value in itself.

Choosing and reading books for group storytime

◆ Make sure that the size of book and the illustrations can be seen by all children.

◆ Check that the book is suitable for the age/stage of children.

◆ Read through the book before trying it out on the children.

◆ Do not start a story until all children are reasonably settled.

◆ Consider using 'props' such as hats or puppets to make a story come to life.

◆ Read with as much energy and expression as possible.

◆ Help children to think about what they are hearing by asking questions.

◆ Ask children to consider what they like about a story.

◆ Focus children's attention on the illustrations, if appropriate.

Using big books with children

It is now possible to buy 'big books', which are as their name suggests! These can be read with groups of children, allowing them to look at the pictures and see the text while the book is being read. Children enjoy using big books as they can feel part of a group and they can quickly learn the text and the storyline.

As big books are quite expensive, some early years settings make their own big books to use with children, preferring to use their book budget on buying several smaller books.

Nursery rhymes and poems

It is now recognised that children who learn nursery rhymes at home and in early years settings learn to read more quickly than those children who have not had this opportunity. The reason for this is not entirely clear, although it is thought that there is a link between a child hearing sound patterns and later being able to distinguish between sounds in words – the key to phonics. Nursery rhymes can help children to develop their listening skills and also will help them feel part of a group. Nursery rhymes often consist of nonsensical words, although they must be quite influential in children's learning as most adults are still able to recollect the rhymes that they learnt as children.

Rhymes can be used during moments when children are waiting for something, for example, to be served with food or before the start of a story. It is a good idea to introduce new rhymes to children on a regular basis, so that children can build up a repertoire of rhymes. This might mean that adults need to read up on some nursery rhymes as it is often easy to be unsure of the second verse of rhymes.

In the same way, poems should be an important part of children's literacy experience. There are many poems written for young children that can help them become aware of words and vocabulary. Poems that have a refrain are particularly good as children can join in and experience the rhythm and pattern. Poems can often be found to complement themes in early years settings.

ACTIVITY

Join in the rhyme

Aim: This activity encourages children to listen very carefully, recognise a pattern and then join in. It encourages children's auditory skills while being a social game.

Resources: None required.

Activity: Working with a small group of children or an individual child, the adult at first quietly claps the rhythm of a nursery rhyme, then very softly starts to hum the tune or say the words. The children have to work out which rhyme it is and then join in.

OUTCOMES FOR CHILDREN

This type of activity links to the following Early Learning Goals

It encourages children to:

◆ listen with enjoyment and respond to stories, songs and other music, rhymes and poems, and make their own stories, songs, rhymes and poems

◆ use language to imagine and recreate roles and experiences.

Helping children to predict storylines

Fluent readers use many strategies which help to predict the text without actually decoding it. For example, a reader might look at a picture to help work out what is going to happen or might work out some words from recognising a previous pattern, such as 'Once upon . . .' Predicting in this way means that readers are using *contextual clues.*

Adults can help children use contextual clues by asking them what they think is going to happen next. Another way is to look at the picture with children and ask them what they think is happening. It is important to stress that this is not cheating. Some adults have been known to cover up the pictures, believing that children should concentrate solely on the text!

ACTIVITY

What happens next?

Aim: The aim of this activity is for children to consider what is likely to happen next. This will help them develop the skills of sequencing and prediction.

Resources: Cartoons, picture books.

Activity: Choose a picture book or a cartoon from which children may be able to guess what is going to happen next. Show the picture to the children and ask them to describe what is happening. Ask if they can guess what might happen next. Then ask the children to turn to the next image to find out if their guess was correct.

OUTCOMES FOR CHILDREN

This type of activity links to the following Early Learning Goals

It encourages children to:

◆ show understanding of elements of stories, such as main character, sequence of events and openings, and show understanding of how information can be found in non-fiction texts to answer questions about where, who, why and how

◆ retell narratives in the correct sequence, drawing on the language patterns of stories

◆ sustain attentive listening, responding to what they have heard using relevant comments, questions or actions.

Helping children to scan text

The English language is read from left to right and children therefore need to get used to moving their eyes in this way. This means that adults can help children by pointing to the text as they are reading a story so that children's eyes travel in this direction. A surprising number of children go on to point to words when they are looking at books because they have seen adults doing this. It is only a small step from this before children who are familiar with a particular book realise that each spoken word corresponds to a grouping of letters. This is sometimes called one-to-one matching.

Adults can also help children's eye movements when they do other activities, such as counting. Objects should be counted from left to right so that this reinforces left to right eye movement.

Making books with children

A good way of helping children understand how books work is to make books with them. A simple book can be made by folding a piece of sugar paper and stapling in a drawing.

Children can draw pictures and adults can write underneath what they have drawn. For example, 'My dog is called Chip.' Children are more likely to recall what is written because they have said it.

Making books has many other advantages. It is a good way of making children feel proud of the drawings and paintings that they have done. It is also a good way of recording a child's stage of development. Parents enjoy seeing their child's work presented in a book form and it means that, at home, children and parents can talk about what the child has done.

Children can also help to make books that tell a story. Small groups of children can each draw or paint a scene from a story that they have been told. The pictures can be put together to make a group book that afterwards can be 'read' by the children.

Making simple books can help children understand how books 'work'

A particularly good activity to do with a small group of children is to ask them to bring in a photo of themselves. Each photo can be put on a page with the child's name. Children will then look at the book and be able to 'read' the name of the child.

Recognition by sight of words in this way helps children to learn to read without them being 'taught' to read. This type of reading is often called contextual reading. It has the advantage that children feel that they are 'reading' and this makes them feel confident.

ACTIVITY

Teddy's day

Teddy wants to make a book of his day at nursery. He wants the children to help him.

Aim: The aim of this activity is to encourage children to sequence the order of Teddy's day and also to make a book which they can use. This activity helps children talk about the order of the day.

Resources: Ten photos of Teddy taken in various places in the setting. The children could choose where these could be taken. (A digital camera would be a great advantage!) Paper, card and a marker pen.

Activity: The children can talk about Teddy's day and then arrange the pictures in order. A simple sentence based on what the children have said can be written underneath. The children can then tell the story of Teddy's day based on the photos.

OUTCOMES FOR CHILDREN

This type of activity links to the following Early Learning Goals

It encourages children to:

◆ explore and experiment with sounds, words and texts

◆ listen with enjoyment and respond to stories, songs and other music, rhymes and poems, and make their own stories, songs, rhymes and poems

◆ retell narratives in the correct sequence, drawing on the language patterns of stories.

Helping children to become aware of print

For most children, their first real step towards reading is identifying their name and some familiar words. There are many ways in which adults can help children to do this. Coat pegs, trays and other belongings can be clearly labelled with children's names. Children can also be given place names at snack and meal times.

It can be a good idea to label children's work when they are there. This means that they are looking while their name is written and because they are being 'exposed' to the letters in their name, they will gradually come to recognise it.

In the same way, children can learn some other everyday words. It is not unusual for children to point to a carrier bag of a supermarket and correctly say the name, even though they are not readers. Adults can help children to identify some familiar words by labelling items around the setting and by drawing children's attention to objects that have a label on them. An example of this is having a tin on which is written 'crackers'. As children learn that there are crackers in the tin, they will gradually recognise and be able to read the word 'crackers'. As is the case with many aspects of development, some children will quickly be able to recognise words while others will not, because children's visual memories and cognitive skills tend to develop at different rates.

Opportunities for children to become familiar with their names and other familiar words

These can include:

- clearly labelling children's work with their names
- labelling children's coat pegs along with a pictorial sign
- playing musical games where children's names are sounded out; for example, her name is S–A–L–L–Y
- showing children their name on a card and asking them to find their name elsewhere
- making a three– or four–piece jigsaw from a name card
- encouraging children to find their name on a list and crossing it off when they have had their snack
- labelling areas of the room such as 'door', 'book corner', 'window'
- hiding children's names in the sand tray and seeing if they can find theirs.

ACTIVITY

Letter snap

Aim: This activity helps children recognise shapes of letters. Eventually children will also be able to call out the sound of the letter.

Resources: Playing cards with letters on them. (It is important that lower case letters are used rather than capitals and that the letters chosen have very dissimilar shapes, such as h, c, x, e.)

Activity: The children each have a handful of cards and put them down one by one. When two letters match, the children have to call out snap. It is a good idea to use only four or five letters to start with so that children are able to recognise them easily.

Note that this activity will only work once children are beginning to understand that letters are symbols that stand for sounds.

OUTCOMES FOR CHILDREN

This type of activity links to the following Early Learning Goal

It encourages children to:

- link sounds to letters, naming and sounding the letters of the alphabet.

Helping children to differentiate between sounds

Part of learning to read is the ability to recognise the link between the sounds of words and letters. Where this fits in the reading process can vary from child to child. Some children are able to start reading by using familiar words in familiar contexts without formally being taught the sounds of letters. For some other children, learning to read using sounds is a starting point.

For most children under the age of four years, learning letter shapes and sounds in a formal way is not appropriate. There are, however, ways of helping children to hear sounds in words and familiarise themselves with letter shapes that will later on help them to learn phonics.

Activities that can help children to differentiate between sounds include:

- alphabet tray puzzles
- I–Spy
- posters and charts with letters on them
- musical activities (see Chapter 13 on creative development, pages 288–94)
- nursery rhymes and songs.

ACTIVITY

What's Teddy doing now?

Teddy wants to play a game with the children. He is making some sounds and the children have to guess what he is doing.

Aim: The aim of this activity is to develop children's auditory skills and also for them to have an opportunity of working together and taking part in a game.

Resources: Teddy plus a number of items that make different sounds (see below) and/or cassette player and tape.

Activity: The children close their eyes while Teddy, via an adult, makes a sound for the children to guess. The children call out their ideas. One child can then be chosen to help Teddy make his next sound. This game could also be carried out by playing children a tape of everyday sounds such as a vacuum cleaner, tap being turned on, etc.

OUTCOMES FOR CHILDREN

This type of activity links to the following Early Learning Goal

It encourages children to:

- explore and experiment with sounds, words and texts.

Ideas for sounds for children to guess/make could include:

- playing a tambourine or other instrument (such as a shaker)
- shaking some keys
- bouncing a ball
- unfolding a newspaper
- undoing a sweet wrapper.

GOOD PRACTICE GUIDE

Good practice in developing children's pre-reading skills

It is important to remember the following points when helping young children with their pre-reading skills:

- make storytime pleasurable
- provide a wide range of good books
- make sure that children have opportunities to share a book with an adult alone and in small groups
- do not force children to sit and look at books
- provide opportunities for children to make their own books
- be prepared to read the same story over and over again(!)
- label items around the room
- point to text as it is read

ACTIVITY

The rhyme family game

Aim: Children need to learn to listen and recognise the sounds in words. This game encourages children to listen carefully to words and notice similarities and differences between them.

Resources: Cards with rhyming words written on them. The cards help adults carry out the activity, but they can also be used with older children (five to six year olds) to see if they can spot the differences in words that are written down.

Activity: The adult calls out four words slowly. Three of these words rhyme and one does not. The children have to listen and decide which one does not fit into the rhyme family.

Ideas for rhyming family cards:

fat	pin	wet	book	can
cat	tin	met	look	pan
sat	fin	let	took	fan
up	pop	hand	five	cow

Note: This activity may be useful to carry out with individual children first so that early years workers can determine which children have the necessary auditory and cognitive skills. Small groups of children can then be put together to play the game.

A warning note!

It is essential that adults check carefully to see what stage a child has reached in the reading process. There is little point in asking a child to sound out letters in a word if that child has not yet understood how books work. In early years settings it is also important to recognise that the desire to learn to read will greatly influence a child's ability to learn to read. A child who enjoys books is more likely to spend time looking at them and trying to decode text. As children need to learn to read in order to succeed in their schooling, it is critical that they are not put off at an early age and made to feel that they cannot cope.

Remember that text is a combination of abstract symbols. Children will only be able to 'crack' the code when their cognitive development has reached a stage of understanding the abstract. Another element in learning to read is being able to remember symbols and word shapes. This again means that children who have difficulty in retaining information are less likely to be able to remember symbols.

Writing

Developing children's writing

Reading and writing fit together, as most children develop these skills side by side. As with reading, writing is a process that cannot be rushed. Children who are pushed to write letters but are not at the stage of recognising them or have poor fine manipulative skills are more likely to develop poor writing habits.

Early years settings need also to be aware of the handwriting policy of the local primary schools as there is a trend towards starting children immediately with joined handwriting (or at least with a 'flick' for where the join will go). Most primary teachers would prefer children to have good fine manipulative skills overall and to be able to hold pencils correctly, rather than to form their letters poorly and incorrectly and not enjoy writing.

Early years settings can help children's developing writing skills in three main ways:

- by developing children's hand–eye co-ordination
- by helping children to hold pencils and other drawing tools
- by providing plenty of opportunities for children to draw and record.

The diagram overleaf shows how to work towards the Early Learning Goals by developing children's writing skills in the three ways listed above, as well as by working on children's pre-reading skills.

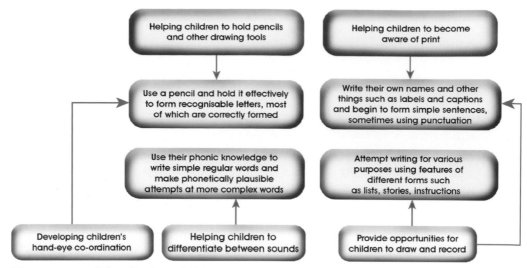

The process of developing children's emergent writing and pre-reading skills feeds into the Early Learning Goals

Developing children's hand–eye co-ordination

Writing letters or numbers requires quite skilled hand–eye co-ordination. A child's feeling of poor co-ordination can often be recreated when an adult tries to write with the 'other' hand! During the process of learning to write, children will also need to copy or to trace letters. This involves hand–eye co-ordination of quite an exact nature.

Children can also be helped to develop their hand–eye co-ordination through a range of activities that are not necessarily linked to writing and recording. The spider diagram overleaf outlines some of the ways to do this.

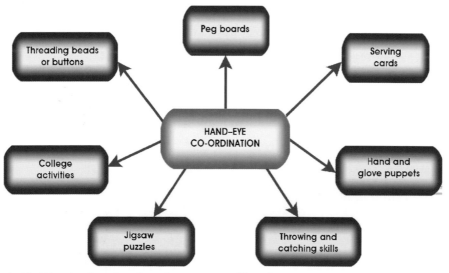

Activities to develop hand–eye co-ordination

Helping children to hold pencils and other drawing tools

Young children start by holding paint brushes and other drawing equipment in a fist clasp. As children become more adept at using drawing materials they should be encouraged to hold them in a pincer clasp. This allows the pencil to be used more accurately. Most children develop this grasp naturally, but other children may need to be given triangular pencils or pencil grips to help them develop this position.

Painting on a large scale can help develop children's writing skills

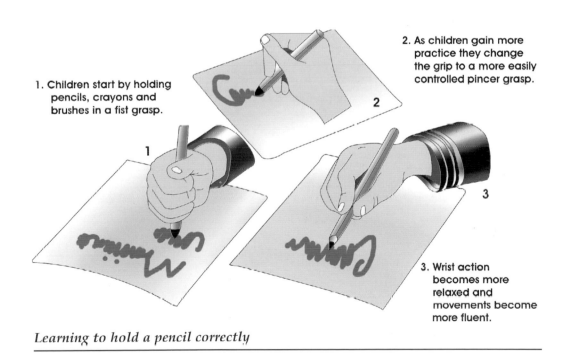

1. Children start by holding pencils, crayons and brushes in a fist grasp.

2. As children gain more practice they change the grip to a more easily controlled pincer grasp.

3. Wrist action becomes more relaxed and movements become more fluent.

Learning to hold a pencil correctly

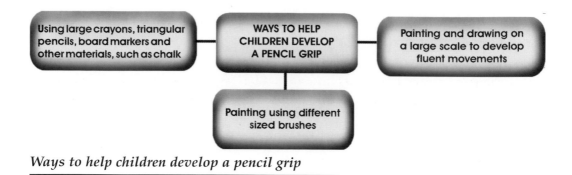

Ways to help children develop a pencil grip

Follow my snake

Young children often enjoy playing in the sand. This activity uses damp sand and encourages children to draw using sticks, lollipop batons and other types of tools.

Aim: This activity helps children to develop hand–eye co-ordination skills.

Resources: Stick, pencils, lollipop sticks.

Activity: A child or an adult draws a simple pattern in the damp sand using a stick. The children have to follow the line until they reach the end when they can draw the head of the snake.

Extension: There are many ways of varying this activity. Where children have started to gain control the adult can draw the line slowly and the aim of the game is then for the children to catch up with the adult's stick.

Tray painting

Aim: This activity helps children to make simple prints. It is also a sensory activity that helps children to feel paint. Children can work in pairs or as individuals.

Resources: Ready-mixed paint, paper, tray or plastic tabletop.

Activity: Spread a thin layer of paint over a tray or tabletop. Too much paint makes it hard to leave a pattern. The children use their fingers to scribble or draw a simple picture in the paint. A piece of paper is placed by the adult on top and is smoothed down by the children. When the paper is lifted, the design is transferred to the paper.

Extension: Once children are able to master this activity they can repeat this activity using a tool such as a pencil or wide brush.

OUTCOMES FOR CHILDREN

These types of activities link to the following Early Learning Goal

They encourage children to use a pencil and hold it effectively to form recognisable letters, most of which are correctly formed.

As children become used to holding pencils and crayons, their hand movements will become more accurate and relaxed.

Activities to help children use their whole hand and wrist will help them develop a good pencil hold. This means that early years workers may need to plan activities which encourage large drawing and painting movements before moving onto activities that require finer movements.

Providing opportunities for children to draw and record

Most children enjoy painting and drawing as through it they are able to communicate and express themselves. The co-ordination and skills needed to help children draw and paint can be transferred to writing. This means that children need to have plenty of opportunities to paint, draw and colour.

At first young children's drawings may look like scribbles, but as children become more co-ordinated and their perception of the world develops, their drawings become more representational as well as more detailed. Once children have gained this co-ordination and also understand that symbols can have meaning, they will be ready to start recording. As with reading, early years settings can give children the desire to record. The word 'record' is being used rather than writing as, at first, children should be given opportunities simply to make marks and have a go at 'writing' for themselves. This is often called **emergent writing**.

Once children have become familiar with holding a pencil and imitating writing, they will gradually form letters that increasingly resemble 'real letters'. Many of these letters will figure in their name as this is a word with which they are likely to be familiar and it has some meaning for them. Once children are aware of letters in text and letter shapes are starting to emerge, adults may consider helping children to form letters correctly. Adults can do this by encouraging children to make anticlockwise circles in sand, with chalk and with paint. Where it is appropriate to show children how to form letters, it is useful to write letters slowly and to talk about how you are forming them. A good game is to take a paintbrush of one colour and to begin to make the letter shape with the child trying to paint over your letter using a different colour of paint.

Opportunities for emergent writing

Adults can encourage children in many ways to have a go at 'writing'. For example, children can write their names on a register as they come into a setting and the home corner can be equipped with pencils, paper and envelopes so that children can pretend to write letters. Children can also be asked if they would like to write about the pictures they have drawn or painted, or the junk models they have made.

The aim of any of these activities is to encourage children to have a go at writing as a way of supporting a play activity, probably imaginative play. In early years settings, most children will enjoy the feeling of pretending to write. Opportunities for writing might include:

- shopping lists as part of playing shops
- writing down patients' medical notes as part of playing hospitals
- registers as part of playing schools
- letters linked to the theme of post offices
- making labels and price tags for shops
- producing railway tickets as part of a theme on trains
- menus for playing cafes.

If there are visitors to a setting, children might also want to contribute to a thank-you letter afterwards.

This child has learnt that print can carry meaning

ACTIVITY

Teddy's postcards

Teddy is on holiday and wants to send some postcards to his friends. He is not very good at writing. Can the children help him?

Aim: The aim of this activity is to encourage children to have a go at writing and learn that there are different purposes for writing. This activity will fit in well with a theme of holidays, and postcards can be displayed.

Resources: Selection of blank postcards, pencils, sticky labels to act as pretend stamps, rubber stamps.

Activity: A table is prepared for children, complete with some postcards that have already been written for children to see. A pretend post box could also be made and children could have a go at rubber stamping their cards when they have finished.

(This type of activity can also be used in school with older children who are reluctant writers, as they do not have to produce much writing to fill up a postcard.)

OUTCOMES FOR CHILDREN

This type of activity links to the following Early Learning Goals

It encourages children to:

◆ attempt writing for various purposes, using features of different forms such as lists, stories, instructions

◆ write their own names and other things such as labels and captions and begin to form simple sentences, sometimes using punctuation

◆ use a pencil and hold it effectively to form recognisable letters, most of which are correctly formed.

Chapter 10 Providing opportunities for mathematical development

Mathematics in the Early Years curriculum

Mathematics plays a vital role in everyone's lives, although some people may have unhappy memories of studying it at school. The ability to count, measure and have some feeling of spatial awareness enables people to carry out everyday tasks, such as shopping, cooking and practical jobs such as wallpapering. Many mathematics teachers believe that if children are given a 'feel' for number, shape and measurement early on in life, they will be able to study mathematics in school with more confidence. This means that early years workers should be providing children in early years settings with practical experiences of basic mathematical concepts.

A hands-on approach to early mathematics

Section 1 looked at some theories of learning. Piaget's theory that children pass through different cognitive stages (see pages 26–31) has particular implications for the way that mathematics is introduced into the Early Years. Piaget's view that young children need to think in concrete rather than abstract terms is widely accepted. In early years settings this means that children need to *experience* mathematics, rather than being taught it in a formal way. This can be done in many ways, for example, children can play shops using toy money or they can think about size by ordering dolls or teddies. Providing good mathematical experiences requires planning and an understanding of how children acquire the concept of number.

Areas of early mathematics

The areas of mathematical experiences in early years settings are:

- counting
- matching

- sorting
- ordering
- making and recognising patterns
- adding and subtracting
- measuring weight, length and time
- volume and capacity
- shape and space.

Other areas of importance considered here are: prediction, the concept of number, recording mathematics, and recognising and writing numbers.

Building vocabulary

In order to be able to think in a mathematical way, children need to hear and be encouraged to use some simple mathematical vocabulary. Adults can help children when supporting their play or activities by using a core of basic words and expressions. Most children will then learn to understand and use this vocabulary. Specific vocabulary is also suggested in different sections in this chapter.

A basic mathematical vocabulary includes the following:

shorter than	biggest	wider than	circle	inside
shortest	smallest	more than	in front of	outside
the difference	pattern	less than	behind	
the same as	match	square	next to	
longer than	shared	rectangle	above	
longest	take away	triangle	below	

Acquiring a feel for number

There are no particular milestones for acquiring mathematical concepts and gaining concepts is often linked to the experiences that children are offered.

If you accept Piaget's belief that children cannot be taught to 'conserve' this means that you must provide them with practical opportunities to experience conservation. Conservation of number is essential if children are going to be able to really understand number, so that they can go on from counting to adding and subtracting.

Finding out whether children can conserve

A simple activity to see whether a child can conserve number is to put out five cubes or similar objects. Ask the child to count them then re-arrange them in front of the child and ask the child how many there are. If the child needs to count them again, it means that there is not yet an understanding of what makes five. In order to help children acquire a 'feeling' for mathematics, it is therefore essential that a practical approach is taken until such time as children are able to think in the abstract, i.e. count objects without touching them or add numbers together in their heads. For most children this will not happen until they are in school. The spider diagram below shows the main experiences that young children need to be offered in order for them to be able to develop an understanding of number.

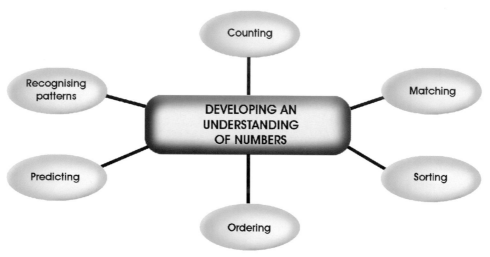

Developing an understanding of numbers

Counting

For many children, their first experience of number is to hear an adult counting. There are many lovely counting rhymes which children quickly learn. Counting introduces children to the idea of numbers, although at first for young children it is just a sequence of sounds. Being able to count does not mean that children have an understanding of number. This may be seen when children forget the numbers or are unable to put out the correct number of objects when asked.

Ideas for counting rhymes

Counting rhymes are one way in which children can learn the 'sounds' of number. It is also an easy and versatile activity to carry out because little preparation is needed and the rhymes can be said at any time of the day; for example, to entertain and stimulate children if they are waiting at home time or for food.

Ten fat sausages sizzling in the pan

Children enjoy this rhyme because they are allowed to clap and shout. It can be used at meal times if children are waiting and also to complement stories about food. If children find it hard to count backwards in twos the rhyme can be changed to 'all of a sudden one went bang,'

Ten fat sausages sizzling in the pan
Then one went pop and another went bang
Eight fat sausages . . .
And then there were no fat sausages left!

Five currant buns in a baker's shop

This traditional rhyme allows children to see how money is used to buy things. It can be a good idea to have some pretend money so that children act out this rhyme. It is also a lovely rhyme to use when a new child joins a setting as his or her name can be used so that other children learn who the new child is.

Five currant buns in a baker's shop
Round and fat with sugar on the top
Along comes . . . (child's name) with a penny one day
Bought a currant bun and took it away.

Five little ducks went swimming one day

Children enjoy singing this rhyme and they can do hand gestures to show how the ducks have gone over the pond and far away. The rhyme can be changed so that other animals can be substituted, for example, 'Five little worms went wiggling one day, down a hole and far away!' This rhyme can also be used for a talk about not going out of sight of adults when in a park or in town: 'How do you think mother duck felt when she could not see her ducklings?'

Five little ducks went swimming one day
Over the pond and far away.
Mother duck said 'Quack, quack, quack, quack'
But only four little ducks came back.
Last verse ends with:
Mother Duck says 'Quack, quack, quack, quack'
And five little ducks came swimming back.

Five little pussy cats playing near the door

This simple rhyme is often enjoyed by children because they may have seen cats or have a family pet.

Five little pussy cats playing near the door;
One ran and hid inside and then there were four.
Four little pussy cats underneath a tree;
One heard a dog bark and then there were three.
Three little pussy cats thinking what to do;
One saw a little bird and then there were two.
Two little pussy cats sitting in the sun;
One ran to catch his tail and then there was one.
One little pussy cat looking for some fun;
He saw a butterfly and then there were none.

Counting rhymes can be extended by using props such as cut-out images for the currant bun or story boards. Repetitive rhymes tend to work well with three year olds, but older children can enjoy slightly more involved rhymes such as 'Five little pussy cats'.

Helping children to count

In order to build children's experience in counting, adults must encourage them to count objects as the next step from just counting out loud. Counting objects by touching or moving them allows children to understand in a concrete way. This is sometimes known as *one-to-one correspondence*. There are many opportunities for children to count during the day. As children also learn by imitation, it is a good idea for adults to demonstrate counting out loud while pointing to objects. When children are counting they should be encouraged to point at or to touch each object. This helps them understand that each number they have said out loud has meaning. It is a good idea to start with less than five objects and gradually find opportunities to count larger numbers.

There are many opportunities for children to count during the day

By the age of four years, most children are ready to start playing board games which involve some counting. It is often a good idea to find a large dice and a very simple board as, at first, children can find it hard to move their counters accurately. It can also be helpful at first to restrict the possible number combinations on a dice so that only 1, 2 or 3 can be thrown. Children need a lot of practice at counting and one-to-one correspondence and it is important not to assume that a child who has mastered this is immediately ready to start writing numbers (see page 221 on reinforcement).

Sorting, ordering and matching

Matching

Matching is a mathematical skill, although it is one that adults tend to take for granted. In order to be able to match, children have to look at an object and compare it to another and decide whether the features are the same. This process leads into many areas of mathematics, for example, the idea of 'equals'(=) means that items are of the same value.

There are many activities that help children practise matching including games such as lotto, snap and happy families, as well as everyday opportunities.

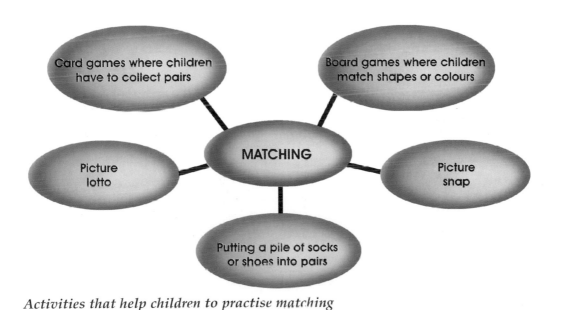

Activities that help children to practise matching

Teddy's wallpaper

ACTIVITY

Teddy wants to decorate his bedroom. He has started to decorate but is in a bit of a muddle because he has five different pieces of wallpaper and he can't work out which one goes with the wallpaper he has already put up. Can the children help him?

Aim: This activity helps children with matching skills.

Resources: Five different squares of wallpaper and Teddy's 'original roll'.

Activity: Show children Teddy's original roll of paper and the five other pieces and ask the children to match the right piece for Teddy.

Varying this activity: This activity can be varied to suit the age/stage of the children. It can be made more demanding by having wallpaper that is quite similar. Another way of doing this activity can be for Teddy to be painting his room and forgetting what shade of paint he has to use.

OUTCOMES FOR CHILDREN

This type of activity links to the following Early Learning Goals

It encourages children to:

◆ use developing mathematical ideas and methods to solve practical problems

◆ talk about, recognise and recreate simple patterns.

Sorting

Sorting is a mathematical process which allows you to compare objects and then decide on features that link them. This helps children learn to be selective and logical. Sorting leads into many mathematical areas, for example, learning about odd and even numbers and grouping shapes according to their features, such as putting triangles and squares into separate piles.

There are many activities to help children practise their sorting skills. Jigsaws offer children the chance to use sorting skills while allowing them to gain an overall sense of satisfaction once they have completed the puzzle. But there are also many everyday opportunities that can allow children to sort. Tidying up at the end of sessions can be structured so that children are sorting while they are tidying. It can help to make the process fun, for example, children can be asked to bring all the red pieces of Duplo to a table or put all the cups from the home corner into the cupboard.

Activities to help children sort

There are many fun structured activities to help children practise their sorting skills. When planning activities for children, you should make sure that three and four year olds are physically touching and moving objects. The example overleaf shows how you might make a game of this.

ACTIVITY

Teddy's washing day

Aim: The idea of this activity is to help Teddy sort out his friends' washing pile. He can't remember who the clothes belong to. Can the children help him?

Resources: A pile of clean clothing that is muddled up in a wash basket.

Activity: The children look at the clothes and decide who they might belong to. Young children might have just a few clothes to sort, i.e. a baby's clothes and an adult's, whereas older children might be encouraged to sort out several sizes of clothing.

OUTCOMES FOR CHILDREN

This type of activity links to the following Early Learning Goals

It encourages children to:

◆ use language such as 'more' or 'less', 'greater' or 'smaller', 'heavier' or 'lighter', to compare two numbers or quantities

◆ use developing mathematical ideas and methods to solve practical problems.

Ordering

Ordering is another ability adults take for granted, although it is a mathematical and logical skill. It is also an essential skill, as children need to have a firm understanding of the position of numbers in relation to each other. There are many activities that can help children to experience ordering. Children can be given objects to order according to their size, such as stacking beakers or different sized teddies. Encouraging children to order objects as part of the tidying process can also be useful; for example, stacking boxes according to their size on a shelf.

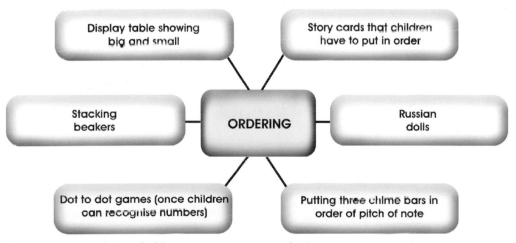

Activities that help children to experience ordering

Using the language of ordering

Children will need to be able to use the language of ordering, i.e. ordinal numbers (first, second and third) and superlatives (best, fastest):

first	second	third	fourth	fifth
last	shortest	quickest	longest	slowest

ACTIVITY

Teddy's three-in-a-row game

Teddy has three musical instruments that he wants to play to the children. When they shut their eyes he is going to play them. Can the children work out the order in which he played them?

Aim: For children to practise listening and ordering skills.

Resources: Drum, tambourine and triangle or any three different sounding instruments.

OUTCOMES FOR CHILDREN

This type of activity links to the following Early Learning Goals

It encourages children to:

◆ use language such as 'more' or 'less', 'greater' or 'smaller', 'heavier' or 'lighter', to compare two numbers or quantities

◆ use developing mathematical ideas and methods to solve practical problems.

Patterns

To be able to recognise and use patterns is an important part of acquiring a good concept not only of number but also of shape and measurement. Patterns are all around us, in nature and in manufactured materials. A pattern is a sequence that is logical and the ability to recognise patterns can help children in many ways, for example, seeing a pattern to all of the multiplication tables.

Activities to help children see patterns

There are many ways of encouraging children to make and recognise patterns. For example, children can carry out threading activities, such as making a necklace which gives them an end product as well as encouraging their fine manipulative skills. Adults can also make patterns for children to recognise, for example, setting a table with alternate coloured plates and asking the children to spot if they can see a pattern.

Music and rhythm can be good ways of encouraging a sense of pattern. Musical activities that make children physically experience rhythm can be arranged, for

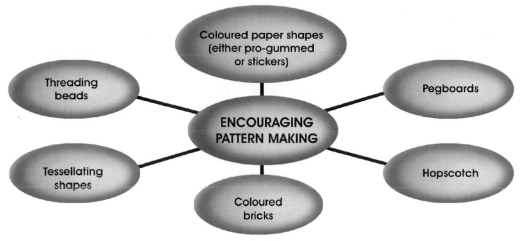

Ways to encourage pattern making in children

example, children can shake percussion instruments in time to a beat. Songs with verses and a chorus can help children to learn about patterns as they experience an alternate pattern through singing verses then the chorus.

Kaleidoscope patterns

There are many ways of making kaleidoscopes. A simple one can be made by putting two mirrors together at right angles and placing the pattern to be repeated underneath. Children will enjoy seeing their pattern being repeated.

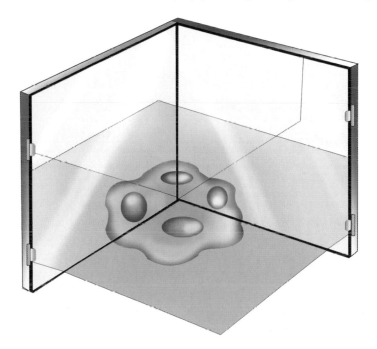

A simple kaleidoscope

Prediction

Prediction is an area that older children can find difficult, although it is an important mathematical skill. Children who can predict an answer or outcome should be able to spot an error in calculations. Giving children experiences of prediction helps their confidence as they can learn that it does not matter if their prediction is not the same as the outcome. Rounding up numbers and getting a rough estimate is one way in which prediction fits the broader mathematical picture.

Helping children to experience prediction is easy to do through everyday situations. For example, children can be asked to guess how many chairs there are around a table and then count them, or how many buttons there are on a coat. It is important that every guess is valued and that praise is given for the guess rather than for the correct answer. Counting the objects afterwards is also important so that children can get a feel for numbers.

How many steps to touch the sleeping lion?   **ACTIVITY**

How many steps will you need to touch a sleeping lion? One child lies down – he or she is the 'lion'. The others have to creep up to the lion, but they must guess how many steps they will take. (Children should be placed around and quite near the lion so that numbers under 10 are used.) Each child says a number and then moves forward the number of steps.

OUTCOMES FOR CHILDREN

This type of activity links to the following Early Learning Goal

It encourages children to:

◆ use developing mathematical ideas and methods to solve practical problems.

Concept of number

As mathematics is part of everyday life it is relatively straightforward to provide practical experiences of number in everyday situations. The role of the adult must be to spot opportunities as they arise and to use them to bring number into the daily routine; for example, an adult may help a child take off a coat while counting the number of buttons on it. There are a few simple strategies which adults can follow to make the most of everyday opportunities.

● Always count objects by touching them or encouraging a child to point to them one by one.

● Count objects from left to right, as this encourages children's eyes to follow in the same way as when they begin to learn to read.

- Encourage children to predict before counting. For example, 'how many books do you think I have put out?'

- Allow children plenty of time to think. Some children take longer to absorb information or to carry out tasks such as pointing.

Reinforcement

Learning the concept of number is a gradual process and children need to experience number in many different ways in order to be completely at ease. This is what is meant by the term *reinforcement*. Reinforcing number activities means that children are given opportunities to repeat them or find out the same information in a different way. It is important that reinforcement activities are valued as there is a danger that adults can assume children have understood a concept and are automatically ready to go on further, when in fact more practice is needed.

Repeating activities builds confidence and helps children to look for short cuts and patterns. For example, a child who has made a pattern by threading beads may do the same activity again, but this time will lay out the pattern first to speed the process up. Children who have counted out the beakers for drinks may be asked to count them back in when all the children have finished. This will teach them that numbers are constant. As they become more familiar with the activity, they could be asked to group the beakers in pairs and then count them.

Reinforcement gives children confidence

Acquiring the 'feel' of number and other mathematical concepts is for most children a slow but steady process. Reinforcement activities, and encouraging children to repeat activities, gives them confidence. It also helps children to acquire other skills, such as persistence, because most children will spend longer carrying out a task that they are enjoying. It is important that when curriculum plans are drawn up there must be opportunities for children to repeat activities, particularly ones that they have enjoyed.

Concepts of addition and subtraction

Links to the Early Learning Goals

By the end of the reception year, most children should be able to:

◆ in practical activities and discussion, begin to use the vocabulary involved in adding and subtracting

◆ find one more or one less than a number from 1 to 10

◆ begin to relate addition to combining two groups of objects, and subtraction to 'taking away'

It is surprising how children quickly gain a concept of subtraction as from an early age they notice if another child tries to take something of theirs away! Children are also able to work out whether someone else has taken another biscuit or has had two turns. This means that although formal subtraction and addition, using written numbers, is not appropriate for the majority of children until they begin school, there is plenty of scope within early years settings for children to learn the language and the concepts of addition and subtraction.

Learning the language of subtraction and addition

The type of vocabulary that children will need gradually to develop is shown below. More formal terms, such as *subtract*, will gradually be learnt if children hear adults using them in context: 'What would happen if we subtracted one, if I took one away?' Most children will not actively be using the extended vocabulary until they are in school.

- *Basic vocabulary*

more than	less than	the same	take away	nothing left	most
add	give	more	altogether	fewer	least

- *Extended vocabulary*

subtract	equals	the difference between	add on

Using everyday opportunities

At first the concept of addition and subtraction will be practised through the daily routine. Young children can learn through being encouraged actively to share equipment, food and play materials. This means that you might ask a child at the dough table to divide a lump of dough between the others, thus creating the opportunity to talk about amounts being the same and asking questions such as 'who has the most dough?'

There are also simple games to use with children which focus on taking or giving. At first young children will prefer only games where they are collecting items as they can be upset if they draw a card or land on a square where they have to give something back.

ACTIVITY

The squirrel game

This is a simple game which links very well into the theme of animals or autumn. It will help children to experience the feeling of adding to something.

Aim: Each child is given an identical size of beaker, cup or box. The aim of the game is to fill the container with nuts.

Resources: Spinner or dice, unshelled nuts such as hazelnuts or walnuts, beakers or other containers.

Activity: Children throw a dice or use a spinner to determine how many nuts they can take. If children are very young the number of nuts can be restricted to numbers under four and a spinner which points to a picture of the quantity of nuts can be used. The winner of the game is the child who fills the beaker first.

OUTCOMES FOR CHILDREN

This type of activity links to the following Early Learning Goals

It encourages children to:

◆ recognise numerals 1 to 9

◆ begin to relate addition to combining two groups of objects, and subtraction to 'taking away'

◆ use developing mathematical ideas and methods to solve practical problems.

Recording mathematics

Over the last few years there has been a trend towards making mathematics more formal. With this comes a danger that children will spend more time writing than actually experiencing mathematical concepts. Recognising and being able to write numbers is best seen as a final step in the mathematical process, rather than being central to a child's early mathematical experience.

It is possible to record a child's work by using photographs of the activity or by asking children to draw pictures of what they have been doing. Some mathematical work can be displayed, for example, putting out on a display table a pattern that a child has made.

You can also keep records by making notes of children's progress, i.e. by keeping records of the activities that children have been doing and also by carrying out structured observations.

Recognising and writing numbers

Links to the Early Learning Goals

By the end of the reception year, most children should be able to:

◆ recognise numerals 1 to 9.

With the trend towards making mathematics more formal has come a move to teach children to write and recognise numbers before they go to school. For some children this is quite hard, as a number is a symbol and therefore an abstract concept. Where children have a good understanding of number as a concept they are more likely to use and write numbers more confidently, as it is always easier to remember a symbol when you understand its meaning. This means that practical activities that encourage children to experience number need to be carried out before children will be ready to recognise and write numbers. The eventual goal is that children at the end of the reception year will be able to recognise numbers from 1 to 9 and so time must be spent in the pre-school years on concentrating on the practical experience of mathematics.

Helping children to recognise numbers

The first step in writing and using written numbers is to be able to recognise them. When children already have a visual picture of the shape of numbers they will find it easier to write them.

Gaining familiarity with the shape of numbers

Many children learn to recognise numbers without being formally taught them. They do this by playing games that have numbers on them, seeing numbers on wall displays and playing shop in the home corner. They can also recognise numbers on front doors of houses and enjoy finding different ones. Adults can help children to recognise numbers by writing down numbers in front of them, for example, they may count the number of children they are working with and write this number down or they may write down how many children need aprons.

Ways of helping children see numbers around them can include:

● displays and signs in the setting that use numbers, for example, '4 people can play in the sand'

● number lines

● pointing out house numbers, bus numbers and other numbers used in the environment

● number lotto or bingo with numbers 1 to 9

● number snap (cards with numbers on).

Written numbers have meaning

Once children are beginning to recognise the shape of numbers, the next step will be to match numbers with objects. This will only be appropriate if children are counting accurately and are starting to have a feel for number. Some children will be ready for this before they start in the reception year, but others will not be at this stage. Below is an example of the type of activity that could be used with children who are ready to match numbers to objects.

Teddy's honey store

ACTIVITY

Teddy is very forgetful. He keeps counting his pots of honey and then forgets how many he has. Can the children help him?

Aim: To help children match numbers to objects.

Resources: A collection of plastic pots and cards with written numbers 1 to 5.

Activity: The children are told a story about Teddy and how he likes to know how much honey he has left. He keeps counting but then forgets later on. The children are asked to count the pots and then put a card with the number on top of them so that Teddy will be able to remember.

Varying this activity: This type of activity can be carried out with individual children or with small groups. The activity can be varied slightly, for example, another day Teddy needs the children to count his cups or shoes. Varying the same activity is important as children will need plenty of reinforcement.

OUTCOMES FOR CHILDREN

This type of activity links to the following Early Learning Goals

It encourages children to:

◆ say and use number names in order in familiar context

◆ count reliably up to 10 everyday objects

◆ recognise numerals 1 to 9.

Measuring

Links to the Early Learning Goals

By the end of the reception year, most children should be able to:

◆ use language such as 'more' or 'less', 'greater' or 'smaller', 'heavier' or 'lighter', to compare two numbers or quantities.

Understanding how to use measure is an important life skill. People measure many things in their lives: time, length, volume and weight. Understanding how to measure is a gradual process and one that can be started in early years settings. Young children do not need to learn how to use standard measurement units such as grams and litres, but adults should be providing them with an understanding of the need to measure and some idea of how to measure.

Providing experiences for measuring

Part of the skill in measuring is being able to make comparisons. Young children can be introduced to making comparisons through everyday opportunities as well as through structured activities.

Everyday opportunities

The main way in which adults can help children to start using comparisons is through their own language. The spider diagram below shows some of the everyday language possibilities.

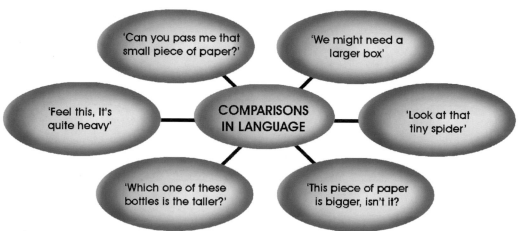

'Can you pass me that small piece of paper?'

'We might need a larger box'

'Feel this, It's quite heavy'

COMPARISONS IN LANGUAGE

'Look at that tiny spider'

'Which one of these bottles is the taller?'

'This piece of paper is bigger, isn't it?'

Everyday language possibilities for making comparisons

There are also many points in the daily routine that can encourage children to make comparisons. At snack time children can pour out drinks and check that beakers have the same amount in them. When deciding who can be first to have a turn or go at something, the traditional method of short straws might be used.

The 'core activities' can also be used to provide opportunities to develop comparison skills. You can ask children to make a large cake and a smaller cake out of dough or to look at two sand castles and decide which one is the larger.

Structured activities

Many books have storylines where size is important and these can be the starting point for discussion. Traditional favourites such as *Goldilocks and the Three Bears* or *Jack and the Beanstalk* help children to think about size. Children can also carry out activities such as finding objects that are smaller or larger than their hands.

Measuring weight

Children experience weighing in many ways, although cooking is usually a favourite activity. For cooking to be a good measuring activity it is important that balancing scales are used, as this is a simple way for children to see how weight can be measured.

ACTIVITY

Quatre, Quatre cakes

This French recipe is interesting because instead of using standard measurements to weigh the ingredients, eggs are used. The recipe makes a mixture that is very similar to traditional fairy cakes, but allows children to be more involved in the weighing process.

Ingredients:

Two eggs

Self-raising flour

Margarine

Sugar

Resources:

Balancing scales

Mixing bowl

Wooden spoons

Small paper cases

Baking tray

Place two eggs on one side of the scales and use these instead of weights. Ask the children to put in spoonfuls of flour until the scales balance. Place the flour in the mixing bowl and weigh out the margarine and sugar in the same way. Then add in the eggs.

Mix all the ingredients together and spoon the mixture into small paper cases placed on a baking tray.

Bake in oven at gas mark 5/190°C for 10–15 minutes or until golden.

OUTCOMES FOR CHILDREN

This type of activity links to the following Early Learning Goals

It encourages children to:

◆ use language such as 'more' or 'less', 'greater' or 'smaller', 'heavier' or 'lighter', to compare two numbers or quantities

◆ use developing mathematical ideas and methods to solve practical problems.

Earlier in this chapter, the importance of encouraging prediction skills with children was mentioned (page 220). When using cooking as a measuring activity, children should also be encouraged to predict. You can ask children to guess how many spoonfuls of flour will be needed to make the scales balance or to feel different weights and guess which one is the heavier.

A balancing scale in the home corner can encourage children to incorporate weighing into their play, by, for example, pretending that they are in a fruit and vegetable shop or that they are cooking.

Measuring length

There are many practical activities to help children experience length. Young children do not need to use rulers or standard units of measurement, but they can use their hands and – more importantly – their eyes. Once again, prediction skills and developing children's mathematical vocabulary are the key elements for providing experiences in measuring length. Children can be shown two or three objects at storytime and asked to decide which is the tallest or shortest. Children can also have fun by jumping over lines or trying to make themselves small or large. Children can count how many steps it takes them to reach different places in the setting. For example, 'How many steps do you need to get from here to the sand tray?'

ACTIVITY

Spider's web

Spider is trying to make herself a web. She has different lengths of string to use. Can the children put the longer strings into a pile to help her?

Aim: For children to measure and sort different lengths of string.

Resources: Pieces of string cut into three different lengths, black piece of card (optional).

Activity: Once children have put the lengths of string into different piles this could be developed into an art activity in which the children make pictures of a spider's web.

OUTCOMES FOR CHILDREN

This type of activity links to the following Early Learning Goals

It encourages children to:

◆ use language such as 'more' or 'less', 'greater' or 'smaller', 'heavier' or 'lighter', to compare two numbers or quantities.

ACTIVITY

Short straws

Can you guess which one of these straws is the longest?

Aim: To help children measure and compare straws of different lengths.

Resources: Sand put into a small tray, straws and scissors.

Activity: Straws of different lengths are poked into the sand tray. Children pick out the straw that they think will be the longest. The children compare their straws.

Varying this activity:

◆ Children can cut straws themselves and play the game with an adult or partner.

◆ Some of the straws are of similar length.

◆ Lengths of string are buried in the sand with just one end showing.

OUTCOMES FOR CHILDREN

This type of activity links to the following Early Learning Goals

It encourages children to:

◆ use language such as 'more' or 'less', 'greater' or 'smaller', 'heavier' or 'lighter', to compare two numbers or quantities.

Measuring time

The measurement of time is a difficult concept for children to understand because it is not something they can see. This means time is an abstract concept and it is not until most children are in their second year of full-time school that they begin to understand how it is measured. Even for many adults time can appear to pass more slowly or quickly depending on what they are doing, so it is probably even harder for a child to grasp the idea of 'five minutes until lunchtime'.

In the early years setting, adults can help children to understand the notion of time by referring to events in the day. By the age of four years, most children will begin to understand what is meant by today, yesterday and tomorrow, although children will not necessarily be able to recollect accurately what they have done in a week.

An awareness of time can be given to children simply by having some chiming or cuckoo clocks in a setting. Children enjoy hearing the chimes and may learn at what times a tune or an action may be seen or heard.

Learning the language of time

There are some activities which can give children the language of time, although young children will not necessarily understand the concept. Being familiar with the language of time will help children to acquire the concept when they are ready.

The language of time

o'clock	yesterday
second	today
minute	tomorrow
half an hour	calendar
hour	diary
day	seasons
week	birthday
month	Christmas
year	other festivals

Opportunities to make children aware of time

- Talk to children during the day about the passing of time and where they are in the day, for example, tell them it's nearly lunch time.

- Use charts to show birthdays and other important events.

- Plan activities around the seasons of the year.

- Use festivals to show that certain times of the year are special.

- Put toy clocks in the home corner.

- 'Hickory Dickory Dock' is a traditional nursery rhyme that can give very young children an awareness of time, especially if a clock is used as a prop.

What's the time Mr Wolf?

ACTIVITY

This is a game for four year olds or for younger children helped by an adult.

One child is chosen to be the wolf, while the other children are several metres away. Children take it in turns to say 'What's the time Mr Wolf?' The 'wolf' replies by choosing a time, such as one o'clock, and turns around. The children then move forward according to the time – one o'clock would be one step while five o'clock would be five paces. The aim of the game is to touch the wolf while his or her back is turned, but there is a twist. The wolf can reply 'dinner time' and then turn around and catch any child who is not fast enough to beat a retreat! A child who is caught then becomes the next Mr Wolf.

Volume and capacity

Many adults find it hard to judge the volume and capacity of objects. Have you ever found that a can of drink fits far more easily into a glass than you had thought? Children can experience volume and capacity in the water and sand trays if they are given some simple pouring and spooning equipment and some guidance. Chapter 7 on 'core activities' looks in detail at ways of using sand and water to stimulate children's experience (pages 141–6).

Specific ideas to help children gain the concept of volume and capacity

- Ask children to predict how many spoonfuls of sand are needed to fill up a cup or beaker.

- Encourage children to explore whether water in a beaker will fit into a different shaped container.

- Ask children to fill up a cup with wooden beads. How many are needed? How many cubes would fit into the same beaker? Is this more or less?

ACTIVITY

Teddy's cubes

Teddy has some cubes and he wants to put them safely into a box. He has two boxes and he does not know which one he should use. Can the children help him?

Aim: To help children gain a concept of capacity.

Resources: Wooden cubes (or other items could be used, such as large buttons). Two boxes – one of which is too small to take the cubes.

Activity: Ask a child to help Teddy by putting the cubes into one of the boxes. Is there enough room for them?

Varying this activity: As children become more skilled at judging which box could be used, more containers could be introduced. In the same way, different items could be used for children to explore capacity, for example, raisins, buttons, clothes pegs.

OUTCOMES FOR CHILDREN

This type of activity links to the following Early Learning Goals

It encourages children to:

- use language such as 'more' or 'less', 'greater' or 'smaller', 'heavier' or 'lighter', to compare two numbers or quantities

- use language such as 'circle' or 'bigger' to describe the shape and size of solids and flat shapes

- use developing mathematical ideas and methods to solve practical problems.

Shape and space

Shape

Young children enjoy using different shapes and are often able to match shapes. There are many creative activities which allow children to experience shape while at the same time learning the names of the basic shapes, such as square, rectangle, circle and triangle. Learning about shape fits in well with creating patterns and children can make pictures or patterns using shapes.

ACTIVITY

Feely bag shape game

This game can be played with small groups of children or with individual children, and can be varied according to the age/stage of the children. Feely bags are fun for children because they enjoy the element of surprise.

Aim: For children to practise the language of shapes.

Resources: Feely bag, collection of wooden bricks of different shapes or other objects.

Activity: Place a brick in the feely bag. Put out several other bricks, including one that matches the shape in the bag. Then:

◆ ask the child with the feely bag to point to the brick that matches the one that can be felt in the bag

◆ or ask the child to describe the brick to the other children so that they can work out which one it is

◆ or ask the other children to ask yes/no type questions about the brick that the child with the bag can feel.

Varying this activity: The children have to guess how many objects are in the bag by feeling them from the outside of the bag. The adult writes the number down on a piece of paper. They then put their hands into the bag and count the objects.

(continued)

OUTCOMES FOR CHILDREN

This type of activity links to the following Early Learning Goals

It encourages children to:

◆ use language such as 'circle' or 'bigger' to describe the shape and size of solids and flat shapes

◆ use everyday words to describe position

◆ use developing mathematical ideas and methods to solve practical problems.

There are games to help children recognise shape and colour, for example, board games where children have to collect all the shapes in order to finish. Jigsaw puzzles are also good for helping children to develop a sense of shape and spatial awareness. There is a strong link to capacity here too, as children learn that some shapes fit better than others into containers. Adults can help children to learn the names of some of the basic shapes by saying them aloud and pointing them out to children. For example, 'Put your finished plates on the rectangular table over there'.

Learning the language of shapes

Children need to be familiar with the language of shapes. The aim is that at the end of the reception year they can recognise familiar shapes such as circles and triangles and also have the vocabulary to name them. Children should learn this language through carrying out their own activities and by hearing adults using appropriate language. Playing shops can help children to gain some of the vocabulary through touching and using different types of packaging. Other 'core activities', such as dough and junk modelling, will also give children the opportunity to use and talk about shapes (see Chapter 7, pages 137–41 and 153–5).

round	curved	smooth	flat	bumpy	corner
triangle	rectangle	square	oval	circle	hard
soft	edges	sharp	oblong	pyramid	cube
ball	sphere	side	face	cone	

Position

Children gain concepts of shape and space from their own physical movements. In addition, adults need to help children learn the vocabulary to enable them to describe position. Overleaf are some key words that children will at first find hard to understand; as they reach five years old they may be able to use the language more confidently and with understanding.

forwards	backwards	sideways	under	over	underneath
closer	behind	next to	left	right	inside
between	upside down	inside out	in front of	on top of	far away

Activities to help children learn about position

There are many activities that will help children learn about position. The best activities with children under five years require them to use their own bodies.

- *Simon says*

This traditional game can be tailored to help children follow instructions and at the same time absorb the meaning of position words, for example, 'Simon says put your hand under your chin' or 'Simon says put your hands on top of your head'.

- *Hot and cold*

This is another traditional game in which 'position' words can be actively used. An object is hidden and one child has to find it. The other children help the child to know whether he or she is close to the object by shouting out 'hot' or 'cold'. If 'cold' is called out, it means that the child is moving in the wrong direction. The role of the adult in this game is to focus the children on the vocabulary by commentating, for example, 'no, it's not underneath the cushion' or 'yes, you are getting closer'.

Teddy's treasure hunt

ACTIVITY

Teddy has organised a treasure hunt. He has hidden one of his special nuts and has given the children a list of instructions to help them find it.

Aim: To help children learn about position.

Resources: Nuts or similar safe objects that can be easily hidden.

Activity: Hide some nuts or other objects and lay a trail of clues. Read the clues out to the children as they find them. For example, 'Teddy says that you must look underneath the big jigsaw box' or 'Teddy says that the next clue is in between the home corner and the sand tray'.

Varying this activity: Children hide nuts and help the adult to find them.

OUTCOMES FOR CHILDREN

This type of activity links to the following Early Learning Goal

It encourages children to:

◆ use everyday words to describe position.

The reflective practitioner

Do I have positive attitudes towards mathematics?

Do I use everyday opportunities to encourage children to count?

Do I plan practical activities that will help children learn concepts?

Do I encourage children to predict and guess?

Do I model mathematical behaviour with children, for example, writing down numbers, guessing, counting?

Are children encouraged to play games and explore construction materials by themselves?

Do children see written numbers in the environment?

Are opportunities for children to use mathematics available in the role play area, for example, shopping?

Are parents aware of the practical approach used in developing early mathematical reasoning?

Are children involved in measuring ingredients during cooking activities?

Do I play simple games using a spinner or dice with children?

Chapter 11 Providing opportunities for knowledge and understanding of the world

This area of the curriculum looks at helping children to explore and consider the world around them. It builds on children's natural curiosity and desire to touch, feel and ask questions about their environment.

This chapter is divided into the following sections:

- providing opportunities for early science
- providing opportunities for early technology (including information and communication technology)
- helping children to explore the concept of past and present
- helping children to explore their environment.

Providing opportunities for early science

Science as a way of thinking

Over the past few years, science has become more of a high profile curriculum area in the education system. The national shortage of scientists and engineers has meant that greater efforts are being made to make science accessible and interesting for children. Science teaching has therefore been extended to primary schools and it is now desirable that an awareness of science is built into an early years curriculum.

Many early years workers worry about providing opportunities for science as they fear that their own personal knowledge of the subject area is limited. So it is important to understand that science at this level is about a way of thinking rather than about the laws of physics! The aim of pre-school science is to encourage children to question the world about them by helping them to predict, observe and consider events and activities. At this stage the role of the adult is not necessarily to teach or to explain, but simply to help children think about what they are seeing and doing.

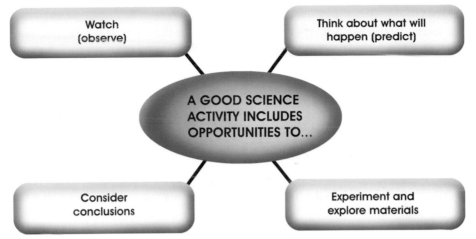

The main ingredients of a good science activity

Many everyday activities can be turned into a scientific experience. Young children need to explore their environment and a good science activity allows them to do exactly that: it helps children to find out and think more about what they are seeing.

Links to the Early Learning Goals

By the end of the reception year, most children should be able to:

◆ investigate objects and materials by using all of their senses as appropriate

◆ find out about, and identify some features of, living things, objects and events they observe

◆ look closely at similarities, differences, patterns and change

◆ ask questions about why things happen and how things work.

Prediction

Prediction means encouraging children to think about what might happen. For example, during a cooking activity an adult might ask the children what they think would happen if a cake was not put in the oven. There are many everyday activities where children can be asked to predict in this way. This helps children to think scientifically as they are questioning the reasons for things rather than simply accepting the world around them.

Helping children to predict

It is important that children are encouraged to predict and that their ideas are valued. Children are constantly learning through their experiences and many of their predictions will be very inaccurate, although often they will be based on the child's own experiences. For example, a child who has never seen a burnt cake will not know that food often becomes dark brown when over-cooked.

Observation

Observation is a skill that allows children to learn more from what they are seeing. For example, by observing a worm, children may notice that it does not have legs; by observing an egg white while it is being whisked, they may see that it changes in colour. Observation allows children to consider changes and differences.

Children need time to observe and will also need an adult to help them focus on details. Adults can use questions to guide observations, for example, 'can you see the lines on the snail's shell?' Young children can often observe more easily when they are alone or in very small groups as they may need to talk about what they are seeing.

The next step from observation is to consider reasons for what has been observed. Young children can often come up with simple explanations that are correct with the help of the adults around them. Explanations that are incorrect are also valid and should not be dismissed out of hand, as the process of considering explanations is of more importance than the accuracy.

In some instances it may be possible to test children's theories, although this next step is more likely to take place within the primary curriculum. Testing theories allows children to check their ideas to see if they work.

Observing helps children learn about the world around them

Language and science

In order to express their ideas, children will need to build up an appropriate vocabulary. There is a strong link between cognitive development and language, which means that children will need to be supported when carrying out science activities. They will have to ask questions as well as put into words what they are seeing. Adults working alongside children should be supportive and at times will actually have to articulate for children what they are trying to express. For example:

Child: Ice has gone.

Adult: That's right, the ice has melted. What is there now?

Child: Water.

The role of the adult in science activities

It is essential that early years workers take to heart the message that you do not have to be a scientist in order to provide opportunities for science. Children rely very much on having an adult to help explore and consider their environment. As there are endless opportunities to add science to everyday life, the adult who lacks the confidence to say, 'I wonder what would happen if we put one of these plants into the fridge?' will be constantly denying children opportunities to learn about the world around them.

It is important to remember that activities and events which seem ordinary to adults are often quite fascinating to children, for example, a child making ice cubes will not know that if you use hot water to make them with, they will take longer to freeze. This means that a science activity can be provided by simply asking children to try making ice cubes with warm water and with cold water and to see which set freezes first.

Tips for providing science opportunities

- Allow time for children to talk and express their ideas.
- Don't be afraid if you are not sure of the reason why – you can always ask someone else or look it up.
- Encourage children to think and develop their own thoughts and ideas.
- Use questions to help children develop their theories.
- Allow children to be active and do things for themselves in activities.
- Remember that many everyday things that you take for granted can be good learning experiences for children.

Ideas for science activities

Although there are endless opportunities to bring science into pre-school settings, there are some themes and activities which lend themselves particularly well to providing a science-based approach.

Water is an interesting material as its state changes according to its temperature. It is good to use in early years settings as children are interested in water and are familiar with it, and water is also easily available. Consider the following ideas for activities.

ACTIVITIES

Water expands when it freezes

Half fill a plastic bottle with water.

Ask a child to put a mark on the bottle to show where the level of the water is.

Put the bottle in the freezer.

◆ Is the ice above the mark?

◆ If you leave the bottle, how long will it take to melt?

◆ When the ice has melted, does the water return to the first level?

Children could do this activity in small groups. Each child can have his or her own bottle and the bottles can be different shapes.

Making ice lollies

This is always a popular activity with children, especially in hot weather.

Prepare a mixture of orange juice and water or another drink mixture with the children, pour the mixture into moulds and add the sticks.

◆ What has happened to the water?

◆ What happens if some moulds are left out of the freezer?

◆ What happens if some moulds are put in the fridge instead?

◆ Is there any difference in the time the lollies take to freeze if the mixture has been in the fridge first?

◆ Why do ice lollies melt in your mouth?

Ice melts

Children can find out that ice melts unless it is kept in a very cold place.

Ask the children to put ice cubes in different places, for example, outside, in the shade, in sunshine, in a dark cupboard, in a glass of water, etc.

Keep checking the ice cubes to see how quickly they are melting.

Why do some melt more quickly than others?

(Continued)

Ice floats

Ice floats because it contains tiny air bubbles.

Freeze some ice cubes or other shapes and put them into a bowl of water, then ask the children to push them down.

◆ What happens?

◆ Can the children hear anything?

(Sometimes in a very quiet room, it is possible to hear the ice crackling. This is because of the trapped air bubbles.)

Water takes on the shape of the container it is in

Pour some water into a rubber glove.

Tie the end of the glove with a rubber band and freeze the glove.

Peel off the glove and look at how the ice has taken on the shape of the glove.

Children can make many ice shapes if they put water into different-shaped plastic containers.

Some substances dissolve in water

Fill several jars or beakers with warm water.

Ask a child to put in a teaspoonful of salt and stir it.

What happens to the salt? (The children can taste the slightly salty water.)

This activity can be repeated using sugar, soap, detergent, gelatine, etc. as well as other substances that will not dissolve.

◆ What happens if cold water is used?

◆ What happens if the water is not stirred?

Science activities to help children learn about plants

Children enjoy growing plants and while they are doing this they can also learn that most seeds need sunlight and moisture to grow.

ACTIVITY

Growing plants from seeds

Put out a variety of seeds.

Ask the children to plant the seeds in several pots.

Water some of the pots – but not all of them.

Put the pots in different places, including some in dark places.

(Continued)

- ◆ What happens to the pots that have not been watered?
- ◆ What happens to the seeds that are not put in the sunlight?
- ◆ Do some types of seeds grow more quickly than others?
- ◆ Do larger seeds grow more quickly in 'normal conditions' than smaller ones?

Science activities to help children learn about materials

ACTIVITIES

Some materials absorb heat easily

Ask the children to pick up some different objects – pieces of wood, stones, plastic, metal.

Ask the children to decide if they feel the same. Do some feel warmer than others?

Stones are interesting as they absorb and release heat slowly, while metals absorb and lose heat quickly.

Floating and sinking

There is a lot of science in this activity, although it is essential to note that the weight of a material does not necessarily determine its ability to float. (If this were so, how would large ships be kept afloat? Beware of telling children that heavy items sink.)

Find several objects of similar weight but not necessarily the same size, for example, a small pebble, coin, twig, clothes peg, plastic lid.

Ask the children to feel the objects and predict which ones will float.

Display together the objects that sunk.

Looking at objects that float

The aim of this activity is to help children make a connection between the items that float and to realise that some types of materials always float.

Collect the objects that float and ask the children if they can think of other objects that are made of the same materials.

Try putting these objects in the water tray. (Normally items made of plastic and wood float as they are less dense than items made from metal or stone.)

Providing opportunities for early technology

Design and technology may seem rather advanced for three year olds, but essentially it involves encouraging children to solve problems using materials. The link between science and technology is strong, as children often learn about science from trying to build or make something. Most young children are resourceful and creative which means that construction toys can be popular with all age groups. Design and technology helps children to develop logical thought processes as well as teaching them about the limitations and strengths of materials around them.

The role of the adult

As with science, children will require time in which to think through the answers to simple problems as well as plenty of materials and support. Sometimes children will not be able to do all that they wish and it is important for children to realise that good ideas do not always work. Adults need to keep a careful eye on children to make sure that they are not becoming frustrated, while allowing children sufficient time to think through what they want to do.

Materials and resources

A well stocked junk box will provide most of the materials needed for technology work. The list below provides an outline of the types of materials and resources that can be made available for children. Some of the items on the list can be expensive, such as sticky-backed Velcro, but may be used sparingly with adult supervision to help children join surfaces.

Ideas for resources

scissors	feathers
glue	stones and pebbles (can act as weights)
sticky tape	rollers

(Continued)

different sizes of cardboard boxes

card

different types of paper

fabric

double-sided sticky tape

crayons

felt tips and markers

pencils

cardboard tubes and rolls

plastic bottles and containers

sponges

threads, wools and cottons

polystyrene packaging

magazines and newspapers

paint

twigs and canes

sticky-backed Velcro

wire

beads, sequins

clay and plasticine

stapler

Helping children to join materials

Most children enjoy making things using materials, but often their good ideas run into difficulty because materials and surfaces will not join together. There are two main ways in which adults can help children. Firstly, adults can make sure that resources such as staplers, sticky tape and strong glue are available, although adults might have to supervise their use. This is important as children can become upset if their 'product' falls apart because the joining method used was insufficient. Secondly, adults can show children some simple joining techniques, such as the ones illustrated below.

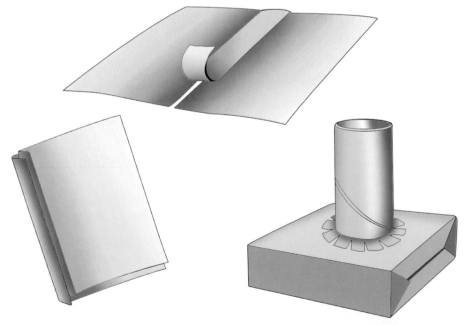

Simple joining methods can help children's constructions and models

Ideas for activities

There are many little problems that can be solved with children which at the same time help them to explore the materials. It is often possible to link projects with themes that are ongoing; for example, one nursery was exploring a theme of pets and was lucky enough to borrow a kitten, so the children were asked to think of making a toy for a kitten. Other fun activities could include the following.

ACTIVITIES

Make a coin float

This is a good activity to do with children who have had some experience of floating and sinking, as it is linked to the theme of water. Show children that a coin sinks if dropped into a bucket or water tray. Ask the children if they have any ideas for how they could keep the coin dry. (It does not have to be a coin, just a small object that would otherwise sink.)

Keep my ice cube cold for me

This is an activity that follows on from previous work done about ice (see pages 240–1). Ask children to think of ways in which you might be able to keep an ice-cube cold.

Make a bed for my teddy

Bring in a teddy or other soft toy. Ask the children if they would like to make a bed or a place for their teddy to curl up.

Wrapping up presents

Children love the idea of surprising people and enjoy wrapping up any kind of present. Activities such as designing and making wrapping-up paper, and then using it, will help children to develop many skills, such as using scissors, selecting the size of the paper, etc.

Teddy's key box

Using a character, such as Teddy, you can ask children to make objects for him. Teddy is always losing his keys. Can the children make a special box to help him keep his keys safe?

OUTCOMES FOR CHILDREN

These types of activities link to the following Early Learning Goals

They encourage children to:

◆ build and construct with a wide range of objects, selecting appropriate resources and adapting their work where necessary

◆ select the tools and techniques they need to shape, assemble and join the materials they are using.

Introducing children to ICT (information and communication technology)

This is an area of the curriculum that is growing in importance throughout society. Children will need to feel confident about using technology. ICT covers a wide range of gadgets and machines including telephones, computers, the Internet as well as some everyday gadgets that have microchips in them. It is important that adults stay up to date and are able to programme and use machines in the setting. Safeguards are needed as some of the technology runs using mains electricity, so it is probably not a good idea for children to be left unsupervised. Where children are using phones and other communication tools such as email, it is also important to protect children from unwanted approaches from adults outside the setting. This again means that you should be showing children how to use the technology and supervising them carefully.

Finally, as this is an area which is rapidly changing, adults need to keep up to date and look for opportunities to try out and feel confident with new equipment such as digital cameras.

Using computers

Computers are in many children's homes and are now a commonplace tool. This means that children need to become familiar with computers, although it is important that young children are still given plenty of opportunities to play using practical equipment.

Choosing software

The key to being sure that computers will provide stimulating learning for young children lies with the software. There are many hundreds of educational programmes developed for very young children, which means that the task of choosing software can seem daunting – especially as some packages are very expensive. Good software should provide children with tasks that are appropriate to their age and allow them to develop confidence in using the computer. Simplified keyboards, often referred to as concept boards, are worth purchasing as they allow children to use the commands more easily.

Tips for buying software

- Buy from suppliers that will allow you to preview the programmes.
- Check that the software will be compatible with your system.
- Find out if the programme can be loaded onto more than one computer (this means that several computers can use it at once).
- Check to see how much 'memory' space is needed for any software.

- Avoid 'borrowing' software as you will be infringing copyright and may also risk loading a virus onto the machine.

Factors to consider

- What will children gain from this programme?
- Will the children be able to use the programme easily? Will they have control of the keyboard, joystick or mouse?
- How much time will be needed for children to use the programme?
- Will an adult need to be present to help children use the programme?
- Can more than one child use the programme at once?
- Is a printer needed?
- Does the software support the anti-discriminatory curriculum?

Using remote programmable toys with children

One way in which children can use technology practically is with programmed toys such as remote control cars, 'turtles' or 'roamers', and pixies. The advantage of these toys is that they still encourage children to be active and practical in their learning. They form the basis of teaching children about programming, as children have to send a command to the toy and then watch the effect of the command. These toys are also useful because they help children to gain spatial awareness skills.

ACTIVITY

Obstacle course

Aim: To help children gain spatial awareness skills and also to develop their skills in programming.

Resources: Simple programmed or remote control toy.

Activity: Chalk a line onto the ground and ask the children if they can get their toy to follow the chalk line. The difficulty of this activity can be increased by simply chalking lines which bend.

Varying this activity: This activity can be varied by drawing a 'track' using two parallel chalk lines and asking children to keep their toy within the lines.

OUTCOMES FOR CHILDREN

This type of activity links to the following Early Learning Goal

It encourages children to:

◆ find out about and identify the uses of everyday technology, and use ICT and programmable toys to support their learning.

Using communication tools

Communication has been an area of huge change over the past few years. Technology has brought mobile phones and emails and it is important that this is reflected in early years settings. You might, for example, use redundant mobile phones as props in the role play area and also organise an activity so that children can send an email over to another setting. As there are health concerns regarding the use of mobile phones it is probably not a good idea to carry out activities that involve using them to make and receive calls and other messages. You can, however, use digital phones and walkie-talkies safely within the setting.

ACTIVITY

Sending a message

Teddy is playing outdoors and wants the children to send a message indoors.

Aim: To help children use ICT and also develop their communication skills.

Resources: Teddy, digital phones which allow for internal calls or walkie-talkies.

Activity: Show pairs or small groups of children how to use the phone or walkie-talkie. Ask a child to stay indoors and wait for a phone call. Ask the other child to make a call indoors using the internal call system or the walkie-talkie. Where children do not know what to say, give them messages from teddy to pass on, for example, Teddy wants to know if anyone is playing in the sand tray indoors.

Varying this activity: Children can be left to explore the technology, although it is important that no outside line is available if digital phones are being used. Children can also use phones and walkie-talkies from different areas outdoors and as part of their role play.

OUTCOMES FOR CHILDREN

This type of activity links to the following Early Learning Goal

It encourages children to:

◆ find out about and identify the uses of everyday technology and use ICT and programmable toys to support their learning.

Using other equipment

This area of learning is also about other gadgets. Some are everyday gadgets such as remote car keys, microwaves and washing machines. Children need to learn about machines and parents could be encouraged to talk to their children as they use them. In the setting, it is also worth investing in a digital camera so children can see photos of themselves instantly and also, with supervision, take some photos.

Helping children to explore the concept of past and present

Most children are not able to tell the time or gain a strong understanding of time in their everyday lives until they are around six years old. The concept of time is a difficult one and helping children develop a sense of time is a gradual process. Children have to understand how time is measured (see Chapter 10, pages 229–30) but alongside this they need to develop an awareness of their own history and the history that is around them in their environment.

Starting with children

For children to develop the concept of past and present, it is important that activities are meaningful for them. A good starting point can be for children to look at themselves, their families and their possessions. This type of work acts as a foundation stage, as once children are able to do this they can move outwards and consider a wider history.

Ideas to help children think about the past

Old and new

One way in which children can be helped to understand the relationship between past and present is by looking at old and new objects. When choosing these it is important that children see objects that have some meaning for them, such as toys, books and clothes. Objects can be handled, described and then classified – old or new. This simple classification will act as a stepping stone because as children get more experienced and older, they will see that some objects which are 'old' are older than others.

- *Toys*

Children are often fascinated by toys that their parents and other people they know played with. They can compare these to the ones they play with and talk about the differences. They can also bring in toys that they played with when they were younger, such as baby rattles and baby balls.

- *Books*

Most children enjoy looking at books. They may have favourite books that they looked at as babies. They are also interested in books that were read to other people they know when they were young. Books also have the advantage that they are easy to classify as old or new because they show their age.

- *Clothes*

Clothes play an important part in most children's lives. Children often have favourite clothes and are always delighted to see clothes that they have now grown out of. Classifying clothes can be quite fun as children can see when clothes are faded or worn.

Marking events in children's lives

Children need to develop an awareness of how to determine the past by placing down markers. Quite early on, children start to use their own markers, such as 'after my birthday' or 'before my sister was born'. You can develop this with themes such as 'growing up' by using photos of children when they were babies and also pictures of them on their birthdays or similar occasions.

ACTIVITIES

Old and new

Aim: The aim of this activity is to help children to classify objects and to describe what they are seeing.

Resources: Two plastic hoops, five or six objects.

Activity: Using a small selection of objects, children consider whether they belong in the old or new hoop, for example, keys – some are new and shiny, others are old and may be rusty.

When I was two

Aim: To help children think about events in their own lives and to develop the concept of past and present.

Resources: Photos, children's drawings and paintings, toys.

Activity: Using photos and other prompts children discuss what they did when they were two years old. Were they wearing nappies? Did they come to nursery? This activity can culminate in a display or interest table.

OUTCOMES FOR CHILDREN

These types of activities link to the following Early Learning Goals

They encourage children to:

◆ investigate objects and materials by using all of their senses as appropriate

◆ find out about, and identify some features of, living things, objects and events they observe

◆ look closely at similarities, differences, patterns and change

◆ find out about past and present events in their own lives, and in those of their families and other people they know.

Finding out about other people's childhoods

An important concept for children to come to terms with is learning that events happened before they were born. Children often ask the question 'where was I?' and you can help them by finding out more about other people's lives. Using other people's childhoods is often a good starting point, because children can relate to this.

- *Using photos*

Staff and parents can bring in photos of when they were children. In one nursery a competition was held to raise money for charity by playing 'Guess Who?', with the adults paying a small entry fee.

- *Using clothes*

Clothes can be brought in to show children what the fashions were – perhaps twenty or thirty years ago. Children can consider the similarities and differences between clothes that were worn in the past and what is worn now.

- *Telling tales*

Staff and parents can talk to the children about their favourite toys and friends in their childhoods. Children will also enjoy listening to tales of when the adults they know were 'naughty' as children.

Helping children to explore their environment

There are many opportunities for children to explore and find out about their environment, both in terms of the natural and built world. Where possible, you should aim to plan activities which directly relate to children's lives. It is also best to take full advantage of what is happening around you; for example, if it begins to snow, children should be given the opportunity to touch and feel the snow flakes.

There are some basic elements in the environment that are useful to explore with children and this section looks at three of these:

- life around us
- weather
- where we live.

Life around us

There are many activities to help children think and discover more about the plants and animals that surround them. It is important here, as with other areas of the early years curriculum, that children are able to relate learning to themselves. Practical activities are therefore likely to be the most useful. Overleaf are some examples of the type of activities that can encourage children to take a closer look at and learn about their surroundings.

Listen around

Aim: To develop children's listening skills and to identify the noises and sounds that surround them.

Resources: None required.

Activity: On a dry and warm day, ask the children to lie down outside and listen for two minutes to the noises that they can hear. Afterwards talk about what they heard and what made these sounds. This activity can be developed by making a listening picture in which children stick or draw pictures of the objects that made the sounds they heard, for example, cars, aeroplanes, dogs barking, birds, people talking.

OUTCOMES FOR CHILDREN

This type of activity links to the following Early Learning Goals

It encourages children to:

◆ observe, find out about and identify features in the place they live and the natural world

◆ find out about their environment and talk about those features they like and dislike.

Other ideas for helping children to explore their environment

Pets

Many families keep pets and children often enjoy talking about pets and other animals. Children can bring in photos of their pets and stories such as *The Tiger Who Came to Tea* (Judith Kerr, Picture Lions: 1991) can be linked in with this theme. A simple pictorial graph can be made to show which pets are the most popular.

Children can talk about where pets live and what their pets need to survive. Visitors from animal charities, such as the RSPCA, can help children to think about what being a good pet owner means.

Plants

It is usually only gradually that children come to learn that plants are living objects. There are many activities that can help children learn about plants and growing, and these are easy to plan for. Most pre-school settings have an outdoor area where children can plant bulbs and seeds and then be encouraged to care for and water them. Indoors, children can plant seeds and beans and watch them grow in cotton wool. In this way children can be helped to learn the vocabulary associated with plants such as 'stem', 'leaf' and 'root', while enjoying taking ownership of their plants. An enjoyable way for children to experience the life cycle of a plant is by planting the seeds of a fruit or vegetable, for example, cutting open a tomato plant, drying the seeds and then planting them.

ACTIVITY

Leaf prints

Aim: To help children observe more closely the differences in leaves.

Resources: Leaves, ready mixed paint, roller, wax crayons.

Activity: In preparation for leaf printing and rubbing, children can collect different types of leaves from the immediate environment. In areas where this is not possible, leaves might have to be brought in. Children can explore the leaves by touching them or ripping them, and also by producing leaf prints. Leaf prints can be made by painting the leaves with ready mixed paint and then pressing them onto a sheet of paper, or covering the leaf with a sheet of paper and rubbing the paper with a wax crayon.

OUTCOMES FOR CHILDREN

This type of activity links to the following Early Learning Goals

It encourages children to:

◆ investigate objects and materials by using all of their senses as appropriate

◆ find out about, and identify some features of, living things, objects and events they observe

◆ look closely at similarities, differences, patterns and change

◆ observe, find out about, and identify features in the place they live and the natural world.

Ways in which we move

Children can consider some of the different ways in which both humans and animals move. This can be developed into a wider topic on transport, with children making their own cars out of cardboard boxes as well as turning the home corner into a bus station or train station. Children can also think about the ways in which different animals move. Pictures of animals can be sorted, for example, into animals that fly and animals that do not. This type of approach can lead into drama and dance, with children acting out the ways in which animals move.

ACTIVITY

Snails move

Aim: To develop children's observational skills.

Resources: Sheet of perspex, a snail.

Activity: Place a snail on a sheet of perspex and ask the children to watch the snail move from underneath. They will see that the snail has no legs. This type of activity can be developed so that children have a go at drawing snails and also make primitive models. It will be important for the snail to be taken back outside at the end of the session and for children to be reminded that most wild creatures prefer to stay outside.

OUTCOMES FOR CHILDREN

This type of activity links to the following Early Learning Goals

It encourages children to:

◆ investigate objects and materials by using all of their senses as appropriate

◆ find out about, and identify some features of, living things, objects and events they observe

◆ observe, find out about, and identify features in the place they live and the natural world.

Weather

In the UK the weather usually plays an important part in daily life. There are many activities that will help children notice the weather and the effects of weather on day-to-day life. Below are some examples of the types of activities that can be carried out.

Collecting rain

On a rainy day, children can have fun using simple rain gauges. These can be put in different places outside and children can pop out from time to time and see how much rain has fallen. Rain gauges can simply be open plastic pots, such as washed-out yoghurt pots, to which the children can attach stickers to show the level of water inside. Children can see whether some places outside are more sheltered than others.

Weather chart

Most settings have weather charts that children can use. Children can also keep a weather diary for themselves over a week. Using stickers can be a popular way of doing this as children enjoy putting stickers onto a page. Older children can draw weather symbols onto stickers for themselves whereas younger children can choose from a selection of prepared stickers.

The sun

Children can have fun finding out that the sun's rays are hot. On a sunny day, a selection of items that can melt can be put outside or by a window indoors. The children can look to see how the sun has warmed and melted them. Items could include chocolate, butter and ice-cubes.

ACTIVITIES

Teddy's washing line

Aim: To help children consider how sun and wind can help to dry clothes.

Resources: Clothes pegs, Teddy's washing, two clothes airers.

Activity: The children must choose where to hang out Teddy's washing. Where should the airers go? Where do the clothes dry best? The children can then keep checking the clothes. Do some types of clothing dry more quickly?

Varying this activity: This activity can form part of a larger project as children can have fun washing Teddy's clothes as well as hanging them out to dry.

Water evaporates

Aim: To show children how the water in puddles evaporates. This type of activity helps children's observational skills.

Resources: Chalk, water to make a puddle (if none are available).

Activity: Draw a chalk mark around a puddle on a sunny day. Ask the children to think about what might happen to the water in the puddle. Look at the puddle later on in the day. Where is the water now?

Ribbon mobile

A simple decoration that very young children can be shown how to make is the ribbon mobile. Children can then see the ribbons move and can learn that the faster the wind moves, the higher the ribbons float.

Aim: For children to learn about the differences in wind speed and their effects.

Resources: Branch with a cord attached (to hang the ribbons by), assorted colours and widths of ribbons.

Activity: The children choose different ribbons to tie onto the branch. The branch is placed outside so that the children can see the ribbons blowing in the wind.

Windmills

Aim: This activity helps children to learn about the power of the wind while providing them with the opportunity to be creative.

(Continued)

Resources: The windmills can be made from thin plastic or from paper. Stickers, felt pens and crayons can be used to decorate them and butterfly clips and straws will be needed.

Activity: The children cut out the shape and decorate the paper before folding and attaching it to the straw or cane, as shown in the diagram below.

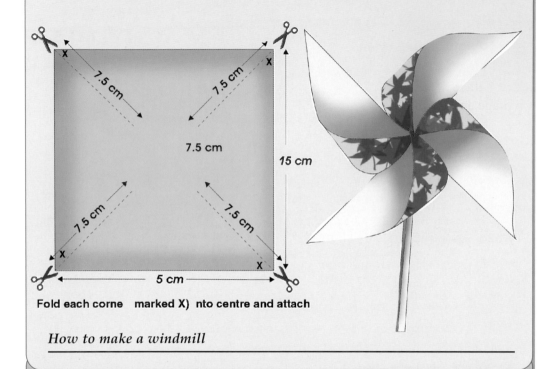

Fold each corner (marked X) into centre and attach

How to make a windmill

OUTCOMES FOR CHILDREN

These types of activities link to the following Early Learning Goals

They encourage children to:

◆ investigate objects and materials by using all of their senses as appropriate

◆ find out about, and identify some features of, living things, objects and events they observe

◆ ask questions about why things happen and how things work

◆ observe, find out about, and identify features in the place they live and the natural world.

Where we live

The immediate environment in which children live is a large part of their lives. They may go to the same shops each week or visit a park or friends on a regular basis. This means that 'where we live' acts as a good starting point for thinking about the environment. There are many ways in which children can be encouraged to talk about and observe their immediate environment, especially as the home corner is often a focus for their play.

Using the home corner

Young children use the home corner to create their own environment or to re-enact their immediate experiences. Adults can help children by encouraging them to make furniture and objects for the home corner using cardboard boxes. Through making objects for their home corner, children tend to become more observant of 'real life' objects. Children can also be encouraged to make their own dens or areas. The benefits of this type of play can be enormous, with children using creative language and negotiation skills as well as learning about ownership.

Out and about

Where possible, adults should try to talk to children about their immediate environment. This is essential as children need to develop their vocabulary. Words that adults take for granted such as 'lamppost', 'door knocker' and 'road sign' have to be learnt and absorbed by children. Going out for walks with children is an effective way of helping them learn more about where they live, even if they go just a short distance. Afterwards, children can be provided with play opportunities for them to use and absorb the information they have gained. This can mean putting out cars and road mats or encouraging children to use doll's houses.

Homes

The theme of 'homes' can be handled in many different ways, depending on the circumstances of the children you are working with. There are many books and stories which touch on this theme and can help children to learn that people and animals live in many different places. Books such as *The Lighthouse-keeper's Lunch* (Ronda and David Armitage, Hippo Scholastic: 1977) or *I Want my Potty* (Tony Ross, Picture Lions: 1988), about a princess, can be used to help children learn about different types of homes. Children can also look at stories that involve animals and homes such as *Percy the Park-keeper* (Nick Butterworth, Harper Collins: 1999) or *The Tiger who Came to Tea* (Judith Kerr, Picture Lions: 1991).

ACTIVITIES

Can you see?

Aim: To help children observe their immediate environment.

Resources: None.

Activity: Going outside, either on a walk or using transport, children are asked to spot objects such as a green front door, a bus stop, a postbox, etc. As children get more skilled at spotting objects, they can choose items for each other to find.

(Continued)

Things I would like in my room

Aim: To help children talk about the toys and furniture needed for a home.

Resources: Magazines and catalogues, paper, glue, scissors and pens.

Activity: Most children enjoy looking at photographs of toys and furniture. In this activity, children look at pictures of different items and talk about what they would like in their bedrooms. Older children can then draw 'their bedroom' and stick photos in it. Where children decide that they would like everything, the adult can ask the child to choose four or five items.

Making a nest

Aim: To help children become aware of the materials needed to build a nest and become more observant of wildlife around them.

Resources: Straw, sticks, paper, grass.

Activity: Children enjoy helping animals and this activity helps children to think about nests. It is helpful if they can look at a nest before starting the activity. Using the materials, the children make a nest themselves. This type of activity is fun to do outdoors because children can gather materials themselves. It is interesting to see that, although the results do not often resemble a real nest, the children tend to enjoy this type of activity and will often co-operate with another child. If children wish to keep their nests, they can be glued onto a piece of paper.

OUTCOMES FOR CHILDREN

These types of activities link to the following Early Learning Goals

They encourage children to:

◆ investigate objects and materials by using all of their senses as appropriate

◆ find out about, and identify some features of, living things, objects and events they observe

◆ ask questions about why things happen and how things work

◆ build and construct with a wide range of objects, selecting appropriate resources and adapting their work where necessary

◆ observe, find out about, and identify features in the place they live and the natural world

◆ begin to know about their own cultures and beliefs and those of other people

◆ find out about their environment, and talk about those features they like and dislike.

The reflective practitioner

Do I provide opportunities for children to explore the properties of materials?

Are objects brought in for children to touch, explore and manipulate?

Do I make sure that children 'discover' for themselves?

Are a wide range of materials available for children to make things with?

Do I support children as they are making things rather than direct them?

Am I comfortable using computers, interactive boards and other types of technology?

Are children given opportunities to play with remote controlled and programmable toys?

Are times available for children to talk to adults about what they have been doing?

Are activities planned for the outdoor area, for example, making windchimes, collecting rain water?

Chapter 12   Providing opportunities for physical development

Developing children's physical skills is an essential element in an Early Years curriculum. Children need to have developed the ability to control their movements in order to do many of the tasks that are expected of them in school. It is also necessary for them to be physically fit to cope with the many demands of the school day, which is usually longer and far more tiring than the early years routine.

Physical activity and exercise are also important in the longer term as children (and adults) need to develop a positive attitude towards physical activity in order to remain healthy.

Early years settings should therefore plan for ways of encouraging children's physical development while at the same time helping children to feel confident about their abilities. In addition, children need to have opportunities to exercise, to develop spatial awareness and to learn to assess risks as part of their learning experiences.

It is important to remember health and safety at all times and careful supervision of young children will be required for all activities involving physical skills. Finally, some children may have special requirements and these need to be catered for sensitively, for example, a child may have a visual impairment. This means that sometimes special equipment might be needed.

This chapter is split into two main sections. The first section gives an overview of the provision of physical activities. The second section looks specifically at ways of providing opportunities to develop physical skills. A final short section then looks at the ways in which children can understand the role that food plays in contributing to physical development and a healthy lifestyle.

Physical development and exercise

Settings can plan opportunities and experiences to help children's physical development, but it is always important to remember that physical development is a process and that children will gain control of their movements at different rates. For example, some children are quickly able to catch and throw a ball whereas others need more support and help. This means that adults must be sure that the opportunities they provide are appropriate to the children they are working with. This is important because children who find a task difficult are likely to lose confidence and then may give up rather than return to an activity.

When planning activities it is helpful to consider the stages of 'normative' physical development to understand what *most* children are able to do at certain stages (while remembering that all children develop at slightly different rates).

Age	Fine manipulative skills	Gross motor skills
3 years	◆ Snips with scissors ◆ Paints circular shapes ◆ Holds crayons with fingers not fist ◆ Strings large beads ◆ Puts on and takes off coat	◆ Runs forwards confidently ◆ Kicks ball ◆ Throws without aiming ◆ Walks on tiptoe ◆ Pedals tricycle
4 years	◆ Puts together 8-piece puzzle ◆ Uses scissors cutting on a curve ◆ Cuts out and pastes simple shapes ◆ Draws a simple house ◆ Prints a few letters ◆ Buttons and unbuttons	◆ Balances on one foot ◆ Jumps down from a step ◆ Throws with aim ◆ Uses a slide ◆ Catches large ball with two hands when thrown from a near distance
5 years	◆ Draws a recognisable picture ◆ Cuts around pictures accurately using scissors ◆ Copies letters ◆ Prints name on paper ◆ Colours accurately	◆ Climbs ◆ Uses a slide confidently ◆ Skips on alternate feet ◆ Moves to music ◆ Bounces and catches ball

Normative physical development in children, 3 to 5 years

This can act as a guide to make sure expectations are not too high, although obviously it is still better to observe individual children to be sure of meeting their needs.

A table that shows normative physical development for children between the ages of three and five is found on page 261.

Developing positive attitudes towards exercise

Good diet and exercise form the backdrop to a healthy lifestyle both in childhood and in later years. Young children tend to be naturally restless and are keen to be active. The aim in the early years is to encourage children to maintain this positive attitude towards physical activity.

The links to social and emotional development

There are many emotional and social benefits to be gained from physical exercise, and if children find it fun and fulfilling, they are likely to develop positive attitudes to physical activity. Children gain in confidence and independence as they begin to master skills such as riding a tricycle or walking on a wall. Some physical activities, such as kicking a ball, help children to release inner aggression and frustrations in a positive way, rather than during their play with other children. Activities such as hitting and kicking balls can help children to feel in control and feel powerful in contrast to their daily lives, where many activities are structured and controlled for them by adults.

There are also social benefits, as many of the opportunities for physical development involve playing alongside and with other children, for example, throwing and catching, playing 'Tig' or taking part in singing games such as 'Okey Cokey'.

The links to cognitive development

It is increasingly being recognised that physical development is closely linked to children's cognitive development. Children will find it easier to concentrate after any type of vigorous exercise, however short. This is because physically the body is more aroused and alert. Physical movements also appear to be involved in information processing. Early physical movements seem to stimulate growth in the brain. This in turn appears to help children to learn to read and organise information. Being able to balance as well as being able to co-ordinate the left and right side of the body appears to be particularly important. Movements such as climbing and crawling as well as hopping and skipping seem to be beneficial and so need to be planned into the routine of the setting.

The benefits of exercise

The need for children to have some exercise every day must not be underestimated. Physical activity helps keep children healthy, strong and mentally alert. It is increasingly recognised that exercise needs to be planned

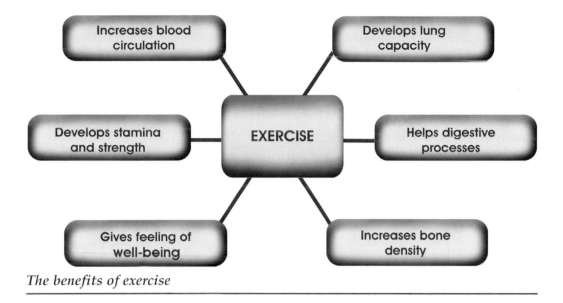

The benefits of exercise

for in a curriculum, because children are generally less fit than they used to be; for example, in the past most children had to walk to school rather than being taken in cars. Studies over the last few years often point to the lack of exercise in childhood as one of the causes of health problems in later life.

Exercise in the early years can be provided for in a fun way and built into children's play opportunities. For example, if children are having fun running around an obstacle course, they will also be getting exercise. It is also useful to remember that young children tend to exercise in a 'stop start' type of way.

Children's exercise should be pleasurable

They often run in short bursts and then rest. This means that they can find it hard to walk for long distances at a constant pace. Understanding children's 'stop start' exercise needs is important when planning activities.

Providing opportunities to exercise and develop stamina

It is important for children to acquire physical stamina and to develop strength as the school day is tiring at first and children will need to be able to cope with its demands, both mentally and physically.

The main point about developing stamina is that it should come from enjoyment. Children who are enjoying an activity will stay at it and develop stamina without realising it. They may run around pretending to be horses or cycle non-stop in a play area believing that they are on a motorway. Therefore, when planning for vigorous play, adults need to make sure that they are allocating enough time for children to develop stamina. Children who are playing in this way can be their own judge of when they are tired, although adults should always be vigilant that children who have asthma are not becoming breathless. (Usually it is the job of adults to prevent children from becoming over-tired because they want to keep on playing.)

Making children aware of the effects of exercise

Adults need to help children to recognise when they are becoming tired and hot, so that they gradually become aware of the changes that happen to their bodies when they are active. This can be done by building in moments of rest within an activity and asking children to think about how they are feeling: 'Touch your forehead – is it hot?' Helping children to make these simple observations provides a foundation for more structured activities later on when they begin full-time schooling.

The effects of exercise

Questions can encourage children to think about the changes that happen to their bodies when they are active. For example:

◆ Listen to your breathing. What can you hear?

◆ Put your hand on your chest. Can you feel your heart pumping?

◆ How do your legs feel? Are they tired?

Overleaf are some examples of activities which will build stamina, develop positive attitudes towards exercise and provide moments for children to consider the effects of exercise on their bodies. They link to the Early Learning Goals as shown.

ACTIVITY

Running cars

Aim: This type of activity is easy to prepare and allows children to build up stamina while having fun. It also offers children opportunities to have moments of rest.

Resources: Chalk, lengths of garden hose or other tubing attached to cardboard boxes – to act as pretend petrol pumps (optional).

Activity: The children pretend to be different cars on the road. They must follow the car in front (which can be an adult); sometimes the cars can go very fast, but sometimes the cars have to go and get some petrol (i.e. stop and rest). A chalk line can be laid down to indicate the road, and bends and other obstacles can be put onto the 'track'.

Rabbits

Aim: This is a good indoor activity which can be played on rainy days. It provides opportunity for vigorous exercise while also allowing children to have moments of rest.

Resources: None required.

Activity: The children hop around and pretend to be rabbits. Rabbits have to be very careful of foxes so when they hear the word 'fox', they must keep absolutely still. If the word 'burrow' is called out all the rabbits must hop to one side of the room as quickly as possible.

OUTCOMES FOR CHILDREN

These types of activities link to the following Early Learning Goals

They encourage children to:

- ◆ move with confidence, imagination and in safety
- ◆ move with control and co-ordination
- ◆ show awareness of space, of themselves and of others
- ◆ recognise the importance of keeping healthy and those things which contribute to this
- ◆ recognise the changes that happen to their bodies when they are active.

Providing opportunities for exercise indoors

Most vigorous activity will take place outdoors, but it is important not to forget that physical activities which encourage gross motor skills can also be carried out indoors. It is particularly useful to have a bank of ideas as there are always times in the year when children cannot go outside because of the weather. Most settings can create a small amount of space by pushing back tables and chairs, which will allow activities to take place.

Dance and drama are perfect ways of helping children to develop a greater awareness of their bodies as well as being enjoyable and fun activities. Children can dance to music in a free way or they may join in with singing games such as 'Head, shoulders knees and toes'. Drama can also be used to extend other work as children can be encouraged to act out parts of a story they have read, for example: 'Can you show me how you think the giant might have walked in *Jack and the Beanstalk*?'

There are many good song books with ideas for singing and dancing games, although children always enjoy learning traditional ones such as 'Oranges and lemons'.

Dance and singing games

Okey Cokey

Farmer's in his den

Ring a ring o' roses

If you're happy and you know it ... stamp your feet (or clap your hands, etc.)

Here we go round the mulberry bush

I'm a dingle, dangle scarecrow

Oranges and lemons

Active games

Follow my leader (see below)

Simon says . . . jump up and down

Musical statues

Football golf (see page 282)

Running cars (see page 265)

ACTIVITY

Follow my leader

Aim: This is an example of the type of game that can be played indoors with children. It is a traditional game that can be varied to suit the needs and age of the children. In this version a musical instrument is used. This activity helps children develop spatial awareness and control of their movements.

Resources: Percussion instrument that is easy to play, such as a drum or tambourine.

Activity: The leader beats out a rhythm and moves around the room. The other children must follow the leader's movements but must freeze when the rhythm or sound stops. The leader turns around each time to see if everyone is still. This can be made into a game so that anyone who carries on moving is out.

OUTCOMES FOR CHILDREN

This type of activity links to the following Early Learning Goals

It encourages children to:

◆ move with confidence, imagination and in safety

◆ show awareness of space, of themselves and of others.

Providing opportunities for children to move safely and develop control

As well as developing stamina, children need to develop some control over their bodies and learn to move safely. This is a gradual process as very young children have limited spatial awareness and only through experience do they develop an awareness of safety and the limits of their own bodies.

Developing a sense of danger and safety awareness

There must always be a balance between enjoyment and risk if children are to gain confidence in their movements. Some children are naturally cautious, sometimes to the point where they are afraid to climb or walk on a wall, whereas other children need to be made aware of risks as they are inclined to ignore dangers.

The role of the adult

Good supervision is essential and adults should aim to allow children some freedom, but must also help children to know their limitations and the consequences of their actions. This might mean that clear rules and boundaries need to be set, so that children know from the start how far they can climb or how many children are allowed on certain pieces of equipment; for example, only one child on the slide at any time.

Children who are enjoying themselves can easily become over-excited. Therefore adults may need to talk to them about their actions, to help them understand that they are putting others at risk. This should be done in a careful and sensitive way, as the aim is to encourage children's enjoyment of exercise and physical activity.

Helping children who are over-cautious

Some children are fearful of climbing or balancing. They like to have their feet firmly on the ground. This means that adults will need to spend some time encouraging and coaxing them to gain confidence. The key is often to build up activities gradually. For example, a child who dislikes jumping off fences or walls can be encouraged to jump off the bottom step of some stairs. Building confidence is a slow process and many children will need the physical reassurance of an adult's presence, for example, an adult holding their hand as they walk on a wall.

Balancing

The ability to balance is a key element in helping children gain control over their bodies. There are many physical activities that involve balancing; for example, riding a bicycle, hopping and jumping. Most children tend to enjoy these types of activities as they are exciting. Children can feel that there is an element of risk and control.

Balancing requires a fair amount of physical co-ordination and control, which is why very young children cannot stand on one leg. There is also a strong link between balancing and vision (try balancing on one leg with your eyes shut).

The ability to balance also improves with confidence and practice and there are many activities that can be provided to help this skill.

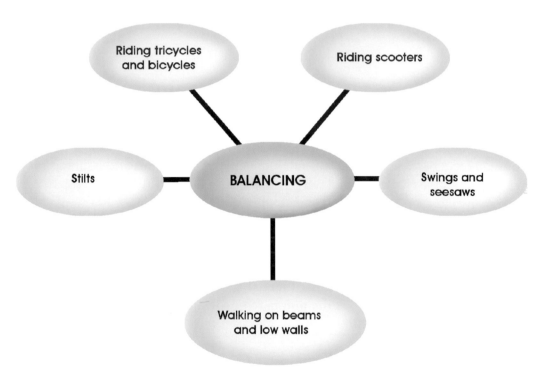

Physical activities for children that involve balancing

Developing physical skills

Most of the activities planned for in other areas of the curriculum will also provide opportunities for children to develop their physical skills; for example, as children paint they also practise their hand–eye co-ordination. Some physical skills can, however, be enhanced by particular activities that have been carefully structured.

CASE STUDY:

Kylie is playing with Cameron on the tricycles. They are racing each other around the climbing frame, oblivious of the other children. Look at the following two different approaches by early years workers.

Conversation A

Adult: Come here at once, both of you! What do you think you are doing? You nearly knocked Alex over! Go and do something else.

Conversation B

Adult: Kylie and Cameron, come here and listen a moment. Right, now I know that you are having a lot of fun at the moment, but you are going rather fast. Why do you think that I have had to stop you?

Kylie: 'Cause we might fall over.

Adult: Yes, that is one reason. It wouldn't be very nice if you had an accident, would it? But you might also hurt someone else. Alex nearly got hurt. I think that you will have to make up another game with the bikes.

Which would work better with the children and make them think about what they are doing? Why?

ACTIVITY

Tightrope walking

Aim: The aim of this activity is to help children to balance and also to improve their general co-ordination and control.

Resources: Chalk (several colours for extension activity).

Activity: A chalk line is put onto the ground. Children have to walk carefully along it without falling off. This activity can be extended for older children by having several lines which interweave, with each child following their own line. This means that children have to become aware of others and negotiate their way past each other.

OUTCOMES FOR CHILDREN

This type of activity links to the following Early Learning Goals

It encourages children to:

◆ move with confidence, imagination and in safety

◆ move with control and co-ordination

◆ show awareness of space, of themselves and of others.

Hand–eye co-ordination

Hand–eye co-ordination affects the accuracy with which children are able to do many tasks involving both fine and gross motor skills. Once children have developed good hand–eye co-ordination, they will be able to use tools, throw and catch, steer and climb. Activities that help children practise hand–eye co-ordination will need to be structured according to their needs, so children may need to practise catching a bean bag rather than a small hard ball, if they are just starting to catch.

Fine manipulative skills

Fine manipulative movements help children control tools and use implements such as pencils, brushes and scissors. There is a strong link between these fine manipulative movements and hand–eye co-ordination as most tasks involve both types of skill; for example, cutting out a shape requires that a child has strength and co-ordination in the hand as well as hand–eye co-ordination. Many tasks that children will be required to do once they are in school require good fine manipulative skills. This means that it is important for children to gain confidence in such skills and also for them to feel able to ask for support without feeling that they have in some way failed.

Using scissors

Using scissors is a difficult skill, although it is one that is often taken for granted. Children need to be able to co-ordinate their hand movements while keeping the paper or card at right angles to the scissors. (You may have seen children who are trying to cut but the paper is sliding through the blades of the scissors.) Children also find that scissors can be uncomfortable to hold and are often unsure which fingers to put where.

There are many ways in which children can be helped to use scissors and enjoy cutting, although most children will need some adult help and guidance until the age of four or five years.

Supporting children's scissors skills

Learning to use scissors can be a frustrating process for children, especially as adults make it look so easy. Early years workers can help children in many practical ways, as described below and overleaf.

● *Give children praise and encouragement*

It is only through practice that children learn to use scissors. This means that they need to be given plenty of praise from adults. Early years workers should also offer to help when they see that a child is starting to become frustrated and has 'had enough'.

● *Make sure that the scissors are the right size and type for the child*

Scissors that are too large will make cutting a much harder process. Left-handed children may need to be given different scissors or shown which side of dual-sided ones to use.

● *Put out dough with scissors*

Many children find it easier to snip dough rather than paper. This means that putting out dough with scissors can be a good first step. As dough is a sensory material, children tend to spend longer snipping and cutting. This in turn means that they become increasingly proficient.

● *Hold the paper for children*

Sometimes children can only concentrate on using the scissors, so if someone holds the paper for them at the right angle, they are more likely to be successful.

● *Make sure that the paper is not too stiff or too thin*

When children have mastered the scissor action and are ready to hold the paper for themselves, they need to be given paper that is easy to cut. Tissue paper or card, for example, are particularly difficult to cut through whereas sugar paper tends to be easier.

● *Give children hand-sized pieces of paper*

Children will find it easier to control their scissors if the paper they are holding is hand-sized. Larger pieces of paper are often creased as children cannot manage the size.

Activities to help children use scissors:

◆ cutting and snipping dough
◆ unstructured opportunities where there are plenty of different types of paper for children to cut up
◆ cutting fringes
◆ cutting and sticking pictures to make greeting cards
◆ junk modelling
◆ collages.

Providing opportunities to develop fine manipulative skills

Many activities that are planned for other curriculum areas, such as creative development, also provide opportunities to develop fine manipulative skills.

Therefore when planning different activities, you should look to see what opportunities for physical development are also being created. For example, weaving, which is looked at in Chapter 13, also develops good hand–eye co-ordination and fine manipulative skills.

The spider diagram below shows how activities that may be associated with other curriculum areas can also be used when planning for physical development.

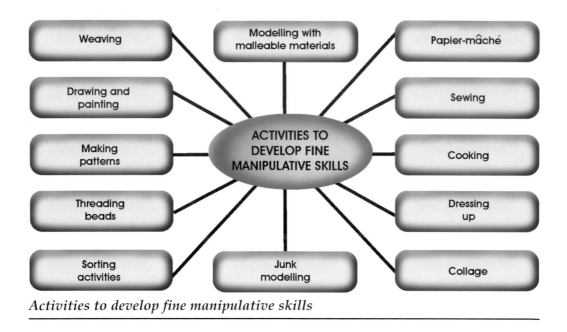

Activities to develop fine manipulative skills

Other activities which develop fine manipulative skills

Cooking

Cooking is a popular activity with children and has many benefits across the Early Years curriculum. In addition, cooking helps children to use their fine manipulative skills and hand–eye co-ordination as they will probably be using their hands in some way, for example, rolling out dough, stirring or whisking mixtures, etc. When looking for recipes to use with children, it is best to choose activities that will allow them the maximum amount of 'hands-on' experience.

Overleaf is an example of how a traditional cooking activity can encourage fine manipulative skills while giving children other learning experiences.

Making gingerbread people

Fine manipulative skills

◆ Using spoon to measure out syrup, spice, flour, etc.

◆ Stirring mixture

◆ Greasing baking tray

◆ Rolling out dough

◆ Using cutters

◆ Transferring onto baking tray

◆ Placing raisins for eyes, buttons

Some links to other curriculum areas

◆ *Personal, social and emotional development*

Helps children feel independent and confident.

Encourages turn-taking and sharing.

◆ *Mathematics*

Helps children learn about measuring, counting and time.

◆ *Language and literacy*

Extends and develops vocabulary.

Provides opportunities for discussion and story (*The Gingerbread Man*).

◆ *Knowledge and understanding of the world*

Helps children to find out more about food.

Gives children the opportunity to learn about properties of materials.

Encourages children to observe and think about the changes they are seeing to the food during the cooking process.

◆ *Creative development*

Helps children learn about texture and shape.

Puzzles

Puzzles not only help children develop spatial awareness and the ability to think logically, they also give children practice with hand–eye co-ordination and fine manipulative skills. Most children enjoy the satisfaction of completing a puzzle and by the age of five years, most children are managing puzzles of at least 10 or 20 pieces. Some will complete much more complex puzzles if they are enthusiastic about the picture; for example, a five year old who is an ardent Thomas the Tank Engine fan may manage a 36–piece Thomas puzzle without help.

Early years workers can help children by making sure that a puzzle is not too difficult for the child (nor too easy). Adults must also look out for signs of frustration that may indicate that a child needs some assistance. As with most activities, children will need praise for their efforts and plenty of time. Many children develop favourite puzzles which they play with over and over again.

Small world toys

Young children enjoy playing with small cars and engines, play people and animals and, although these toys are not often associated with physical development, they encourage children to use their hand–eye co-ordination and fine manipulative skills. These skills are developed as children move these toys around; for example, a figure may be put into a car and the car pushed around a track. Children also develop and practise their language skills at the same time as immersing themselves in an imaginary world.

Providing opportunities for small world play

Wherever possible, a good range of small world toys should be available to children, who often have favourite types to play with. You will see children lying on the floor for long periods talking and moving them around. It is important not to underestimate the value of this type of play as children are also developing their language skills and ability to concentrate while having much enjoyment and learning to entertain themselves. Early years workers can help children by making sure that there is plenty of floor space available as this type of play activity can often 'spread', as well as allowing enough time for children to develop their games.

If possible, an early years setting (and Reception classes) should have a range of the following equipment for small world play:

- interlocking train sets (such as Brio or Duplo)
- Duplo/Lego sets with animals and people
- Playmobil vehicles and people
- toy cars, dumper trucks, tractors
- toy animals including farm and zoo sets
- play mats with roads, railways and farms printed on–these are very useful props.

Strengthening hand preference

Hand preference is important as not only does it allow for one hand to become more skilful, but it also seems to play a part in cognitive development. Children who have not developed a strong hand preference are, for example, more likely to have difficulties in processing information and learning to read. While hand preference appears to be biologically determined, how strong it becomes is partly a result of the experiences that are provided. Ideally you need to plan activities that encourage one hand to be active and the other to act as a stabiliser. Years ago, in the everyday routine of a house, children were more likely to be making these movements; dusting and polishing were good examples of this. Activities such as threading beads help to develop hand preference: one hand holds the bead and thus acts as a stabiliser while the other pushes the thread through the bead and works as the active hand. Other activities that can help children to develop and strengthen hand preference include:

- hanging up coats on hangers
- pouring drinks
- cooking activities such as spreading butter onto bread, cutting fruit
- washing and drying equipment such as beakers, plates.

Developing children's gross and locomotive skills

In order to be able to move with confidence and use large play equipment, children's gross and locomotive skills need to be developed.

Gross motor skills allow children to carry out tasks with whole limb movements such as throwing, large painting and lifting. Gross motor skills can help children to control their bodies, which means that they can learn to balance, pedal and swim. Children who have good gross motor skills are able to enjoy a variety of play experiences as they can climb, hop, jump and participate in group games, such as chase and imaginative play.

There are some skills that children and adults value which require good gross motor co-ordination and development, such as riding a bicycle or skipping with a rope. These types of skills are built up gradually and early years workers will need to plan activities that will allow children to work towards mastering them.

Outdoor play

Gross motor skills, stamina and general co-ordination can be developed during the daily routine of the early years setting. Most settings have periods in the day where children play outdoors. This is valuable time for children as they are often able to play in an unstructured way and choose what they want to do. This may mean that some children decide to charge around on tricycles whereas others want to kick balls or use climbing apparatus.

Early years workers can help children enjoy this time by providing play materials such as skipping ropes, balls and even props for children's games, such as shopping baskets and tickets. A good variety of equipment will help children concentrate for longer periods and allow them to vary their play.

Where large pieces of equipment such as swings or climbing apparatus are not available, early years workers may be able to make outdoor play more challenging by improvising a little.

● *Creating an obstacle course*
Plastic hoops, benches and even large cushions can be used to make obstacle courses for young children.

● *Using chalk to create trails*
A lot of fun can be had using chalk to create trails for children. Simply chalk in dotted or straight lines for children to walk or run along. Children can then use them to follow each other or as part of their pretend play. Children can also follow the trail on tricycles or while pushing prams or trolleys.

● *Making stilts*
Stilts can be made by using strong cans or tins and threading rope through them (or plastic stilts can be quite cheap to buy). Children enjoy the fun of walking with them as they immediately become taller.

ACTIVITY

All aboard!

Aim: The aim of this activity is to allow children to develop their gross and locomotive skills in a fun way. This activity can be extended as children become more confident in their movements. It also helps children's listening skills as they have to move quickly on cue. This activity can be played indoors as well as outdoors.

Resources: This depends on what is available, but items such as mats, benches and play tunnels are very useful.

Activity: The children are running or walking around in the 'sea' and when they hear the cry 'all aboard' they must find somewhere to go where their feet are not touching the floor. This might mean getting onto a mat, a folded-up newspaper or a bench, or into a play tunnel. If this game is being played outside, a whistle could be used to give the signal.

OUTCOMES FOR CHILDREN

This type of activity links to the following Early Learning Goals

It encourages children to:

◆ move with confidence, imagination and in safety

◆ move with control and co-ordination

◆ show awareness of space, of themselves and of others

◆ use a range of small and large equipment

◆ travel around, under, over and through balancing and climbing equipment.

Using large apparatus with children

Large apparatus helps children to develop many physical skills, and where a setting cannot provide large apparatus such as swings or slides, it may be possible to visit a local play area which does have this type of equipment. The chart below gives a summary of the benefits of many types of large apparatus.

Type of equipment	Play and development potential
Trampolines	Children enjoy bouncing and this allows them to develop their sense of balance while having fun. Jumping and bouncing strengthens leg muscles and builds stamina.
Seesaws and rockers	Children enjoying working in pairs and can enjoy the sensation of moving from side to side. Balance and co-ordination skills are improved. This activity can teach children about weighing and balancing.
Play tunnels	Play tunnels can be used in many ways. Children can use them as places to hide as part of a game. They can also be used as part of an obstacle course and they can link into other pieces of equipment such as tents. Play tunnels can develop co-ordination between the arms and legs as well as general agility.
Slides	Slides help children to learn to climb and build up confidence in balancing. Children enjoy the sense of achievement from completing the movement. Children enjoy the sense of risk-taking and challenge as they climb.
Swings	Swings give children much pleasure as they enjoy the rhythmic movements. As they learn to co-ordinate their movements they build up strength in the legs and upper body as well as the ability to balance when they learn to swing by themselves.
Climbing frames	Co-ordination and balance are developed through climbing. Leg and arm muscles are strengthened and children enjoy the challenge and the feeling of adventure. A climbing frame can be used as part of a game, i.e. it becomes a house or ship. Co-operative play is often seen when older children are using climbing frames. Young children will need to be carefully supervised.

(Continued)

Type of equipment	Play and development potential
Ropes and rope ladders	Children enjoy learning to climb up ladders. This helps their sense of balance and co-ordination. Children enjoy the challenge of this activity. Ropes can be used for swinging on and this strengthens arm muscles. Ropes can be used as part of children's games.
Sit and ride toys Tricycles Go-karts Bicycles	These are versatile and popular with children. They can make moving around part of their games and encourage children to play co-operatively together. Many skills are developed, including the ability to judge speed, steer and pedal. Leg muscles are strengthened and general co-ordination is developed.

Types of large equipment for physical play and the play potential for children

Riding a bicycle

This is a skill that most children want to achieve. Riding a bicycle requires balance, strength in the legs, good hand–eye co-ordination and the ability to judge speed and distance. It is a good example of how children can build up their stamina, concentration and hand–eye co-ordination in a fun way. Children also develop spatial awareness as they try to steer accurately.

Early years workers can help children by giving them plenty of opportunities to practise riding on tricycles, scooters, pedal cars and bicycles. Children will need lots of encouragement when they fall over or find it difficult to steer.

It is important that children have confidence in themselves before moving to more demanding tasks, such as going from a tricycle to a bicycle. Seats may need to be lowered so that children can

Tricycles help develop children's balance as well as confidence

put their feet on the ground. This is especially important when children are trying to ride without stabilisers as they often use their feet as brakes. Most children will leave early years settings being able to use a tricycle or bicycle with stabilisers competently, but most will not be riding a bicycle alone until they are about five years old or more.

Learning to ride a bicycle

This involves the following stages:

- sitting on a wheeled toy pushing with feet, for example, in a sit and ride car
- gaining experience in steering, for example, manoeuvring prams, trolleys
- pushing with feet and steering at the same time, for example, using tricycles, scooters
- pedalling with feet, for example, using tricycles, go-karts
- pedalling and steering competently avoiding objects, for example, using tricycles
- pedalling, steering and using brakes, for example, using a tricycle
- gaining experience of riding a bicycle, for example, using a bicycle with stabilisers or an adult supporting.

Opportunities:

- free play with different types of wheeled toys available
- simple obstacle courses to practise steering
- imaginative play opportunities where children can use tricycles, etc. as part of their play.

Resources needed:

- a large hard-surfaced area for children to practise
- well-maintained wheeled toys, tricycles and bicycles
- safety helmets if appropriate.

Throwing and catching

Children enjoy throwing and catching even though it is not an easy skill to acquire. By the time they leave early years settings, most children will be able to throw and catch — providing that the ball is large and the distances involved are relatively small. As with many other skills, children will gradually become more competent and confident with practice. Adults can help children by planning throwing and catching activities for children in a progressive way. The box below and overleaf shows steps that can be used in this planning.

Throwing and catching

Providing opportunities for throwing:

- rolling balls across a floor
- throwing a variety of balls, including soft foam balls
- knocking down objects on a wall using foam balls

(Continued)

- throwing bean bags into plastic hoops on the floor
- throwing bean bags and balls through hoops placed at waist level
- throwing bean bags to an adult nearby
- throwing large balls to an adult or child nearby.

Providing opportunities for catching:

- catching balls that are rolled along a floor
- catching bean bags from a nearby adult
- catching balloons
- catching soft balls
- bouncing and catching a football.

ACTIVITY

Paper balls

Aim: This indoor activity allows children to practise their throwing skills without any risk of harming themselves or others.

Resources: Sheets of thin scrap paper, large basket or tray.

Activity: The children screw up sheets of paper into balls and have to throw them into a large basket. As children become more skilled the size of the target can be reduced. Children can also have pretend 'snowball fights' using paper balls, which can be fun on a rainy day to let off steam.

Frog hoops

Aim: To encourage children to practise throwing and jumping.

Resources: Plastic hoops, bean bags.

Preparation: Plastic hoops are put out close together but not touching. They can be spaced out depending on the age of the children.

Activity: The children are given a bean bag each. They stand in one hoop and hop or jump to another hoop only when they have thrown their bean bag in it. This is a non-competitive game, although it can be adapted as a race where children have to move from one side to another.

OUTCOMES FOR CHILDREN

These types of activities link to the following Early Learning Goals

They encourage children to:

- move with confidence, imagination and safety
- move with control and co-ordination
- show awareness of space, of themselves and of others
- use a range of small and large equipment
- handle tools, objects, construction and malleable materials safely and with increasing control.

Batting and hitting

Most children seem to gain much satisfaction from being able to hit a ball with a racket or bat. The reason for this may be an enjoyment of releasing aggression in a relatively harmless way, providing that they do not break a window! Batting and hitting follow on from being able to throw and catch. There is quite a lot of skill in being able to aim and hit a ball as it requires good hand–eye co-ordination as well as good judgement in assessing the speed of the ball.

Early years workers can help develop this skill by providing children with bats or rackets that are easy to hold and have a large surface area. A good range of bats, clubs and rackets is now available for young children. They often have small handles and are light in weight. It is also a good idea to provide children with soft foam balls to avoid potential accidents.

Good adult supervision is essential as there is always a danger that children will hit another child while swinging a racket or bat. It is also easy for children to become frustrated if they are not having much success and possibly throw the bat in anger. As with all physical skills that require hand–eye co-ordination, children will need plenty of praise, time and space to become confident.

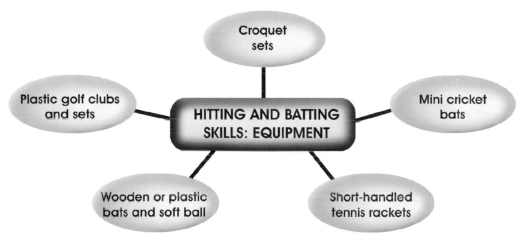

Equipment to help develop children's hitting and batting skills

Kicking balls

Young children can enjoy kicking balls around, although until they are about five or six years old they will find it difficult to play a game, such as football, with organised rules. In early years settings, children will simply enjoy the feeling of satisfaction and releasing aggression that kicking allows.

At this stage most children will be kicking and then running after a ball, rather than being able to control it with their feet. Quite often a child will kick the ball and then run and pick it up. It can be a good idea to make sure that all children have their own balls, to avoid arguments. Early years workers should probably not insist that the ball has to stay on the ground all the time.

Children have a lot of fun with this type of activity, which also develops their leg muscles, stamina and co-ordination skills.

Football golf

ACTIVITY

Aim: The aim of this activity is to give children an opportunity to develop their kicking skills while building prediction and spatial skills. This game can be played indoors if there is enough space.

Resources: Plastic hoops, ball (size and style dependent on age of children and where this activity is to take place).

Activity: Several plastic hoops are laid flat on the floor/ground. The children have to kick their ball into the hoop. This means that when the ball is near the hoop, the children have to learn that they must kick it very gently to get it in.

OUTCOMES FOR CHILDREN

This type of activity links to the following Early Learning Goals

It encourages children to:

◆ move with confidence, imagination and safety

◆ move with control and co-ordination

◆ show awareness of space, of themselves and of others

◆ use a range of small and large equipment.

The role of food in keeping healthy

Children need to learn about and understand the role played by a good diet in keeping them healthy. This is a gradual process, with children first starting to explore the importance of food in their lives. Early years workers have to be sensitive when discussing diet as children are not often in a position where they can choose the food they are eating; it is therefore a good idea to concentrate on helping children to learn about food. It is important to remember that culture will determine how and what some children eat, and that other children may have food intolerances or allergies.

Ways in which children can learn about food

The following activities will prove popular with children while they learn about food and the importance of a healthy diet.

Food I like/dislike

Children can cut out pictures of food or draw foods that they like. This can be extended by doing a survey of favourite foods and making a picture bar graph of the results (this also links in with early mathematics).

Food tasting

Children can enjoy tasting foods that may be unfamiliar to them, such as tropical fruits, vegetables and other dishes. Work on festivals and the seasons can provide a starting point, for example the Chinese New Year and some Chinese-style dishes.

Food testing

Children can have fun deciding which food product tastes the best. Three food products such as white rice, brown rice and wild rice are laid out; children decide which one tastes the best. Examples of foods that can be put on test include different cheeses, crisps and apples. This activity helps children find out that there are variations in food types.

Printing with food

Oranges, peppers and potatoes can all be used to help children with printing activities. Printing with fruits and vegetables helps children to observe food closely. It may also have a creative and artistic value.

Grouping foods

Children can learn how foods are grouped into different 'families'. Foods such as dairy foods, fruits, vegetables and pulses are grouped together. Children can have hands-on experience by sorting 'real' foods, such as fruits and vegetables, as well as sorting pictures of foods.

Foods that animals like

Children can find out about the different types of food that animals eat. This activity can be extended by making/preparing food for animals, for example, collecting leaves for stick insects, making seed cakes for birds.

Feeling food can be an enjoyable tactile experience for young children

ACTIVITY

Feeling food

Aim: This is a tactile and fun activity for young children to try. The activity can help children to explore different food groups and also learn about foods with which they may be unfamiliar. It can be varied and adapted according to the age of the children.

Resources: Cardboard boxes with a small circle cut out so that children can put their hands in, but cannot see what they are feeling; plastic bowls; food stuffs such as dry pasta, semolina, different types of bread, jelly.

Activity: The children put their hands into the boxes and feel what is inside. They have to describe what they can feel and guess what it is.

OUTCOMES FOR CHILDREN

This type of activity links to the following Early Learning Goal

It encourages children to:

◆ recognise the importance of keeping healthy and those things which contribute to this.

Note: Always check that the children have no allergies before carrying out any activities which involve touching and tasting food.

The reflective practitioner

Do I provide plenty of opportunities for children to play outdoors?

Is there a range of equipment for outdoor play, for example, hoops, tricycles, balls?

Are toys and equipment rotated to ensure that children do not get bored?

Are games played indoors that encourage children's gross and locomotive movements?

Do I join in games and support children as they play?

Are children given opportunities to use tools to develop hand–eye co-ordination?

Are activities provided that will help children strengthen their hand preference?

Is water provided for children during the day and are children encouraged to drink after exercising?

Creative development as a curriculum area not only encompasses children's ability to express themselves creatively using a variety of media, but also develops in children an awareness and appreciation of different aesthetic forms. This means that children need to be provided with opportunities to appreciate different types of music, visual art, poetry and drama as well as being given the chance to express themselves creatively.

In some ways creative development can be considered as the development of the inner soul of a child – allowing children to use their imagination and focus on their emotions. Throughout history, cultures all over the world have used the arts to express their identities. The need to express oneself and the ability to respond to beauty seem to be peculiarly human traits. Encouraging and developing children's creativity is therefore essential in helping them to be fulfilled in their future lives.

Early Learning Goals

These goals relate to the stimulation of curiosity and engagement with a wide range of sensory experiences. They focus on the development of children's imagination and creativity and their ability to explore, express and share ideas and feelings through different forms of communication. The diagram on page 287 shows how the Early Learning Goals link with areas of creative development.

Creative development is not only about being creative

There are two sides to creative development as a curriculum area: encouraging children to express themselves using a variety of media, and providing opportunities for children to appreciate and develop critical awareness of the world around them, including the artistic work of others.

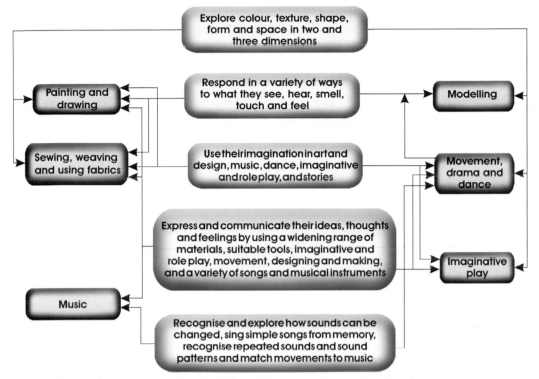

How the Early Learning Goals link with areas of creative development

There is a strong link between creativity and emotional development. The ability to express emotions and to get in touch with oneself are facilitated by music, dance, drama and visual representation. In the early years of a child's life when communication is hampered by the lack of oral language, opportunities to express feelings and emotions are particularly essential. For years, therapists (particularly Anna Freud and Erik Erikson) have used art and music with disturbed children as a way of allowing them to express themselves. It is interesting to note that for some children the urgent need to draw and make visual representations seems to ebb after they have gained fluency in their language and become more articulate.

This chapter looks at the following areas of creative development and the role of the adult in providing opportunities for them:

- music
- movement, drama and dance
- painting and drawing
- modelling
- sewing, weaving and using fabrics
- imaginative play.

Music

Children seem to be born with a sense of rhythm and can enjoy music from a very early age, for example, playing Mozart may soothe a crying infant. This relationship has been linked to the mother's instinctive rocking of her children and the heartbeat heard in the womb. Babies also respond very positively to the human voice; and mothers have sung to their children for generations.

Music plays a part in many people's lives. Although many people today do not play musical instruments or sing, it is likely that they listen to or hear music during their day-to-day routine. It is easy to forget that music is part of a country's culture and tradition and that, through music, children can be given a sense of their own cultural identity as well as exploring that of others.

Listening to and appreciating music

Early years workers have an important role in introducing babies and children to a variety of different types of music. This is particularly essential where children are being cared for in all-day settings. It is easy to use the same tapes each week, but adults should be exposing children to the widest possible range of music. This might include classical music, opera, reggae, jazz or folk music, Indian music, African music, etc. By doing this, adults are giving children the opportunity to respond to different sounds and helping them to distinguish between styles.

Where possible children should be able to listen to a range of musical styles, not forgetting the simple songs and rhymes that are recorded especially for children. This is not difficult to do as there is a wide variety of music available and a plan of music to be played each week can be programmed in alongside the activities for children.

Helping children listen to music

In many situations where music is played, it is more often heard rather than listened to. Helping children to listen to music can improve their overall listening skills as well as helping them to enjoy music more.

The role of the adult is not to sit children down and make them listen to music, but more to ask children what they can hear; for example, an adult may say to a child, 'Can you hear any drums or loud sounds?' or, 'Do you think that this is a loud or a soft part?' When playing music for children it is important to remember that, like most activities, children need time and opportunities for repetition. They may need to hear the same song or piece several times before they become familiar with it (just as adults do). In the same way, although an adult may have heard Prokofiev's *Peter and the Wolf* on countless occasions, a child listening to it for the first time may become excited and want to hear it over and over again.

ACTIVITY

Hands up

Aim: The aim of this activity is to focus children's attention when they are listening. This type of activity can be varied and used with most pieces of music.

Resources: Tape recorder or CD player.

Activity: Tell the children to listen out for either one particular instrument or type of sound in a piece. The children must put their hands up as they hear it. This activity can be varied by asking children to stand up or cross their arms when they recognise a sound, or children can be asked to listen out for several different sounds with each one having its own signal.

Ideas for this activity:

Listen for brass instruments, drums or interesting sounds such as dramatic sounds in Haydn's *Surprise Symphony*. Listen for certain words or choruses.

Listen out for very loud or soft parts in pieces.

OUTCOMES FOR CHILDREN

This type of activity links to the following Early Learning Goals

It encourages children to:

◆ explore colour, texture, shape, form and space in two and three dimensions

◆ recognise and explore how sounds can be changed, sing simple songs from memory, recognise repeated sounds and sound patterns, and match movements to music.

Creating opportunities for children to make music

Young children need opportunities to make sounds and music. Two of the most common ways of doing this in early years settings is by using percussion instruments and through singing.

Singing

Most early years settings make special time for children to sing and the musical rhymes that children learn in their infant years stay with them for life. Nursery rhymes have been proven to lay a good foundation on which reading skills can be taught. It is thought that the rhyme and patterns that are a feature of nursery rhymes help children to distinguish sounds and patterns in their early reading.

Singing also has many other benefits for children and should be a positive presence in their early lives. Children can enjoy recognising tunes and feeling part of a group when they are singing. Songs can be used to make and change atmospheres. A child who is feeling homesick may feel more part of a group if there is a familiar song to join in with. Fractious children can be calmed by hearing and joining in with a lullaby or gentle song.

Resources for singing

There are many excellent song books available, so that songs can be chosen according to the theme of the setting. Some books also come with tapes, although once a song has been learnt it is often better not to use a tape recording. 'Live' songs are usually preferable as the pace and tone of the song can be adapted to the mood of the children. A comprehensive nursery rhyme book is a good investment for any early years worker.

The following list of song books and resources for singing is certainly not exhaustive, because there are so many to choose from, but can provide a good starting point:

Kate Umansky, *Three Singing Pigs* (A & C Black, London)

Niki Davies, *Everything's Growing* (IMP Publishers, Woodford Green, Essex)

Niki Davies, *It's Time to Wake Up* (IMP Publishers, Woodford Green, Essex)

Eileen Diamond, *Let's Make Music Fun* (IMP Publishers, Woodford Green, Essex)

Jane Sebba, *Ready Steady Sing* (Faber Music, London)

David Gadsby and Beatrice Harrop, *Flying a Round* (A & C Black, London)

Sheena Roberts, *Playsongs* (Playsongs Publications, London)

ACTIVITY

Stop with me

Many games can be played while children are singing. This type of game can be played with many ages of children.

Aim: This is a simple game that helps children to concentrate as well as join in with singing.

Resources: None required.

Activity: A leader starts to sing a song or nursery rhyme that is well known to the children. Once the children are joining in, the leader suddenly stops singing and the children have to try and stop as soon as they can.

OUTCOMES FOR CHILDREN

This type of activity links to the following Early Learning Goal

It encourages children to:

◆ express and communicate their ideas, thoughts and feelings by using a widening range of materials, suitable tools, imaginative and role play, movement, designing and making, and a variety of songs and instruments.

Percussion instruments

There are two types of percussion instruments: tuned and untuned. Examples of tuned percussion instruments are xylophones, chime bars and the glockenspiel. Tuned percussion instruments enable children to pick out a melody or make up a tune. Untuned percussion instruments include drums, tambours, cymbals and shakers; they are often used to mark out a rhythm.

Ideally, settings should have a range of both types of instruments. In the same way that songs can reflect cultural identity, percussion instruments can also be part of a culture. Children should have the opportunity to explore and play as many different instruments as possible, regardless of their own cultural background.

Using percussion instruments with young children

It is common to find that there are different views about how percussion instruments should be used with young children. In some settings, instruments are left out so that children can access them as part of their play and can use them quite freely. This can mean that at times other children's quiet play is interrupted if children are banging instruments nearby.

Other settings have a more structured approach, believing that children need to learn that musical instruments are not toys and should be respected. In settings where this is the practice, music is often 'timetabled' and children make music in small groups rather than as individuals. This can mean that children do not have as much time with instruments as they would like, and do not get the chance to use all the instruments as they have to wait for other children. Each approach has its own advantages and disadvantages, as can be seen in the table below.

Structured approach	Unstructured approach
◆ Instruments are not damaged ◆ The correct beaters are used with instruments ◆ Children look forward to a 'special time' ◆ Staff can help children to use instruments more easily ◆ Children do not take the instruments for granted	◆ Children can explore instruments at their own pace ◆ Music can be integrated into children's play ◆ Children can use the instruments for longer periods

Noise or music?

Whatever the approach of the setting towards the access and availability of instruments, the issue of whether children are making noise or music has to be considered. Adults have to be aware of their own attitude to children making sounds. Some adults find it hard to cope with groups of children who are all banging different instruments at different tempos; their natural reaction may be to ask children to be quiet or to take the instruments away, allowing only a few children at a time to play. Sometimes the noise of so many sounds at once can make adults feel that they are not in control of the situation because the sound that they are hearing is not a tidy one. Unfortunately, children do need time to explore the instruments and so it is necessary to find a balance between allowing musical chaos to ensue and organising children to the extent that they are unable to enjoy and have fun with instruments. As is the case with the debate over free versus structured play, most settings find that they decide to allow for both organised and unstructured musical experiences.

Many settings that have structured music sessions start by encouraging children to make as much noise as they want. This means that children may then be ready for some more organised musical activity.

Children need time to explore musical instruments

Ideas for percussion games for children

Great fun can be had by playing games with a musical bias with children. Most of the games mentioned on pages 293–4 encourage children's listening skills and help them to explore some of the concepts in music, for example, fast and slow, soft and loud, echo, and so on.

(Continued)

◆ *Rice in a jar*

Partially fill a jar with rice.

Shake the jar.

Tell the children to shake their fingers when they see/hear the rice move.

Tell the children to keep their fingers still when the rice is still.

Variations:

1. Hide the jar. Can the children shake their fingers when the rice is moving without seeing the jar?

2. Introduce other sounds such as a comb, bell or buzzer.

3. Allow the children to take turns with the jar or other object.

◆ *Name the instrument*

A child goes behind a screen and chooses a percussion instrument, then plays it in short bursts. One child is then chosen to identify the instrument. The other children can give clues to help, for example, it is big, it is made of metal.

◆ *How many sounds . . .*

The children are seated in a circle. An instrument is passed around and the children sing 'Extraordinary _____, Extraordinary _____, how many sounds can you make?' When the song stops the child holding the instrument has to find a different way of making a sound with it. You can use conventional instruments as well as homemade ones.

◆ *Simon says*

Similar to the traditional game, this can be played in two different ways.

1. Instead of saying 'Simon says', a pattern is clapped. When no pattern is clapped the children should not follow the action.

2. Following on from the first idea, all the actions are replaced by sounds made by the body, i.e. clapping, stamping, humming, etc.

◆ *Hot and cold with instruments*

An instrument is hidden and one child is asked to find it. The other children play their own instruments loudly when the child is close to it and softly when the child is 'cold'.

◆ *Stand up, sit down*

The adult plays a pattern on a drum over and over again. A child who is hidden plays a shaker. When the shaker is being played at the same time the children stand up and when the shaker stops the children sit down.

◆ *Pass the beater . . .*

The children sit in a circle and a beater is passed round to the song, 'Pass the beater, round and round, when it stops you must make a sound'. The child with the beater must go to the middle and play the instrument.

(Continued)

(Any instrument could be used, such as a triangle or tambourine as well as other percussion instruments.)

◆ *Listen to this . . .*

The children are in a circle. An instrument is passed round and the children chant 'Listen to this . . . Listen to this . . . You can give an answer . . .' accompanied by the leader on a drum. On the word 'you' the child holding the instrument gets ready to play it and must play a short rhythm. If the answer is quiet, the next chant is said quietly.

◆ *Order in the court*

The children are in a circle and they play their instruments and chant 'Order in the court . . . Order in the court . . . The judge is eating beans . . . His wife is in the bath tub . . . counting submarines.'

When they get to 'submarines' the children stop playing and count '1, 2, 3, 4', and then start again.

◆ *A variation on the theme of Old Macdonald*

Instead of Old Macdonald, you could have 'Tiptoes Nursery (i.e. the name of the setting) had a band, ee-i-ee-i-o, and in that band there was a drum . . . With a bang, bang here and a bang, bang there . . . Tiptoes's Nursery had a band, ee-i-ee-i-o', etc.

These types of activities link to the following Early Learning Goals

They encourage children to:

◆ recognise and explore how sounds can be changed, sing simple songs from memory, recognise repeated sounds and sound patterns and match movements to music

◆ respond in a variety of ways to what they see, hear, smell, touch and feel

◆ use their imagination in art and design, music, dance, imaginative and role play, and stories

◆ express and communicate their ideas, thoughts and feelings by using a widening range of materials, suitable tools, drama, movement, designing and making, and a variety of songs and instruments.

Movement, drama and dance

An area that complements music is movement, drama and dance. Children respond well to rhythm and can express their innate creativity by using their bodies and dancing. Through music and dance children also gain confidence and co-ordination in their movements.

The role of the adult

Movement, drama and dance work with this age group usually has to be a timetabled activity, because few settings will have the space available for children to move and dance as and when they wish. This does not mean that the activity needs to be highly structured, as young children will gain most by being given a minimum of instructions, such as: 'Listen to the beat of my drum. Can you move in time with it?' This type of instruction allows children to be safe in moving around but still allows for self-expression. For safety reasons children will have to know when to stop moving. This can be learnt as part of a game at the beginning of sessions: 'When you hear me ring the triangle you must sit down. Let's see who can remember this'.

It can be a good idea for children to watch each other move and dance. With large groups this gives individuals more space and prevents children from having accidents, while allowing children to exchange ideas. Children should be praised for their participation rather than for any particular skill, as there is an element of physical readiness and development in moving to music.

In order to encourage creativity it is not necessary to 'teach' children set movements or patterns as the aim of this type of session is to allow children to use their own imagination to explore movement and music. In the same way, although sessions could be videoed to record the children's work, it should *not* be performance-led at this stage, as constant rehearsing takes away the very spontaneity that makes movement and dance a creative activity.

It is important for adults to bring in as many different types and styles of music and ideas for dance as possible. Some cultures have very strong traditions in dance and the accompanying music or percussion beats can inspire children.

Using movement, drama and dance across the curriculum

Music can be selected to fit with themes in early years settings; for example, a theme about animals can be extended in these sessions by playing pieces from Saint-Saëns' *Carnival of the Animals*. Below are some starting points for ideas that may fit in with themes. Remember that most young children respond particularly well when they have props to work with and can make props themselves.

Ideas for drama, dance and movement activities

◆ *Hatching out*

This is a lovely activity to accompany a theme of birds, especially if children have seen chickens or other birds being hatched. It fits in well with spring-time activities.

Imagine you are a bird just hatching out of a shell. You have been tucked up in your egg and now, bit by bit, you are pushing out of your shell. You have managed to break out! You stretch a little and then you need a rest.

(Continued)

◆ *Flying in the air*

This activity can fit in with a theme about flight or about birds. Music such as 'Walking in the air' from *The Snowman* can be played as well.

You are a large bird, perhaps an eagle or a hawk, and you have long, strong wings that you use to glide around with. Stretch and flap your wings and now glide through the air, making sure that you have plenty of space. Sometimes you may need to land and find a perch to have a rest on. (A signal such as a tambourine tells the children that they must 'land'.)

◆ *Clowns*

Most children love the idea of clowns and circuses and have seen pictures of clowns. This type of activity can be used with face paints and real dressing-up clothes as children can put on large shoes to practise walking in.

You are a circus clown, getting dressed in the morning. What would you put on first? You put on your big trousers and floppy shoes. Can you walk in your big floppy shoes? You must make sure that you are wearing your smile. Have you practised waving at everyone?

◆ *Head bakers*

Children enjoy the idea of cooking and making food. This type of activity fits in well with themes on food and can be easily varied.

You are the head baker and you and the other bakers have been asked to produce a very special dish. What dish are you going to make? Go and collect all the different ingredients that you will need. How many people are needed to make it? Stir all the ingredients together. Does your dish need mixing, kneading or spreading? What does everyone think of it once it has been cooked? Does it smell nice?

◆ *Fantastic cars*

The humble cardboard box is loved by most children. Boxes can be climbed into to make boats, buses, cars and trains, and can form the basis of some very enjoyable drama and movement work. Music such as the theme from *Chitty Chitty Bang Bang* can be used.

You have been given a special car. It is able to do many things. What can your car do? Does it hoot, fly or can you make it into a home? Does it need petrol or something else to keep it running? Have you tried cleaning your car?

These types of activities link to the following Early Learning Goals

They encourage children to:

◆ use their imagination in art and design, music, dance, imaginative and role play, and stories

◆ express and communicate their ideas, thoughts and feelings by using a widening range of materials, suitable tools, imaginative and role play, movement, designing and making, and a variety of songs and instruments.

Painting and drawing

Painting and drawing are very satisfying activities for young children. When young children draw and paint they are often completely absorbed in the process, enjoying the physical sensation as well as the satisfaction of being in control of what they are doing.

This idea of being in control of what they are trying to produce can even be seen as the key to creativity in young children. This means that where possible the adult needs to act as a provider rather than a controller if children are to gain the most when painting or drawing. It is interesting to note that young children rarely ask an adult to help them while they are painting or drawing, needing assistance only for practical reasons such as running out of paint or not having enough paper.

As painting and drawing is also a 'core activity' see also Chapter 7, pages 146–9.

Materials

Where possible children should be given many opportunities to try out different paint and drawing materials, for example:

◆ watercolour paints	◆ rollers	◆ felt tips
◆ pastels	◆ fine brushes	◆ markers
◆ chalks	◆ thick decorator's brushes	◆ leaves
◆ charcoal	◆ sponges	◆ string.

Providing opportunities for painting and drawing

Children should have plenty of time and opportunities to experience different paint and drawing techniques. They will need to be able to use different types of equipment, for example, small rollers or sponges. Adults can help children to use different paint techniques by planning activities around them, for example, preparing an activity where children use string to make marks or use chalk to draw with. By doing this children learn how to make different textures and patterns and learn about the effects of different materials. From this exploratory work, children can then go on to incorporate these textures and techniques into their future designs and work. This in turn makes the experience of painting more interesting and satisfying for them.

The role of the adult
Working alongside children

It is important that adults do not worry about their own artistic abilities. The aim is not to teach children to paint and draw, but simply to provide them with opportunities and interesting experiences. It is good practice to join in painting activities by painting or drawing alongside children. This shows children that artwork is valued, while often allowing adults to enjoy the experience of painting themselves.

Encouraging children to learn from the process

Adults should resist the temptation to make painting and drawing an area where end products are always made. A final picture is not necessarily an indicator of a good learning experience, and you should be encouraging children to enjoy and learn from the experience. This means that a child who has spent some time mixing paint using sponges may have learnt a lot about colour and texture even though a final picture was not the outcome. For children it is the process rather than the product which must be valued.

Giving children time

If painting and drawing are seen as valuable learning experiences, children will need to be given as much time as they need to finish their pictures. Too often settings will offer painting activities in a conveyor-belt fashion, with groups of children being shown a technique or being asked to paint something and then ten minutes later told that they have finished and it is time for another group to do this activity. Such an approach may ensure that all the children in the setting have had a turn, but on the other hand does not allow children enough time to linger and explore painting.

Wherever possible children should be given as much time and equipment as *they* need to paint and draw, rather than being told that they only get one turn or one piece of paper.

Encouraging children to reflect

In order for children to become more sensitive and aesthetically aware, adults need to help children to reflect on their experiences. This may mean that adults talk to children about what they are doing by asking questions such as, 'Which is your favourite colour?' or 'How did you make this pattern?'

Adults should also encourage children to look at other children's work so that they can learn from each other. One child may have mixed an interesting colour, while another might have made an exciting pattern using a sponge.

Avoiding judgements

Adults need to be aware of the dangers of making judgemental comments – whether positive or negative – about children's work, such as, 'I like your house' or 'What a pity that you haven't used more blue'. Judgements on children's work often lead children to becoming more focused on what they are producing rather than on the process. It can mean that some children tend to paint and draw in order to gain an adult's attention, rather than for the pleasure of using the materials. It can be a good idea to ask the children what they have enjoyed most about the session and praise them for their thoughts and effort.

Enjoying the process of creativity is important!

Displaying work

Children gain a great deal of satisfaction from seeing their work displayed. Displays should include not only figurative pictures but also work that is more experimental. So a child who has used sponges to print with can find that this piece has been mounted and displayed, as well as the more usual pictures of 'my house'.

Areas of experience and opportunity

Painting and drawing can be planned for on a weekly basis and children can explore different skills and techniques. The activities described on pages 300–2 give children the opportunity to try out the different skills and techniques. Do not worry if children have already tried them before as most children benefit from repeating activities at different times. You can also vary the types of paper, paint and other resources, so that children get different results.

ACTIVITY

Colour collages

Aim: The idea is to help children explore colour by doing a painting that has as many shades of one colour as possible.

Resources: Ready mixed paints – red, yellow, blue and white. A tray or plastic plates. Sponges, brushes, string and other objects that may make marks. A large piece of white paper.

Activity: Put some of each of the colours on a tray or on plates. This helps children to dip in the materials more easily and makes it easier to wash up at the end of the activity. Choose one colour as the theme and make sure that there is more of this colour than the others, i.e. for a red picture put out plenty of red paint.

Encourage the children to cover the paper with as many different shades of the same colour as possible, made from dipping their materials into the red paint and then into another colour.

They can make many different marks, for example, by twisting the sponge, using their fingers and hands.

This should give children a red picture with shades of pink, orange, purple.

These paintings may be used afterwards as a basis for further collage work or as a background for a display.

Tip: Using a kitchen tray or polystyrene meat trays makes it possible for children to mix colours more easily. The trays are easily washed and wiped afterwards.

Combing colours

Aim: To show children how primary colours can mix together to make new colours. This is a quick activity and children may want to have more than one turn.

Resources: Pieces of cardboard, i.e. from cardboard boxes. Ready mixed paint – red, yellow and blue. Paper.

Preparation: Cut the cardboard into rectangles that are comfortable for children to hold.

Cut out small triangles on one of the long sides of the rectangles, to make a comb.

Activity: Ask the children to squeeze lines of paint across their paper. An adult can do this for younger children if necessary. Three or four lines in any direction are sufficient. The children then use their combs across the paper, crissing and crossing. This makes the lines of paint mix and creates a pattern.

Matching colours

Aim: For children to understand that colours come in different shades.

Resources: Paper. Paints – red, yellow, blue and white. Paint brushes (medium sized). Colour cards from DIY stores (optional).

(Continued)

Activity: The children are asked to mix up a colour of paint and put a blob of it on their paper. They must then try and match it either to a colour of an object in the room or to a colour on a colour card. Children can choose a name for the colour they have made.

Varying this activity: This activity can be varied by choosing a colour from a colour card or of an object in the room and asking the children if they are able to match it themselves.

Wax resist

Aim: This activity helps children to discover some of the properties of water-based paint.

Resources: Wax crayons or candles. Large-headed paint brush (for example, one that is normally used for gloss painting). Powder paint mixed with water.

Preparation: Mix up the powder paint with water so that it makes a 'wash'. The paint needs to be quite thin so that the wax can show through it. Dark colours such as black and blue tend to work the best.

Activity: The children scribble or draw using wax crayons or candles. They need to press quite hard. The wash is applied over the picture, the brush going from side to side. It is important that the children only go over an area once, otherwise the wax does not show through. Children tend to love this part of the process because it seems like magic. This technique can be used to complement a topic such as fireworks or sealife.

Fruit and vegetable printing

Aim: This activity helps children to see that everyday items can be used for printing.

Resources: Ready-mixed paint. Trays or plates. Selection of fruit and vegetables, such as peppers, tomatoes, oranges.

Preparation: Cut the fruit and vegetables in half or in slices. (They can be left to dry out a little.) Pour paint onto trays or plates to make it easier for children to apply the paint.

Activity: The children dip fruit or vegetables into a colour and print with them. This activity is also a good opportunity to examine fruit and vegetables.

Marbling

Aim: This activity helps children to understand that oil and water do not mix.

Resources: Marbling inks. Deep tray. Water. White paper. Paper or plastic straws.

Activity: Fill a deep tray with water. (It may be worth buying a tray just for this purpose as some inks can be difficult to remove. Cat litter trays are ideal.) A few drops of ink are added to the water. The children can swirl them with a straw. A piece of paper is laid on top of the water and then lifted out again. A print is made of the swirling pattern. This activity fits in well with a topic on water as children can see that the ink stays on top of the water.

(Continued)

Paper batik

This activity can be linked to a theme about fabrics. Children can see fabric batiks and their paper batiks can be displayed alongside.

Resources: Large wax crayons; paper such as duplicating paper or cartridge paper (not newsprint or sugar paper); a 'wash' made from watercolour paint or ready mixed paint and water; a large paintbrush.

Activity: Draw or scribble a design on the paper using wax crayons. Encourage the children to press firmly. Crumple the paper up (this is the part that the children really enjoy).

Dip the paper into a bucket of water. Remove the paper and carefully flatten it out. You can put it onto a wad of newspaper.

Using a large paintbrush, wash over the paper. The paint avoids the waxed areas and falls into the creases.

Once the paper has dried, the wax colours can be polished by rubbing gently with a soft cloth.

Sand paper prints

Aim: This is a simple way of letting children make a print.

Resources: Sand paper, wax crayons, roller, ready mixed paint, paper.

Activity: The children draw or scribble onto the sand paper. The roller with paint then covers the sand paper.

A piece of paper is then gently put onto the sand paper and smoothed down.

The paper is peeled back, showing a print of whatever has been drawn.

OUTCOMES FOR CHILDREN

These types of activities link to the following Early Learning Goals

They encourage children to:

- explore colour, texture, shape, form and space in two and three dimensions
- use their imagination in art and design, music, dance, imaginative and role play, and stories
- express and communicate their ideas, thoughts and feelings by using a widening range of materials, suitable tools, imaginative and role play, movement, designing and making, and a variety of songs and instruments.

Appreciating art

It is important that children not only paint and draw but that they also look at other people's work. Creative development involves helping children to appreciate and respond to visual art. This means that children can be shown other children's work as well as seeing posters and postcards of famous paintings and drawings. It is important for children to see as many types of paintings and drawings as possible, as the more they see, the more they will develop their own taste and style.

Remember that when considering what types of work to show children, they should be looking at pictures from a variety of cultures. This shows children that all types of work should be valued and considered as well as broadening their artistic horizons.

Helping children to appreciate artwork

Adults can ask children what they like or dislike about a painting, which colours they like and how it makes them feel. Children may also be encouraged to notice how an artist has used colour or shapes in a work.

Helping children to talk about what they are seeing means that children will have to develop a broad vocabulary, which will include some of the following words.

Vocabulary for artwork discussions

dark	bright	tones	smooth	sketch
light	dull	depth	artist	oil painting
bold	soft	background	painter	print
pale	warm	rough	portrait	colour

Learning through drawing

Children can learn through looking at objects and then drawing them. This is known as *observational drawing* and helps children to look more carefully at objects around them. This in turn helps them to be more accurate in their drawing and allows them a greater satisfaction. Chapter 7 on core activities looks at the importance of maintaining children's confidence in their artwork, and giving children opportunities to draw in this way can help them to remain confident.

An example of a four-year-old's observational drawing

As children tend to think and learn as they draw, objects can be chosen that will also support other curriculum areas, particularly knowledge and understanding of the world. For example, if the theme of the setting is 'feet', children may choose to draw their shoes.

Involving local artists

Many areas have local artist groups who are keen to promote art in the community and inviting artists into the setting can be very successful. Children are able to see that art is valued and can learn from watching an artist at work. Some settings display the work of local artists, whereas others may have 'an artist in residence' who will work alongside the children. In some areas of the country small grants are available to help these types of schemes.

Modelling

Producing a model is another way of helping children to represent their world and express their creativity. Children enjoy modelling as they are using their hands and can actually feel what they are creating. There are many ways of providing for modelling in early years settings and it is important that children are given opportunities to experience as many of these as possible. Planning different types of modelling activities can therefore be built into a term's curriculum plan.

Modelling activities

These will include the following:

- papier mâché
- clay
- dough
- plasticine
- junk modelling.

Each of these materials has different properties which means that children need to experience as many of them as possible. (See also dough and junk modelling, pages 137–41 and 153–5, in Chapter 7 on core activities.)

The role of the adult

Dough and other types of malleable materials, such as plasticine, are often provided in early years settings as part of the routine because they are easy for children to use and do not require too much adult supervision. Other types of modelling, such as papier mâché and clay, will need more adult support and therefore may be used as part of a structured activity. For example, small groups of children may make bowls rather than each one making their own object. This allows children to gain some familiarity with the material, even though they cannot explore it fully. Where children are able to have one-to-one adult support, they should be encouraged to develop their own ideas for modelling, although they may still need to be shown some techniques, for example, learning to join pieces of clay together or using wire to make a base for papier mâché.

Whatever the type of material used for modelling, adults will need to encourage children and support them, as sometimes children become frustrated because they have not developed all the skills or co-ordination they need. Many projects will need to be finished over several sessions, as clay or papier mâché will need time to dry. An important element of the adult's role is to help children maintain their enthusiasm for a project. Children who finish projects will have learnt many other skills such as perseverance, patience and concentration, which they can transfer into other areas of their learning.

Providing equipment

A wide range of equipment is needed if children are going to be able to explore materials fully. This is particularly important where the same materials are set out regularly, for example, dough and plasticine. Providing children with different tools will help them work in different ways, which will make the activity more satisfying. Useful equipment will include:

cutters	scissors	combs
knives	rolling pins	rollers
brushes	modelling tools	paints

Making jewellery – brooches and badges

Most children enjoy things that glitter and the idea of treasure or jewels. Using odds and ends children can make large badges and brooches. Pasta, glitter, sticky paper and feathers are examples of the types of materials that can be stuck onto pieces of card. Proper badge pins can be bought from most large art and craft stores.

ACTIVITY

Making pendants (or medals)

Children can make pendants or medals by using either clay or salt dough.

Resources: Salt dough, modelling materials, paint, varnish, straw or other tool to make the hole.

Activity: A small piece of salt dough or clay is rolled out and shaped to the final size of the pendant or medal.

Using a straw or other tool, a hole is made near the top of the pendant.

After it has dried out the pendant is decorated with paint and can be varnished by an adult.

The pendant is threaded onto a piece of wool, string or ribbon.

OUTCOMES FOR CHILDREN

This type of activity links to the following Early Learning Goals

It encourages children to:

◆ explore colour, texture, shape, form and space in two and three dimensions

◆ respond in a variety of ways to what they see, hear, smell, touch and feel

◆ express and communicate their ideas, thoughts and feelings by using a widening range of materials, suitable tools, imaginative and role play, movement, designing and making, and a variety of songs and musical instruments.

Sewing, weaving and other work with fabrics

Some of these types of activities will require significant adult support but children can find them very satisfying. Every culture has a tradition of making and using fabrics and so children should not only be given opportunities to work with different types of fabrics but should also be encouraged to appreciate them. This can be achieved by bringing in different fabrics for children to feel and look at. Fabrics can be draped as part of a display or framed and mounted. Fabrics from a variety of countries and cultures should be shown so that children can see different styles and colours, for example, batik cloths from Africa or painted silks from Asia.

Resources

A good range of equipment and resources can help both adults and children enjoy using fabrics to be creative. These can include:

- *Fabrics*

    nets   hessian   cottons

    silks   binker   muslin

- *Trimmings*

lace	twine		tapes	buttons	string
braid	wool		zips	feathers	grasses
ribbons	embroidery threads		feathers	sequins	tinsel.

Fabric collages

Collage can be a good way of introducing children to the feel and beauty of fabrics. Children enjoy making collages using a selection of materials. Collages can be put together using a theme, for example, the colour blue, or by making up a picture.

A good selection of fabrics is essential to make this an attractive sensory experience. Adults may need to help by cutting up fabrics if children cannot cope with the scissors. Lace and trimmings are often popular with children as they are easier to cut and interesting in shape. It is a good idea to use a small area of paper with young children, so that they do not feel overwhelmed by an apparently large task.

ACTIVITY

Colour collages

Aim: To encourage children to look at textures and shades. The activity can be used alongside a theme on colours. It can also be extended by asking children to sort and glue according to shades of colours.

Resources: Materials, fabrics, laces and trimmings of one shade of colour such as red; sheet of card or strong paper to act as a backing.

Activity: This can either be done as a group activity or all children can have their own square of paper to work with. The children are asked to use the materials to make a 'red' collage. It is useful if a red sheet of paper can be used for the backing as then any gaps are less apparent.

(Continued)

Sewing

Sewing can be a creative activity for children as well as giving them a good life skill. Children enjoy selecting items to sew onto fabric and choosing different colour threads. When they have finished they also have a product that they have created themselves.

Young children can manage to sew if given large blunt needles and loosely woven fabric such as binker. Children can sew on sequins and beads, as well as trying to do different stitches. Although children can often be quite independent in their sewing, good adult supervision and support is necessary because of the safety implications of children using needles. Remember that sewing can have links to mathematics because children learn about pattern if they are trying to complete regular stitches.

Weaving

Weaving is a tradition in most communities. Weaving is also a mathematical experience for children as they gain an understanding of pattern. It is possible to weave with strips of paper as a starting point with children. It is also possible for children to weave something as a group. A loom can be made and children can add a row to it when they wish. At first children will need some adult help to understand what they need to do, but as they gain in confidence they will need less adult support. Weaving can be done with strips of fabric and grass as well as the traditional wool. The activity described below and overleaf shows how paper can be used for simple weaving by children.

ACTIVITY

Paper weaving

Aim: Children can carry out simple weaving using paper.

Resources: A4 piece of paper, paper of different colours and textures cut into strips.

Activity: Prepare a paper loom for the children by stapling strips of paper lengthwise onto another piece of paper. Weave other strips of paper across the paper loom. Fold back and glue down the edges.

(Continued)

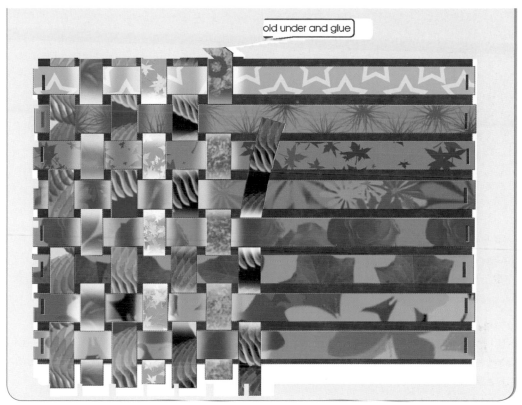

Paper weaving

Imaginative play

Imaginative play happens when children take on roles and act them out. In early years settings this frequently happens in the home corner, although children can also play in this way with 'small world' toys, such as train sets and Playmobil characters, or when they are outdoors. It is easy to forget that this type of play is indeed creative as children are expressing themselves freely and are in control of their play. The only difference between this type of play and 'acting' is that children do not learn lines or have rehearsals.

In many ways this can be the most popular type of play among children as there are no rules imposed by adults and children are free to take on whatever role they wish. This means that some children choose to be heroes (like Bob the builder or Superman) while others wish to be parents or adults (often, teachers!). The benefits of this type of play are examined in Chapter 7 on core activities, pages 149–52, which also looks at ways of extending imaginative play.

Making and using puppets

To encourage children to play imaginatively, adults can help them to make and use puppets. Most children enjoy puppets and helping them to make their own can enhance their play. Children can either play with puppets by themselves or they can hide behind some sort of a screen, which could simply be a curtain. In some settings there are puppet theatres, although it is possible to make a simple puppet theatre by cutting out part of a cardboard box.

Ideas for puppet making

◆ *Sock puppets*

These are very easy to use and to make. Children need to have a sock and can then sew or glue on eyes and a nose. They can pretend to make the puppet speak by opening and closing its mouth. A long sock can be made to look like a snake.

◆ *Finger puppets*

Children can make traditional finger puppets from felt, although most children will need a lot of adult support for this. It is always possible to give children partially made puppets onto which they just add the feature that they wish.

Where time is short or children are too young to make their own finger puppets, a face can be directly penned onto a child's finger.

◆ *Hand puppets*

Most hand puppets that are used in early years settings are shop-bought, because it would be quite difficult for young children to make one. However, it is possible to use a glove as the basis of making some animals, such as a tortoise.

Hand puppets are always popular with young children

(Continued)

◆ *Spoon puppets*

A wooden spoon or stick can form the basis of a puppet. Spoon puppets are easy to make with young children and easy for them to hold and use. The head of the spoon acts as the head and fabric is rolled around it to make the body.

These types of activities link to the following Early Learning Goals

They encourage children to:

◆ use their imagination in art and design, music, dance, imaginative and role play, and stories

◆ express and communicate their ideas, thoughts and feelings by using a widening range of materials, suitable tools, imaginative and role play, movement, designing and making, and a variety of songs and musical instruments.

The reflective practitioner

Do I paint, collage or model alongside children so that I act as a role model?

Is there a range of materials available for children?

Are children encouraged to make choices about the materials that they use?

Are children expressing their own ideas?

Is the focus on children exploring materials rather than on producing an 'end product'?

Do I support children rather than direct them as they are working?

Are children given plenty of time to follow their ideas?

Do I make sure that all children's work is valued?

Do I put out the musical instruments for children to enjoy and explore?

Is a range of music from a variety of cultures played in the setting?

Do I talk to parents about the value of this area of learning?

Appendix

The following Early Learning Goals diagrams are also available to download from our website: www.heinemann.co.uk

Mathematical development
- use language such as 'more' or 'less', 'greater' or 'smaller', 'heavier' or 'lighter', or compare two numbers or quantities
- use language such as 'circle' or 'bigger' to describe the shape and size of solids and flat shapes
- use everyday words to describe position

Physical development
- use a range of small and large equipment
- handle tools, objects, construction and malleable materials safely and with increasing control

Knowledge and understanding of the world
- investigate objects and materials by using all of their senses as appropriate
- select tools and techniques they need to shape, assemble and join the materials they are using

DOUGH

Personal, social and emotional development
- be confident to try new activities, initiate ideas and speak in a familiar group
- maintain attention, concentrate and sit quietly when appropriate
- continue to be interested, excited and motivated to learn
- dress and undress independently and manage their own personal hygiene
- select and use activities and resources independently

Communication, language and literacy
- use talk to organise, sequence and clarify thinking, ideas, feelings and events

Creative development
- explore colour, texture, shape, form and space in two or three dimensions
- respond in a variety of ways to what they see, hear, smell, touch and feel
- express and communicate their ideas, thoughts and feelings by using a widening range of materials, suitable tools, imaginative and role play, movement, designing and making, and a variety of songs and musical instruments

Dough and the Early Learning Goals

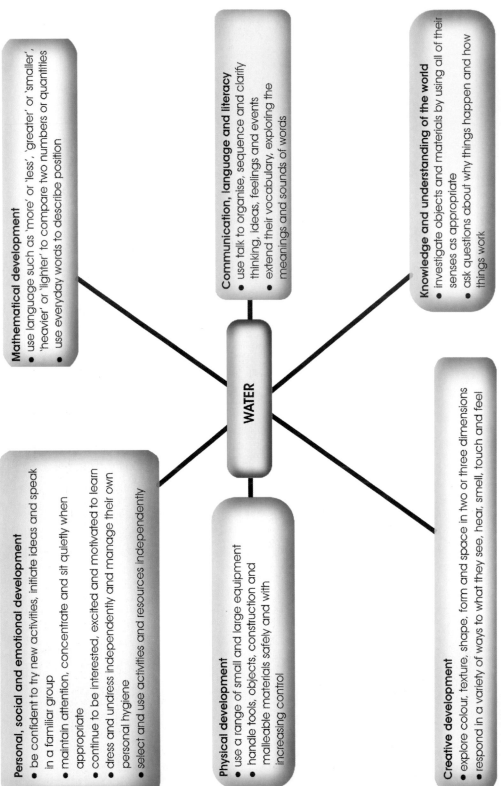

Mathematical development
- use language such as 'more' or 'less', 'greater' or 'smaller', 'heavier' or 'lighter' to compare two numbers or quantities
- use everyday words to describe position

Communication, language and literacy
- use talk to organise, sequence and clarify thinking, ideas, feelings and events
- extend their vocabulary, exploring the meanings and sounds of words

Knowledge and understanding of the world
- investigate objects and materials by using all of their senses as appropriate
- ask questions about why things happen and how things work

Personal, social and emotional development
- be confident to try new activities, initiate ideas and speak in a familiar group
- maintain attention, concentrate and sit quietly when appropriate
- continue to be interested, excited and motivated to learn
- dress and undress independently and manage their own personal hygiene
- select and use activities and resources independently

Physical development
- use a range of small and large equipment
- handle tools, objects, construction and malleable materials safely and with increasing control

Creative development
- explore colour, texture, shape, form and space in two or three dimensions
- respond in a variety of ways to what they see, hear, smell, touch and feel

WATER

Water and the Early Learning Goals

Mathematical development

- use language such as 'more' or 'less', 'greater' or 'smaller', 'heavier' or 'lighter' to compare two numbers or quantities
- use everyday words to describe position

Communication, language and literacy

- use language to imagine and recreate roles and experiences
- use talk to organise, sequence and clarify thinking, ideas, feelings and events
- interact with others, negotiating plans and activities and taking turns in conversation
- extend their vocabulary, exploring the meanings and sounds of new words

Knowledge and understanding of the world

- investigate objects and materials by using all of their senses as appropriate
- building and construct with a wide range of objects, selecting appropriate resources and adapting their work where necessary

SAND

Personal, social and emotional development

- be confident to try new activities, initiate ideas and speak in a familiar group
- maintain attention, concentrate and sit quietly when appropriate
- continue to be interested, excited and motivated to learn
- form good relationships with adults and peers
- select and use activities and resources independently
- dress and undress independently and manage their own personal hygiene

Physical development

- use a range of small and large equipment
- handle tools, objects, construction and malleable materials safely and with increasing control

Creative development

- explore colour, texture, shape, form and space in two or three dimensions
- respond in a variety of ways to what they see, hear, smell, touch and feel

Sand play and the Early Learning Goals

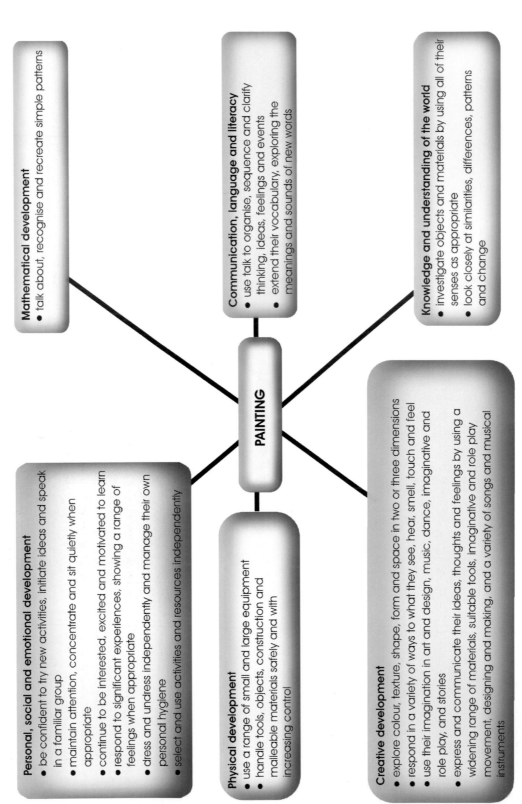

Painting and the Early Learning Goals

Mathematical development
- say and use number names in order in familiar contexts
- use everyday words to describe position

Communication, language and literacy
- use language to imagine and recreate roles and experiences
- use talk to organise, sequence and clarify thinking, ideas, feelings and events
- sustain attentive listening, responding to what they have heard by relevant comments, questions or actions
- interact with others, negotiating plans and activities and taking turns in conversation
- extend their vocabulary, exploring the meanings and sounds of words
- speak clearly and audibly with confidence and control and show awareness of the listener, for example, by their use of conventional greetings 'please' and 'thank you'

Knowledge and understanding of the world
- build and construct with a wide range of objects selecting appropriate resources and adapting their work where necessary
- look closely at similarities, differences, patterns and change

Personal, social and emotional development
- be confident to try new activities, initiate ideas and speak in a familiar group
- maintain attention, concentrate and sit quietly when appropriate
- continue to be interested, excited and motivated to learn
- have a developing awareness of their own needs, views and feelings, and be sensitive to the needs, views and feelings of others
- respond to significant experiences, showing a range of feelings when appropriate
- form good relationships with adults and peers
- work as part of a group or class, taking turns and sharing fairly, understanding that there needs to be agreed values and codes of behavior for groups of people, including adults and children, to work together harmoniously
- select and use activities and resources independently
- dress and undress independently and manage their own personal hygiene
- consider the consequences of their words and actions for themselves and others

Physical development
- use a range of small and large equipment
- handle tools, objects, construction and malleable materials safely and with increasing control

Creative development
- explore colour, texture, shape, form and space in two or three dimensions
- respond in a variety of ways to what they see, hear, smell, touch and feel
- use their imagination in art and design, music, dance, imaginative and role play, and stories
- express and communicate their ideas, thoughts and feelings by using a widening range of materials, suitable tools, imaginative and role play, movement, designing and making, and a variety of songs and musical instruments

HOME CORNER/ DRESSING UP

Home corner/dressing up and the Early Learning Goals

Mathematical development
- use language such as 'more' or 'less', greater or 'smaller', 'heavier' or 'lighter' to compare two number or quantities
- use everyday words to describe position
- use developing mathematical ideas and methods to solve practical problems

Communication, language and literacy
- use talk to organise, sequence and clarify thinking, ideas, feelings and events
- interact with others, negotiating plans and activities and taking turns in conversation
- extend their vocabulary, exploring the meanings and sounds of new words

Knowledge and understanding of the world
- investigate objects and materials by using all of their senses as appropriate
- ask questions about why things happen and how things work
- build and construct with a wide range of objects, selecting appropriate resources and adapting their work where necessary
- select the tools and techniques they need to shape, assemble and join the materials they are using

JUNK MODELLING

Personal, social and emotional development
- be confident to try new activities, initiate ideas and speak in a familiar group
- maintain attention, concentrate and sit quietly when appropriate
- continue to be interested, excited and motivated to learn
- select and use activities and resources independently
- dress and undress independently and manage their own personal hygiene

Physical development
- show awareness of space, of themselves and of others
- use a range of small and large equipment
- handle tools, objects, construction and malleable materials safely and with increasing control

Creative development
- explore colour, texture, shape, form and space in two or three dimensions
- use their imagination in art and design, music, dance, imaginative and role play, and stories
- express and communicate their ideas, thoughts and feelings by using a widening range of materials, suitable tools, imaginative and role play, movement, designing and making, and a variety of songs and musical instruments

Junk modelling and the Early Learning Goals

Mathematical development

- use language such as 'more' or 'less', 'greater' or 'smaller', 'heavier' or 'lighter' to compare two numbers or quantities
- in practical activities and discussion begin to use the vocabulary involved in adding and subtracting
- use language such as 'circle' or 'bigger' to describe the shape and size of solids and flat shapes
- use everyday words to describe position
- use developing mathematical ideas and methods to solve practical problems

Communication, language and literacy

- use talk to organise, sequence and clarify thinking, ideas, feelings and events
- interact with others, negotiating plans and activities and taking turns in conversation
- extend their vocabulary, exploring the meanings and sounds of new words

Knowledge and understanding of the world

- investigate objects and materials by using all of their senses as appropriate
- ask questions about why things happen and how things work
- build and construct with a wide range of objects, selecting appropriate resources and adapting their work where necessary
- select the tools and techniques they need to shape, assemble and join the materials they are using

CONSTRUCTION TOYS

Personal, social and emotional development

- be confident to try new activities, initiate ideas and speak in a familiar group
- maintain attention, concentrate and sit quietly when appropriate
- continue to be interested, excited and motivated to learn
- form good relationships with adults and peers
- work as part of a group or class, taking turns and sharing fairly, understanding that there needs to be agreed values and codes of behavior for groups of people, including adults and children, to work together harmoniously
- select and use activities and resources independently

Physical development

- Use a range of small and large equipment
- handle tools, objects, construction and malleable materials safely and with increasing control

Creative development

- explore colour, texture, shape, form and space in two or three dimensions
- use their imagination in art and design, music, dance, imaginative and role play, and stories
- express and communicate their ideas, thoughts and feelings by using a widening range of materials, suitable tools, imaginative and role play, movement, designing and making, and a variety of songs and musical instruments

Construction toys and the Early Learning Goals

INDEX